To Nathe

Christmas 2013.

With love,

Babi & Grampy

SO I BOUGHT AN AIR FORCE

So I Bought an Air Force

The True Story
of a Gritty Midwesterner
in Somoza's Nicaragua

W. W. Martin

So I Bought an Air Force
by W. W. Martin

Two Harbors Press
212 3rd Avenue North, Suite 290
Minneapolis, MN 55401
612.455.2294
www.twoharborspress.com

ISBN: 978-1-938690-36-5
LCCN: 2013909038

Production Editor: Patrick Aylward
Cover Design: Christopher Gyorgy

To my best friend,
my brother Glenn
and
to my wife,
Patricia Daggett Martin
my favorite navigator who is so much more

CONTENTS

AUTHOR'S NOTE   IX

PROLOGUE   3

Chapter 1:   CRASH   5

Chapter 2:   PLANES FOR SALE   13

Chapter 3:   BITTEN BY THE FLYING BUG   16

Chapter 4:   MACHINE GUNS AND MERCENARIES   24

Chapter 5:   DOUBLE-CROSS   36

Chapter 6:   A FAMOUS CHICAGO GANGSTER   50

Chapter 7:   HIRED PILOTS: PART I   60

Chapter 8:   COCKPIT TALES   64

Chapter 9:   HIRED PILOTS: PART II   69

Chapter 10: B-26 BRONCO-RIDING   73

Chapter 11: HIRED PILOTS: PART III   83

Chapter 12: JUAN BONILLA   103

Chapter 13: WHITHER THOU GOEST...   106

Chapter 14: OF TRANSPORTS AND TRAINERS   119

Chapter 15: NICA DAYS   125

Chapter 16: TICO TROUBLES   131

Chapter 17: A GIFT FOR THE GENERAL   138

Chapter 18: THROUGH THE FENCE   142

Chapter 19: TRAVELS WITH BILL   148

Chapter 20: A FOREIGN AFFAIR   174

Chapter 21: THIS NICARAGUAN LIFE   178

Chapter 22: JIMMY ANGEL'S GOLD   183

Chapter 23: THUNDERBOLT DOWN   187

Chapter 24: COUNSEL FROM THE COMMANDANT   189

Chapter 25 **An Evening with the Dusters**   198

Chapter 26 **Chila**   203

Chapter 27 **Martinez the Cab Driver**   210

Chapter 28 **Into the Mangrove Jungle**   214

Chapter 28 **Yankee Blues**   223

Chapter 30 **El Gato**   228

Chapter 31 **Wheels Up**   235

Epilogue   241

Acknowledgments   253

Index   255

About the Author   259

AUTHOR'S NOTE

This is a true story written almost fifty years after it happened. The memories of the people, the planes, the smells—they are all still vivid to me. Of course, the extensive documentation I kept—crash reports, newspapers, receipts and photographs—has been invaluable. I have identified all the major characters by their real names, but have changed the names of certain minor ones in order to avoid embarrassing them.

So I Bought an Air Force

Prologue

Fifty years ago, the American public was on edge. Fidel Castro's overthrow of the Batista dictatorship and establishment of a communist government in Cuba had brought the Soviet threat to the United States' southern doorstep. The 1961 Bay of Pigs fiasco was followed the next year by the Cuban Missile Crisis, intensifying Americans' fear of a nuclear attack. For almost two weeks in October of 1962, the country held its collective breath as President Kennedy and Russian Premier Khrushchev negotiated the removal of the Soviet warheads that were pointed at the U.S. mainland.

The U.S. had staked out a presence in Central America through alliances with various nations that were themselves nervous about the spread of communism and specifically the downfall of their own governments. A May 10, 1961 telegram from the U.S. State Department to "Certain Diplomatic Posts in the American Republics" tersely summarized the view of the Kennedy administration: "Castro-communism...can be expected [to] attempt [to] infiltrate and subvert established governments and to disrupt positive development programs. It is essential [to] build up defenses against this danger so Latin American countries can get on with development plans."*

Nicaragua was a staunch U.S. ally. The Somoza strongmen,

---

*Office of the Historian, U.S. Department of State, *Foreign Relations of the United States, 1961-1963,Volume XII American Republics*, ed. Edward C. Keefer, Harriet Dashiell Schwar, and William Taylor Fain (Washington D.C.: Government Printing Office, 1996). Document 75. http://history.state.gov/historicaldocuments/frus1961-63v12/d75.

Anastasio Somoza Debayle, the head of the Nicaraguan armed forces, and his brother, Luis, the president of Nicaragua, received military equipment, training, and aid for their country from the U.S. military and the CIA. In exchange, the Somozas supported U.S. activity in the region, including allowing the U.S. to launch its B-26s for the Bay of Pigs invasion out of an airfield in Puerto Cabezas on Nicaragua's northeastern coast.

The embrace of the Somoza dictatorship posed a potentially tricky diplomatic issue for the U.S. State Department, which worried about a public relations disaster at the United Nations as well as the Organization of American States. The Somozas could, however, be counted on as fiercely anti-Castro partners in the fight against communism, and the CIA dismissed the State Department's concerns.*

Kennedy is quoted in a September 10, 1962 State Department telegram: "It continues to be the policy of the United States that the Castro regime will not be allowed to export its aggressive purposes by force or the threat of force. It will be prevented by whatever means may be necessary from taking action against any part of the Western Hemisphere."† Six months later, my story begins.

---

* Jack B. Pfeiffer, *Official History of the Bay of Pigs Operation, Volume II, Participation in the Conduct of Foreign Policy*, October 1979, p.100. http://www.foia.cia.gov/bay-of-pigs/bop-vol2-part1.pdf.
† Office of the Historian, U.S. Department of State, *Foreign Relations of the United States, 1961-1963,Volume XII American Republics*, Document 99. http://history.state.gov/historicaldocuments/frus1961-63v12/d99.

Chapter 1

CRASH

The silence was eerie. The giant propeller spun noiselessly in front of the dead engine. A chill spread over me even as the fierce tropical sun beat down through the Mustang's canopy. A mile and a half below in the Gulf of Fonseca, two freighters plowed through the dark blue water. I felt strangely calm as the plane began to lose altitude, the air whistling past the fuselage. Reaching down with my left hand, I pulled back on the release levers and jettisoned the heavy drop tanks. The plane buoyed up as the half ton of fuel hurtled toward the deep water below. I quickly put the prop in high pitch to minimize drag and trimmed the plane for its optimal glide speed.

I cut the switches and pulled the mixture control to off. From my altitude I could see for miles, and the gulf was empty except for the freighters. I had to make a fast decision—ditch or try for land? The Nicaraguan shore looked to be about twenty miles away. If I were going to ditch, those cargo ships would be my only chance for a rescue. If I rode the plane down, I'd have to have enough momentum to make a pass over the bridge of one of them to make sure the crew saw me. Even so, I knew the plane's underbelly air scoop would suck in water the instant it hit—the manuals warn the Mustang sinks in 1 1/2 to 2 seconds. I didn't have any flotation gear. Could I get my high-top boots off before they filled with water? Probably not. *Shit.* I would try for land.

As the dark green mass of the Nicaraguan mainland loomed in the distance, I could make out a narrow piece of shoreline that looked flat; hitting any sort of ridge on landing could flip the plane. I knew pilots back home who'd put planes down on the shores of Lake Michigan. But they were coming in at 45 miles per hour with aircraft a fraction of the Mustang's weight. I tugged on my harness straps, pulling them as tight as they would go and put my sunglasses in my pocket. *What an expert I'm becoming on crashing,* I thought wryly.

White-capped waves were breaking on the beach. I was now maybe two hundred feet above the water, the plane sinking steadily. The rapidly approaching shore looked smooth as far as I could see. I slid back the canopy; the roar of the rushing air deafened me. I skimmed along at a hundred miles an hour just barely above the white sand. Not knowing if my harness would snap, I covered the gun sight mount with my left hand to protect my face, and then taking a deep breath, I gently eased the plane down.

The prop hit with a muffled thud. I wrenched the stick forward and felt the first deceleration, the Mustang's nose pitching down violently. A searing pain flashed along my spine, and my head snapped forward with a hard jolt. The plane slid in at the water's edge, skipped once, and then plowed two hundred feet down the beach, a torrent of sand, pebbles, and sticks flying up through the air on either side of the fuselage. The plane began to slow, grating against the sand, and finally came to a stop in about eight inches of water.

* * * * *

"Court rules for the defendant." Bang! The judge's gavel came down. The lawyers for the other side exchanged slight smiles and began gathering up their papers. My brothers and I sat frozen. Mel, our attorney and a college friend, looked ashen. His shoulders slumped in his rumpled blue suit as he shoved papers in his worn leather brief bag.

"Shouldn't have fucked with the big boys, sonny," sneered our former supplier as he passed in front of our table. I watched as he and his high-priced New York lawyers walked together out of the courtroom, the footsteps of their custom shoes clicking on the wooden floor.

There was a loud buzzing in my ears. I heard the court recorder say something to the judge through a din of white noise. The courtroom emptied out quickly, everyone evidently moving on to the rest of the day, as if nothing had happened. My younger brother Glenn sat motionless. My older brother Gene picked up his coat and hat. "Nice going, Will." The sarcasm was biting. "Damn bastards," he muttered as he walked out.

I was a 34-year-old Chicagoan. My brothers and I had owned the largest specialty vehicle dealership in the U.S., selling ambulances, school buses and funeral cars. We'd also set up the first leasing company in the business and our large body shop provided custom modifications for buyers. I was president of the company. Gene was in charge of sales, and our kid brother Glenn did some of everything. We had an excellent reputation and our buyers were loyal. We'd built the company from the ground up, and I was very proud of the business. Even my wife's father, the wealthy owner of a national truck line, gave me grudging respect.

The previous year we'd landed an enormous sale, but because of a bone-headed mistake in our leasing contract, we'd exposed ourselves financially; I hadn't been smart enough to set up holding companies that would have shielded one part of the business from another's liabilities. Our manufacturer, wanting in on the lucrative leasing portion of the business, seized on the contract omission and exploited it. If we didn't play ball, he'd give the franchise to another group. I consulted my college friend Mel, and he assured me we had a solid legal case. He was wrong.

We had to liquidate the company. I was devastated. I'd let down my younger brother Glenn; he and his wife had a new baby and a two-year-old. Gene, my bachelor older brother, announced he was going out on his own and moved to New York. What to do now? I was bitter and disillusioned.

It was early 1963. My wife Pat and I had been enjoying suburban living with our two young daughters outside of Chicago on a couple of wooded acres in a beautiful home. My life had turned out better than I'd ever dreamed possible, at least until the lawsuit.

I'd grown up on Chicago's South Side in a working-class neighborhood in a small two-story frame house with my parents and older brothers Gene and Norm. When I was eight, my brother Glenn was born. During the winters there were two more people, as my mother's parents would come down from their farm in northern Wisconsin to live with us in order to escape the bitterly cold weather up there. Our house would later be torn down when the Dan Ryan Expressway was built.

Like my mother, Dad had also grown up on a Wisconsin farm. He was the third of eleven children. His father, a tall, powerfully built German, had a blacksmith shop on his farm and did smithing for the whole area. When Dad was a teenager, he and my grandfather would go into the woods during the winter and repair chains and harnesses for the loggers and put ice shoes on the big draft horses. During the harvest season, Dad operated the steam engine on the thresher; working with machinery was the only part of farming that interested him.

Drafted in the First World War, Dad came to Chicago for basic training and got to know the city. The war ended before he was shipped overseas, and he headed back reluctantly to the farm. After marrying my mother, however, he moved with her to Chicago. A skilled mechanic, Dad found work with the White Motor Company, eventually rising to the position of shop superintendent.

One day a position opened up at the White Motor Company that would have been a promotion for my dad, but he was told he wouldn't be considered for it because he didn't have a college degree. Dad quit and within a year bought a garage and went into business for himself. I was eleven at the time and thought it was thrilling to have all those cars around. I learned to drive that year, and when I was fourteen, bought my first car, a 1931 Model A Ford. I used a duplicate of my older brother Gene's license until I could legally drive.

Dad's garage was at 55th and Ingleside in Hyde Park and he offered mechanical repair work to his customers as well as car storage.

He was an honest businessman and had a strong sense of patriotism. During World War II, no passenger cars were made for the civilian market, and replacement parts were almost impossible to get. When a customer's car was towed in one day with a broken clutch linkage, my dad took off the broken piece, and using it as a pattern, fabricated a new one. To the customer's astonishment, the bill was only two dollars; my father believed it was unethical to raise prices during wartime. He had tried to re-enlist, but the military turned him down due to his age.

Ours was very much a patriarchal household. Dad often spoke German with our mother, but not with us, and we had no interest in learning it. On Sundays, attendance at the Methodist church with our mother was mandatory; Dad worked seven days a week.

The neighborhood schoolyard was a rough and tumble place. My elementary school classmates were a cross section of Chicago South Side ethnicities: mostly white–Germans, Swedes, Irish, Italians–with a handful of African American kids mixed in. I got into a lot of fistfights and was sent home regularly, usually with a note to bring a parent in for a meeting with the principal. I was double-promoted twice, probably because I'd outgrown the lower grade desk.

Although we didn't have a phonograph, there was a lot of music in our house. Mother played the piano and organ, and my brothers and I had all learned to play instruments as kids. Mother taught me to play the piano. She insisted I perform for guests and at church functions, which I hated, and one day I just quit playing.

It was when I discovered boogie-woogie that I headed back to the piano. Boogie-woogie, a style of piano blues with repeated bass patterns in the left hand and a strong beat, was a lot more fun to play than Methodist hymns. From boogie-woogie, I moved on to the jazz standards. I found girls liked piano players and I began to have a lot of fun with music.

When I was in seventh grade, I joined my two older brothers working for my dad at the garage. We ranged in height from six foot two to six foot four inches. Perhaps due to our size, our father seemed to lose track of our ages, and we were expected to do a man's work while still kids. There wasn't good ventilation in the garage, and the heavy carbon monoxide would build up, especially in the winter when the big doors were closed. When we got dizzy, we would be sat down outside and handed a ginger ale to drink on the theory it would make us burp out the carbon monoxide. It never occurred to us to complain; Dad worked as hard or harder than we did.

By the time I entered high school, the war had created a manpower shortage, so I was now working every other night straight through until morning. After a quick breakfast following a night shift, I would go to high school and then sleep that night before repeating the cycle. My grades dropped as I had trouble staying awake in class. But it wasn't until I fell asleep at the wheel and wrecked a customer's '41 Plymouth that my mother intervened and that particular work schedule was rethought.

I attended an all-male public high school. Tilden Tech had about four thousand boys and was known for its champion football and wrestling teams. With my work at the garage curtailed, I started wrestling. Our coach, Bob Hicks, was famous for producing tough competitors, and I was on several all-city and state championship teams. When it came time for college, the entire Tilden team was offered Big Ten scholarships, but by then my right knee was shot so I couldn't accept. I began taking courses at Wilson Junior College.

My junior year I transferred to Northwestern University. I lived at home and took classes at the downtown Chicago campus, paying my tuition by grading accounting papers at night. I naively assumed Northwestern would accept my junior college credits toward my accounting major. When Northwestern refused, with a semester to go, I transferred and finished up at less expensive Bradley University.

After college, I knew I didn't want to work as an accountant. My brother Gene and I decided to start our own company, and because we knew about cars, we started the specialty vehicle business. We worked hard but we made money, and life was suddenly very good. Glenn was still in school when we launched the business, but joined us later.

Through a college friend, I got into sailboat racing on Lake Michigan. I was tall, lean, and had long arms, so I found myself welcomed on to big sailboats as crew. I liked both the competition and the camaraderie. I joined the Chicago Yacht Club because it bothered me I could never pay for a round of drinks at the bar there—you had to be a member to run a tab.

It was November of 1956, and the club was holding its annual end-of-sailing-season awards dinner. I had been crewing on one of the larger racing boats that year. It was an elegant party with an orchestra. About midnight the musicians finished playing and began packing up their instruments. The guests stood around on the dance floor, the sound of tinkling ice cubes mingling with laughter. I looked for my date, and saw her talking to someone across the room. Sitting down at the piano, I started to play some Gershwin. A tall good-looking blonde slid over next to me on the piano bench. Wow, was she ever lovely.

"Hello, I'm Pat Daggett," she said with a smile. "I like your piano-playing."

"I'm glad you do. Who are you with?" I asked.

"He's over there." She gestured lightly with her head toward a group by the staircase. She didn't seem too concerned about him.

Barney, the club's longtime bartender, gave me a sly wink when I walked up to the bar to order drinks. "She's a looker, that one," he commented as he slid the glasses toward me. I smiled and picked up the two scotches.

Pat had been brought up with the rule you left with the guy who brought you, but I made sure I got her phone number before she did. Six weeks later, at Christmastime in front of the fireplace at the Yacht Club, I asked Pat to marry me.

When she said yes, suddenly the entire club seemed to know, and glass after glass of champagne arrived at our table with best wishes from members. I drove Pat home, and afterward as I was headed back down Lake Shore Drive, flashing blue lights appeared in my rear view mirror. "You in a hurry?" asked the Chicago cop as I rolled down my window.

I pulled out my wallet. "Take whatever you want," I said, handing it to him with a grin. "I just got engaged!"

The cop shook his head, helped himself to some bills, and handed back my wallet. "Go on home and go to bed, son," he said gruffly. "And hey, take it easy on the speed."

Pat and I were married the following summer. Two years later, we had our first child and moved to a lovely suburb surrounded by forest preserve and farm fields. Our new house, a redwood contemporary on a couple acres, was designed by a well-known Chicago architect and had been written up in the *Chicago Tribune*. The huge living room windows looked out onto a vast expanse of green and in the spring, two thousand daffodils bloomed in a clearing among the giant red oaks. A big brown barn with a post-and-rail corral stood on the lower part of the property near the road. I bought a dark bay mare, Ginger, and would go riding early in the morning in the forest preserve with Sam, the small black and white rescue dog Pat and I had adopted.

A second daughter came along. Pat was a stay-at-home mom and active in local charities. Neighbors would drop in, and no one locked their doors. On warm summer nights after the girls had been put to bed, Pat and I would sit together on the back porch, with just an oil lamp for light, holding hands and talking quietly about the day.

By now I had my pilot's license. Pat and I had spent part of our honeymoon looking at planes and had bought a single-engine Navion before we bought the house. With my sleek, solid Navion, I now loved flying. I loved the sensation of flight at the moment when the Navion lifted off and we were airborne. I enjoyed the little challenges—a perfectly balanced turn, holding a steady heading in rough air—and I took satisfaction in a good approach, a neat landing. I would fly Pat and the girls up to Minnesota to visit my in-laws and marvel every trip at the hundreds of beautiful northern lakes that I could see for miles at altitude. When I traded my Navion for a twin-engine Apache, Pat and I took it on many trips around the country and went island hopping in the Caribbean with her brother Marvin and his wife Bette. It didn't seem life could get much better.

Overnight, the lawsuit changed all that. With the court judgment, our perfect existence was shattered. I was damn near broke. Devastated by the loss of my company and with a dwindling bank account, I tried to figure out what to do next.

Chapter 2

PLANES FOR SALE

It was early March of 1963. I was looking through an issue of *Trade-A-Plane*, an aircraft-for-sale newsletter, when I noticed a small ad. It announced the Nicaraguan government was closing out its fleet of P-51 Mustangs and P-47 Thunderbolts. I paused. These were World War II-era fighter planes, but I could resell the planes in the U.S. if the price were right.

I called upstairs to Pat. "Do you know where Nicaragua is?"

"Someplace in Latin America, I think," she answered, "Why?"

As Pat came down the stairs, I marveled again at my good fortune in marrying her. She had been supportive through the break-up of our company and was now doing her best to keep an open mind as I struggled to find a new business. We had been married almost six years.

I gave Pat a quick rundown on the *Trade-A-Plane* ad. She knew I wanted to make a fresh start. "It might be worth looking into," she said, trying not to sound dubious.

I sent a letter of inquiry. A few weeks later, a brief airmail note arrived from a Sumner B. Morgan, stating that the Nicaraguan Air Force, the *Fuerza Aérea de Nicaragua,* or FAN, was selling all its piston-engine planes because the U.S. military was sending Nicaragua jets.

"The greater majority of these aircraft are in active service and ready to go and would need only a day or two for the removal of armaments and the paperwork necessary for a ferry flight north. General condition is very good." I wrote back for more information.

Shortly thereafter, I received a phone call. The line crackled with static. "This is Sumner Morgan. I'm calling for Will Martin," announced a crusty voice. He was calling on a radiophone, so one person would talk, wait, and then the other person would talk. If both talked at once, it wouldn't work.

"This is Will Martin. I'm interested in your planes. Can you tell me more about them?"

"Not over the phone. You have to come down here to talk to me," replied Morgan abruptly. "Let me know when and I'll meet you." There was a click and the line went dead.

I talked to my brother Glenn. He was by nature more cautious than I was. More sensible, I think he would have said. "Will, this seems like an awfully long way to go. What do we know about Nicaragua? Where are we going to get the money?"

"We don't need a lot of money to start and we've still got a little cash in the bank. I'm going to set it up so we just buy one or two planes that we can sell up here. We take the profits and buy more planes. We can do this. This guy Morgan said the planes are in good shape." Glenn eventually agreed we should at least find out more.

My total knowledge of Nicaragua came from the song, "Managua, Nicaragua" ("…what a wonderful spot / There's coffee and bananas and a temperature hot"). But I dug out my passport, made a reservation on Pan Am, and called my bank. An officer there spoke reassuringly, "I was in Nicaragua last year and American dollars are accepted everywhere. Lots of people speak English. You won't have any problem." I was relieved since I didn't speak Spanish.

I called to give Morgan my arrival time. "I'm six four with a brown crew cut," I advised him.

Morgan grunted and said he'd be there.

"I'll just go down and look the situation over. I'll probably be back by Saturday," I assured Pat. "And Glenn will be here if you need anything." My brother and his wife Bobbe lived a few miles from us.

A few days later I was on my way to Central America. "Coffee, Mr. Martin?" inquired the pretty Pan Am stewardess cheerfully as the DC-7 leveled off at altitude.

"No thanks."

"Can I get you anything else?" she persisted.

"How 'bout a scotch on the rocks."

"Coming right up!" She returned a few minutes later with a glass. "Going to Nicaragua for business or pleasure, Mr. Martin?" she asked, leaning close to my face as she set down the drink.

I looked at her and smiled. "I'm going down to buy an air force."

Chapter 3

Bitten by the Flying Bug

I was about fourteen and out joyriding in my dad's new Packard with my brother Norm when I spotted a sign: HOWELL AIRPORT– AIRPLANE RIDES–$5. We pulled in the gravel parking lot and I strode up, trying to look manly. I announced I wanted a ride.

Willy Howell, the heavy-set owner behind the counter, said gruffly, "Five dollars, pay in advance." I reached in my pants to pull out five of the six dollars burning a hole in my pocket. Willy waved at a guy working on an engine. "Charlie, take this lad up for a ride."

"Okay, Willy," Charlie answered, wiping grease off his hands with an equally greasy rag. I had read all the *G-8 and His Battle Aces* books and was disappointed he didn't look like a real aviator with a scarf and goggles. We walked over to one of the planes. "Get in," he said, pointing to the front seat. I hesitated, and he explained, "I fly this from the rear seat." As I climbed in, I thought the plane looked awfully flimsy close up.

Mr. Howell came over and hollered, "Switch off!"

Charlie confirmed, "Switch off!"

Mr. Howell swung the prop through a couple times and shouted back, "Switch on!"

Charlie yelled, "Contact!" and Mr. Howell swung the little prop through several more times until the engine started with a loud rumble. This was my first introduction to engines without mufflers. The little plane shook like a dog shedding water. With cars, a heavy vibration meant trouble. I was beginning to doubt the wisdom of this whole idea.

We bounced along to the end of the runway where Charlie paused to fiddle with the controls. "Ready?" he yelled.

"Ready," I shouted back nervously. The little plane swerved from side to side as it rolled down the runway and finally lifted off the ground. We flew slowly over a golf course, and I could see a golfer tee off. We were still over the course when the golfer walked up to take his second shot. After flying around a few minutes at about 1,000 feet, we landed, bouncing back to the line of planes.

"Howd'ya like it?" Charlie asked as he helped me unbuckle my seat belt.

"I like motorcycles better," I said bluntly as I climbed out of the cockpit. Charlie turned his back and walked away. Obviously I wasn't a prospect for flying lessons.

Years later, I tried flying again. I took a few lessons in a trainer plane, but my size 14 feet kept slipping off the small pedals, and the plane didn't feel very solid. It wasn't until I spotted a Navion for sale at an airport on my honeymoon that I got excited. All shiny silver metal with a huge canopy that slid back like a WWII fighter—the Navion was a *real* airplane.

The rationalization to justify the expense came quickly. The factory supplying the vehicles for our business was located in a small town in Ohio, far from easy commercial transportation. If customers could be flown to the airstrip near the factory, however, they could pick up their vehicle and drive back to Chicago in the same day. The solution seemed clear: all I had to do was learn to fly and buy an airplane. Instead, I bought the airplane and then learned to fly.

That Navion became my first plane. Since I didn't have my license, a pilot friend delivered my new possession to the small field where I planned to base it. Rubinkam Airport maintained a short southwest gravel runway and a shorter grass strip straight south. A group of airport bums hung around the modest office lounge, critiquing every takeoff and landing, though they never actually flew themselves that I saw. An excellent Navion mechanic worked on the field, and Al Zumallen, the tall, reserved airport operator, gave flying lessons. His chatterbox wife and mother-in-law ran the office and could be depended on to offer their opinions about everyone and everything.

When I told Al that I wanted to get my license, he started to explain he had several aircraft and instructors available. I interrupted politely. "I'd like to learn to fly in my own plane."

Al rubbed his chin. "That'd be pretty unusual. A plane as complicated as a Navion is usually reserved for pilots with several hundred hours." I explained I had experienced a lot of trouble with smaller planes. After more conversation, he gave up and agreed to instruct me in my own plane himself.

As Al and I walked over to the plane for my first lesson, I started to climb up on the wing to get in. "Wait a minute, Will. We have some things to do first," said Al. I got back down. He stuck his head in the cockpit. "Run your hands down the edges of the prop to feel for nicks," he called out. "By the way, I just checked to make sure the magneto switch was in the off position—wouldn't want the prop to catch you by surprise," he explained. I told him the prop felt fine. "Good," said Al, "A nick in the prop can lead to a crack and calamity."

He then opened the left engine cowling and pointed: "Look for leaks—hydraulic, gas, oil. Make sure nothing is loose." I peered in. The oil level was fine, so we closed the cowl. Next we walked over to the left wing to check the aileron and flap movement, then to the tail assembly for the rudder and elevators. We repeated the checks on the right wing and right engine cowling.

Al knelt down and opened the gas drain to check for contamination. While we were bending down, he told me to always check the wheels, struts, and tires. "Look in the gas tank and see if you have gas," he said. I thought he was kidding. He wasn't.

Inside the plane, the cockpit check was straightforward: all switches in the proper position, gas selector on correct tank, throttle set one and a half inches forward, prop control and mixture control full forward. We ran the flight controls through full movement to make sure no gust locks had been left on. The last thing we did was to look out in front of the plane and holler, "Clear!" I hit the starter switch, and after the prop turned a few times, I flipped on the magneto switch and the engine caught. All of this took about twenty-five minutes and every time we flew, we did the same thing. I got the message.

The four-place Navion, with its variable pitch propeller, big 205-horsepower engine, and retractable wheels and flaps, was considered sophisticated for a novice pilot. The full instrument panel had a turn-and-bank indicator, artificial horizon, and directional gyro. With the then state-of-the-art radios, a Narco four-channel Super Homer VHF transmitter and Omni indicator, along with a surplus ADF and left/right indicator, it was a hot airplane for a beginner to fly.

I began lessons with Al and another instructor at Rubinkam, Bruce Raymond. Whether it was Bruce or Al in the co-pilot's seat, they would always appear very relaxed, first talking through, and sometimes demonstrating, the procedure they wanted me to do. Smooth movement of controls was emphasized and I would try to copy the instructor as best I could. In between lessons, I studied for the written flight exam, reading about weather patterns, navigation, traffic rules, flight control mechanics, and so forth. Although I easily passed the written flight test, I decided to take ground school because there had been things I didn't know on the exam.

The Navion, as it turned out, was a good plane to learn in. It was a little heavier, and gusts of wind didn't buffet it like they did the very light fabric-covered planes I'd tried earlier. The cockpit was comfortable, and although it had more systems, like the retractable gear and so forth, none were a big deal as the panel setup was very logical. I read everything I could about Navions, and I soloed after seven hours of instruction.

After logging forty hours, the minimum required to take the flight test for a license, I met with the FAA examiner, a gray-haired, no-nonsense sort of man. "Set a course for Minneapolis," he ordered as soon as we were airborne. I hastily laid out the heading and checked the navigational landmarks along the route. After a few minutes, he began calling out new headings: "head due south…now east…now west… now north." We did some slow flights and stalls. Then he announced, "Back to the airport." We landed. "Give me your paperwork," the examiner said curtly and disappeared into the airfield office. Had I passed or not?

When the FAA examiner reappeared, he shook my hand, mumbled a gruff "Congratulations," and signed my logbook. At that moment, Glenn drove up with Pat. I nodded, and they started loading suitcases in the baggage compartment of the Navion. The examiner looked shocked. "What are you doing?"

"We're going up to Minnesota to spend Christmas with my wife's parents."

"But…but…you just got your license," he stammered.

"Is something wrong? Am I legal to fly or not?"

"Yes but…." He shrugged and threw up his hands.

Within weeks, I was flying customers to the factory in Ohio and back the same day. After returning late one afternoon, I was tying the plane down on the tarmac when three of the airport whiz-bangs strolled up. None of them offered to help, but just stood around watching me.

"Say Will," one of them announced, "I hear Navions are a hydraulic nightmare." When I ignored him, he leaned on the plane and continued, "Say Will, what would you do if you lost hydraulic pressure and the wheels didn't come down?"

I didn't bother explaining that the wheels would still drop, since the landing gear is forced down by large springs when activated. Without looking up from my work, I replied, "I'd use the radio."

"Why?"

"To tell whoever was around to call my brother."

"What good would that do?" His companions furrowed their brows.

I yanked the last knot tight and came up out from under the wing. "I'd tell him to insure the airplane," I said and walked away.

None of the students used aircraft radios at Rubinkam. In fact, the training planes didn't even have them, because the current wisdom held it was too dangerous for inexperienced pilots to fly into controlled airports. Flying between Rubinkam and the uncontrolled field near the Ohio factory, I never needed to call a tower so it didn't matter.

I usually left the factory in Ohio early enough to arrive home well before nightfall. But one afternoon I was delayed. It was fall and as I was flying back, it got dark a little earlier than I expected. In the twilight, Rubinkam Airport was difficult to find. It was soon pitch-black and my familiar landmarks had melted away in the darkness. Finally, to my great relief, I spotted the yellow light outside the Rubinkam office. But the runway lights weren't on. Where was the runway? I buzzed the field and cycled the prop, hoping the noise would rouse someone to turn on the lights. No luck.

There was now a hard knot in the middle of my stomach. My hands were so sweaty they were slipping on the controls, and I kept wiping them on my slacks. I realized I wasn't going to be able to find the narrow runway in the dark. I could see in the distance the stream of planes with their blinking lights heading into Midway Airport, at the time the world's busiest. I tuned in the radio and fortunately, 118.7, Midway's very high frequency channel, was one of my four pre-sets.

The tower operators sounded like tobacco auctioneers. An incoming flight radioed, "United-2423-landing-Midway-Lake-Calumet." Lake Calumet was apparently the reporting point, since it was a big dark spot surrounded by city lights and easy to find. After a rapid exchange with five or six other planes, the tower operator briskly directed the United flight, "23-follow-DC-4-on-final-31-right."

The United captain answered "23." There evidently wasn't time to give all four numbers. I realized if you weren't sharp, you might miss your call sign and have to wait for the controller to work you back into the stream of numbers.

I saw the lights of a big transport ahead of me and after its pilot identified himself as over Lake Calumet, I took a deep breath and jumped in: "Navion-4187-Kilo-landing-Midway-Lake Calumet."

The controller fired back, "87-Kilo-follow-the-DC-3-number-four-to-land-keep-your-speed-up."

Wow! I was with the big guys! I didn't slow up until I was about a city block out, then pulled up the nose, closed the throttle, dropped the wheels, lowered full flap, and dove for the runway. It was a good landing and since it was clear everyone got the hell off the runway as fast as possible, I turned on to the first taxiway to a fixed base operator.

I never went back to Rubinkam. Midway Airport had the best tower operators in the world. After a few months, they knew my number and always squeezed me in. I was proud to tell people my plane was based there.

Several years later, a P-51D Mustang, one of the most famous fighters of World War II, landed at Midway. I had just put away my Apache. I stood mesmerized as the sleek, powerful machine taxied by. Fast and highly maneuverable, the Mustang had served as a combat aircraft over Europe and Japan. The "D" model, with its clear bubble canopy and advanced armaments, was the most widely produced version. Built by North American Aviation, the P-51D had arrived in Europe in the spring of 1944. It had quickly proved a ferocious combatant against the German Luftwaffe, shooting down almost five thousand enemy planes by the war's end. I had seen pictures of Mustangs in the newspaper as a kid. And now there was one right at Midway. I hesitated and then walked across the tarmac toward the parked warbird.

The pilot was standing next to the plane, talking to the owner of the radio repair shop. I stepped forward and introduced myself. The pilot's name was Bob Gore. "I've read a lot about Mustangs, but have never had a chance to get up close to one," I explained, eyeing the big prop next to me. "Would you mind if I took a look in the cockpit?"

"Sure. Go on up!" invited Gore. He was a friendly guy and proud of the plane. He showed me the handholds to get onto the wing, and he followed me up. We leaned over the side of the cockpit and he pointed out the various trim wheels and the landing gear handle. I was surprised how tiny the cockpit was. I could see there hadn't been any fat combat pilots flying this thing!

The Mustang was designed to be single-place, but Gore had removed the auxiliary gas tank behind the pilot's seat to make room for a small second seat. "Would you like to go for a hop?" he asked after a few more minutes of chatting.

Moments later I was dropping into the narrow second seat. I pulled the metal and canvas shoulder straps and seatbelt tight and

Gore handed me a headset. There was an intercom, so we were able to talk to each other. The smell of the warm metal and fuel wafted up as Gore shouted, "Clear prop!" He gave me a thumbs-up as the canopy slid forward and closed over us with a click. The engine coughed a puff of blue-gray smoke, sputtered, and suddenly all twelve cylinders caught with a deep-throated rumble. I was glad for the headset.

The radio shop owner's pants legs were flapping from the prop blast as the plane swung around. Covering his eyes with his left forearm, he waved and went back in his shop. The pilot taxied to the edge of the runway, paused, and held the brakes to do his engine run-up check. My chest cavity vibrated as the enormous engine roared angrily and then subsided. Gore slowly turned the plane on to the runway.

The Mustang started its rollout, picking up speed as it tracked down the runway, airport buildings blurring. The uptilted nose leveled off and with a whining roar, the plane tore into the sky. We skimmed the Indiana beaches going a breathtaking six miles a minute. The pilot pulled up sharply, creating a G-load that pinned me in my seat and pulled my eyeballs toward the floorboards. Then he dropped the plane through a smooth arc, sending my stomach soaring into space. Finally he rolled the Mustang and I suddenly saw blue sky below me and green earth above me. He completed the aileron roll, bringing the sky and earth back to their proper places and before I knew it, we were touching down again at Midway. Back at the hangar, I thanked Gore profusely and walked away on wobbly legs, wishing very much that I had a Mustang.

Now, three years later, I was headed thousands of miles from home to purchase a small squadron of these magnificent fighters. I looked out the window at the Gulf of Mexico's bright blue water and lost myself in thought as the plane flew toward Nicaragua.

Chapter 4

MACHINE GUNS AND MERCENARIES

It was early afternoon when the airliner touched down at Las Mercedes Airport. I stepped through the cabin door and reached for my sunglasses as the hot white sunlight hit my face. The other passengers and I carefully made our way down the metal stairs and across the tarmac to the airport terminal, a flat-roofed brick and stucco building. There was a strong smell of gasoline in the hot, heavy air.

The temperature inside the terminal simmered at more than 100 degrees, and my long-sleeved shirt clung to my back. Everyone appeared to be at least a foot shorter than I was. I felt conspicuous and uncomfortable. The immigration and customs officials wore military uniforms and carried large, serious-looking sidearms. No one stared directly at me, but instead cast furtive glances my direction.

A tall, lean man with thinning hair and a deeply lined face strode up and asked gruffly, "Martin?" He didn't introduce himself, but it had to be Sumner Morgan, the man who had placed the ad in the *Trade-a-Plane* publication. He looked to be in his sixties. He wore a long white cotton shirt hanging out over dark trousers. It looked comfortable and cool.

Morgan took me roughly by the arm and propelled me to the head of the line where he spoke in rapid Spanish to a short, dark, and very tough-looking fellow who turned out to be Captain Garcia, Chief of Immigration. Captain Garcia didn't say a word, but stared hard at me with unsmiling eyes. Then he grunted to an aide who stamped my passport and passed my luggage through quickly.

We climbed into Morgan's gray 1948 Buick and drove into Managua, the capital. The paved streets had many speed bumps. I saw only older model cars and trucks. Beat-up yellow school buses converted for public transportation and the occasional horse and rider shared the road as well. Ads for big international companies such as Kodak, Shell Oil, Esso and American Express dominated the billboards. Most of the buildings we were passing had walls covered with pastel-colored stucco topped with red clay tile roofs. Few were more than two stories tall. Tangles of electrical and telephone wires crisscrossed above the intersections. Morgan suggested I stay at the Gran Hotel, the best in town.

"Where do you stay?" I asked.

"Estrella—it's a native hotel."

"I'd like to stay there," I said quickly.

A few minutes later, Morgan maneuvered the car into a tight, fenced-in area next to a modest-looking hotel, a real chore without power steering. "Best not to leave a car on the street," he explained.

A U.S. expat and a bachelor, Morgan spoke only when asked a direct question and then he dispensed his words sparingly. His impassive expression never changed much. He addressed me as "Bub," which I didn't like. He said that as a civilian, he worked as the head mechanic for the Nicaraguan Air Force's fleet of Cessnas. Morgan let me know that during WWII he had test-flown and ferried P-47s around the U.S., logging a lot of flying time and seaplane hours as well. This was his way of signaling he had serious flying experience and wasn't just a mechanic.

The Estrella Hotel's exterior had pale green, pink, and blue walls; a row of wire stars decorated the roofline. The hotel didn't have a solid front door. Instead, we passed through the open-air metal security gates with their ornamental grids of aluminum curlicues and starbursts and into an inner courtyard.

At the front desk, no one spoke English. Morgan translated for me and the clerk handed me a room key. "Don't expect any water in the shower until night, Bub," Morgan warned. "And then it'll be cold. But that's ok," he assured me, "'cause it's always hot here." I couldn't tell if he was joking. By way of invitation he added, "See you in the dining room about six."

My room had a narrow bed with a thin mattress, rough cotton sheets, a dresser with a cracked mirror, and a single forlorn chair. The sink in the small bathroom contained globs of the previous guest's shaving cream. It was clear that the management didn't take cleanliness too seriously, but since I planned to stay only a day or so, it suited me. I put down my bag and stretched out on the bed, trying to get comfortable.

Downstairs at dinnertime, the restaurant's wooden tables were covered with oilcloths anchored by catsup bottles. There was no menu since everyone was served the Special of the Day. The food looked to be a mixture of black beans, rice, and mystery meat that tasted surprisingly good. I was hungry.

Morgan and I ate in silence. I heard high-pitched laughter, and looking up, saw a couple of the waiters giggling together by the kitchen door. I looked at Morgan questioningly. He shrugged. "They are what you think they are. Here in Nicaragua, labor law says the management has to pay maternity benefits, so the hotel figures they can avoid the expense by hiring these guys."

After dinner I told Morgan I was going to sit in the hotel's inner patio awhile. The night in Nicaragua was cool and beautiful, and the sky was clear and filled with stars brighter than I had ever seen. Pat and my life back home were very far away. What had I gotten myself into? I didn't know the language, I didn't know the culture. What had I been thinking? I was exhausted and went up to bed.

The next morning Morgan drove me out to the airport. Three airlines—Lanica, which was owned by General Anastasio Somoza Debayle, the head of the Nicaraguan military; TACA, an El Salvadoran line; and Pan Am—all shared the airport with the Nicaraguan Air Force, which everyone referred to by its Spanish name initials, FAN. There were several large steel hangars with dark pink roofs and a few low buildings for air force offices. An officers' club with an outdoor pool stood separately. As we passed through the gate at the restricted military end of the field, I noticed machine gun placements sunk into the ground on the far side.

Morgan stopped at the security checkpoint where a young guard was leaning on a Browning automatic rifle almost as tall as he was. He knew Morgan but came around to my side to peer in, pointing the gun straight at me as the car engine idled. The sight of this kid with such a powerful gun struck me as ridiculous, and I stifled a grin. The guard nodded curtly and turned away.

Morgan shifted gears and the car proceeded on to the base. Looking straight ahead, Morgan bawled me out, "Bub, lemme tell you something. You can be just as dead if you get shot by a greenhorn as by a professional soldier. Remember you're in their country, and the rules are different." I accepted the rebuke meekly.

We walked down the flight line. Scattered under the tropical sun were P-51 Mustangs, P-47 Thunderbolts, C-45s and a civilian twin-engine Aero Commander. The gleam had faded, but time could not diminish the classic beauty of these magnificent machines. Some looked as though they were ready to fly, and others sat in various stages of repair or disassembly, parked helter-skelter with parts scattered on the ground. I shook my head.

"Nicaraguans don't go to the parts room when they need a replacement. They just pull it off the nearest plane," Morgan explained, reading my mind.

"Why do those Cessnas have such huge tires?" I asked, pointing at several wrecked Cessnas languishing in one of the hangars.

"Down here, pilots will land, or try to land, on almost anything. Them's tail wheels from DC-3s, and they make it easier to land."

"Why are they selling these planes?" I asked.

"'Cause they keep killing themselves. Crashed five of them. Last week, a pilot took off, or started to, in a '47 and the damned fool pulled straight up, stalled, and crashed about half way down the runway. Wrecked the plane and killed himself." Morgan spat contemptuously.

After showing me around the field, Morgan took me in to meet the commandant of the Nicaraguan Air Force, Colonel Saavedra. After a quick introduction, Morgan disappeared. Francisco Saavedra was a handsome dark-haired man with a full face and a military flat-top cut. He looked to be in his mid-forties. He spoke very good English. Although Morgan had handled the initial contact, I quickly realized this was the guy making the decisions on the airplane sale.

The colonel explained the deal: "The FAN wants to sell all their P-51s and P-47s for cash. We will prepare the planes for the ferry flight, and you can pay for them as you take them," he said.

This was what I had hoped, since I would not have to commit a lot of money upfront. "I can work with that," I replied.

The colonel added, "We are also looking to buy some T-28s and B-26s from the United States. Do you have the capabilities to provide those aircraft?"

I nodded. "I'd like to look over your planes, but I am definitely interested." We shook hands.

Next to Saavedra's office was the U.S. Mission. The United States maintained a military presence at the field headed by Colonel Richard Mansfield. A major, two captains, and a number of NCOs reported to him. Colonel Mansfield was career Air Force, having won his spurs in World War II. He looked to be in his early fifties. "The mission's purpose," he explained, "is to advise the Nicaraguans."

The mission operated only one plane, a DC-3 polished to such a high gloss that it looked as though it were chrome-plated. The Americans apparently never flew with the Nicaraguans; I wondered just what they did do there and what they advised about.

I wandered through a large, dusty parts warehouse, opening drawers and poking around old engines. It was noon and blisteringly hot. I sat down on an engine crate, trying to make sense of the situation. Which were the planes for sale? What would it take to get them ready to ferry? Morgan's ad had said the planes could be ready to go "in a day or so," but that looked pretty optimistic.

I spent the next weeks climbing up and around the FAN's airplanes, asking questions and trying to figure out which planes were in fact airworthy. Other prospective buyers from the U.S. came and went, staying two or three days. Apparently they thought they were going to trade colored beads to the natives, because when they realized the terms of sale were U.S. dollars, FOB Managua, they took the next flight out. Once I figured out the primitive phone system, I called Glenn and asked him to check prices on engines and parts that might be needed to get these planes flying. Days and weeks dragged by.

On Sundays, the only day I wasn't at the field, Morgan and I would sometimes drive into the countryside. The roads were unpaved outside the city. Men swinging machetes cut tall grass alongside the road. The tropical climate with its rich volcanic ash made good farming, particularly for sugar cane, though farms, or *fincas*, were small. The hilly areas were used for grazing cattle. In the privacy of the car, Morgan relaxed and actually carried on a conversation.

"How come the telephone poles are made of concrete?" I asked. "There seems to be lots of timber around for poles."

Morgan smirked, "'Cause the Somoza family owns the concrete factory. And Lanica Airlines. And the Mercedes dealership. And the shipping lines. And a radio station and newspaper. And lotsa land. If you start a business, and it's a good one, pretty soon you find that a Somoza is your partner."

"But how did they get so much power?" I wondered.

Morgan swatted at a fly buzzing against the dashboard. "When the Marines left in the '30s, the U.S. put General Somoza, the old general that is, in charge, mostly 'cause he spoke English. He bought lots of German-owned land and businesses here for cheap during WWII. Now the family pretty much has a share in anything worth having. Old Tacho got himself shot at a party in '56, and his sons ended up running the country—Luis as president and his younger brother Tachito heading the military."

"And the U.S. went along with that?" I asked.

"Oh, they fussed a little, but pretty much they figure they need strong men in this part of the world to keep order," he said. Morgan showed thinly veiled contempt for North Americans and the U.S. government. "Tachito went to West Point; he and his family know how to get along with the U.S. military. All the Somozas hate Castro, and that's good enough for the U.S."

Morgan never did tell me how he ended up in Central America.

He had said that he moved airplanes around for Republic Aviation in the States during WWII, but didn't account for the gap between that time and the present. He did not drink, smoke, or have any social life that I could see. About the only personal reference he made was to his policy of never having sex the night before flying. "Weakens a man," he grunted. His hotel room was bare. As far as I knew, he never went back to the States for visits.

Morgan was silent the rest of the way into Managua.

By this time, Glenn had called all over the United States and Canada to get prices on T-28s and B-26s and cabled them to me. I put together a proposal for Colonel Saavedra: I would provide the parts not in their inventory necessary to make the Nicaraguan planes ferryable to the States, with the FAN supplying the labor. As a separate deal, I would sell them T-28s and B-26s. Saavedra smiled agreeably and promised to respond "mañana."

More time went by, with one day hotter than the one before. I had now been in Nicaragua about a month. I'd adopted the local dress of a long cotton *guayabera* shirt worn over khaki slacks, and I was deeply tanned. I was beginning to give up hope that I'd ever get an answer from Colonel Saavedra, much less a favorable one. A couple more days and I'd call it quits, I decided.

I was sitting outside a hangar the next day reviewing an inventory list when suddenly I felt dizzy and nauseated. Morgan happened by, took one look, and dragged me over to the only source of clean water on the field, a garden hose.

"Bub, you can't sit out in that sun without a hat," he scolded as he poured water over my head. "You got some sunstroke. I'll run you back to the hotel."

I was still shaky the next day but decided to go out to the field for just an hour or so. It was the only day I didn't shave.

I was checking out propellers in the parts room when a Nicaraguan sergeant came in and to my astonishment, saluted. "Come with me," he ordered.

Out on the tarmac, Colonel Saavedra and a pilot waited in a Cessna 180, engine running. I wedged myself in the rear seat beside the sergeant who was cradling a Browning automatic rifle. The FAN must have found a great price on them. Everyone seemed to have one.

We took off, and as the plane banked eastward, the colonel announced, "We are going to see the General!"

I nodded, my stomach tightening. Of all the days for me not to shave.

The colonel was in a jovial mood, pointing out the window to areas of interest. "We are over Lake Nicaragua," he said. "The only freshwater lake in the world with sharks," he added cheerfully.

After about an hour, without warning, the plane made a steep turn, diving for what looked like farmland. The pilot flared out and we hit hard as he made a three-point landing. I could see why Morgan had so many Cessnas to fix.

By the time we stopped rolling, several jeeps had appeared alongside of us. "Get in," barked one of the soldiers to me, jerking his head toward the front jeep. I got in. Colonel Saavedra sat down next to me. A second jeep, full of armed soldiers, followed. I realized with a sinking feeling that I was surrounded by machine guns and I was the only unarmed guy in the convoy. The road dipped in several places so steeply that the jeeps had to crawl uphill in low gear. I wondered why General Somoza couldn't afford a better road.

We stopped in front of a low, rambling ranch house with tall communication towers in front of it. "Wait here," said the colonel, "I will come for you when the General is ready."

It was early afternoon and the sun was blazing. I eased myself down on a wooden bench under the watchful eyes of five soldiers in green military fatigues. Unlike the young guard at the airport gate, they looked as though they knew how to use their guns. A pack of Dobermans lounging in the shade raised their heads, eyeing me suspiciously. I could see men moving about on the surrounding hills. I now understood the steep ups and downs of the road; no question it would be very difficult to get to the General without a real firefight.

After about fifteen minutes, Colonel Saavedra reappeared and motioned for me to come inside. The living room was dimly lit and the air conditioner hummed as it blasted cold air. When my eyes became accustomed to the darkness, I saw the room was simply furnished with rustic wooden furniture. A large refrigerator, a status symbol in Nicaragua, dominated one wall. Lounging in a hammock was a beautiful woman I recognized from newspaper pictures as the General's wife, Hope. She acknowledged me with a wave, and I nodded respectfully, but we were not introduced.

I had seen General Somoza several times at the airport in Managua, but never up close. He looked to be in his early forties, about six feet tall, with a slight paunch. He had heavy black-rimmed glasses and was wearing khakis and a crisp shirt. His dark hair was slicked back. He spoke unaccented English. "Welcome to my ranch. Won't you please sit down?" he said, extending his hand toward a park-type bench sitting in the middle of the room. He sat down across from me. He could have passed for the CEO of a Fortune 500 company.

"Colonel Saavedra has outlined your offer. But before we discuss that, please tell me a little about your background."

I told him I had majored in accounting in college. Briefly I related how my brothers and I had developed a million-dollar business selling and servicing specialty cars in Chicago. I didn't want to get into the lawsuit, so I merely told him that when the manufacturer stopped making the chassis, we had gone out of business.

We discussed the airplane contract for a while, and then the most powerful man in Latin America pulled three bottles of Coke out of the refrigerator, popped the tops and served them. My mouth was dry and I drank it quickly. General Somoza turned to Colonel Saavedra and said, "This sounds like we are on the right track. Why don't you and Mr. Martin work out the details and get going on the planes you want. I'd like to talk to Mr. Martin for a few more minutes, and then he will join you."

After Colonel Saavedra excused himself, the General asked, "So, Mr. Martin, what are your plans after this project?"

Surprised and flattered, I said I was looking for other opportunities. "Perhaps I could supply you with construction equipment," I said.

He nodded approvingly, his eyes boring into mine. "Maybe Nicaragua is a good place for you to do business. Let's talk again when you finish this deal." With that, he stood up and the meeting was over.

Two days later, I came to a final agreement with Colonel Saavedra and found myself officially in the munitions business. We set a price for twenty-one Mustangs, two P-47s, two twin Beech C-45s, and all of their spare parts. As a separate deal, I would sell them five T-28s and two B-26s, plus spare parts. The T-28, a post-WWII trainer, had two seats. I reasoned I could send two pilots down in a '28, and they could each bring back a plane. In my letter to Pat that night, I wrote I'd won the business with the Nicaraguans and that I'd be home soon.

That evening at dinner, I told Morgan I had sealed the contract.

"Who you gonna get to ferry the planes, Bub?" he asked. He knew I didn't know how to fly any of them, and that I had no intention of learning.

"There are all kinds of pilots around. At any airport there're fellows talking about their war heroics, just waiting to fly one of these birds again," I said confidently.

Morgan looked thoughtful. "You know, Bub," he said slowly, "flyin' down here ain't like flyin' in the States." He motioned to the waiter for coffee. "There's no navigation aids like Omnis or stuff like that. You got to map read. You should also know that if you do go down in that tough terrain, ain't nobody gonna go look for you. And if they did, they wouldn't find you. You go down in the jungle, and the trees just open up and close after you. You could fly right over the wreck and never see it. Lotsa planes been lost down here and never found."

I listened respectfully. But with good planes and skilled pilots, both of which I would have, I was sure my plan would work. I confided that General Somoza was encouraging me to go into business in Nicaragua.

Morgan snorted. "Lotsa people thought they could work with Somoza and most of them aren't around anymore. It's a lot easier to get into bed with him than to get out." That was all he would say.

Many of the Nicaraguan pilots had gone to the U.S. for advanced flight training. When I asked Colonel Saavedra if I could hire any of his pilots to ferry planes to the U.S., he thanked me but said he couldn't permit that. He paused and thought a moment. "You might talk to Jerry DeLarm. He's a local guy with dual citizenship for the U.S. and Nicaragua. He flew with the U.S. Air Force."   •

The word apparently got around because the next day I was stopped coming out of a hangar by a small wiry man dressed in tight black pants, a white shirt and a black cowboy hat. His eyes flickered over me and a little smile crossed his face. I could see he was missing some teeth. "Mr. Martin?"

"That's right."

"I'm Jerry DeLarm," he announced. "I hear you need a ferry pilot. I fly a '51 better'n anyone else in Central America, maybe in the U.S. too."

He said he was an American who had lived most of his life in Central America. He spoke fluent Spanish. He hired out to the highest bidder in revolutions. "Sometimes," he bragged, "I fly for both sides."

So, he was a mercenary. He seemed to want to impress me. "I got lots of connections in Nicaragua an' other places down here. I could be a big help to you," he added.

I wondered. Soldiers of fortune weren't known for their moral rectitude. But did it matter? The guy was just going to deliver planes. He wouldn't look me in the eye, though, which bothered me.

"I'll let you know," I promised. Later, I cornered Morgan. He knew these people and he knew airplanes. "Who's this DeLarm character? Can he fly a '51?"

Since Morgan's normal expression was a scowl, it was hard to know what he was thinking. "I'd say he flies a '51 or '47 better'n anyone I've seen," he said.

"What's his background? He looks like he's out of the local mafia."

"Listen, Bub," he said crisply. "When you've lived here as long as I have, you learn you're better off not asking too many questions or knowing too many answers. You lookin' for a Sunday school teacher or a pilot?"

Morgan changed the subject.

I was ticketed to leave the next day on Pan Am for the States. I hired DeLarm to bring up a Mustang and told him I'd have a T-28 for him to fly back. There was no reason for me to ever come back to Nicaragua. Home sure sounded good.

I paid for the first Mustang, which the mechanics assured me would be ready to ferry in a few days. I told DeLarm I would contact him as soon as we had a T-28 ready to send down. I was back on my feet.

Chapter 5

DOUBLE-CROSS

Glenn and I sat down with a big pot of coffee at his kitchen table. He had found plenty of T-28s on the market, but B-26s were in short supply. The original Martin B-26s had a reputation for being dangerous to fly. Our contract, however, specified the more stable Douglas '26s, originally called A-26s. This was our first experience with war surplus aircraft dealers and individuals. Glenn observed this group made used car dealers look like saints; there was no line they would not cross to make a sale. He was beginning to get cold feet.

"Let's go over the deal again," Glenn said, pouring more coffee, "and see if this whole thing still makes sense."

"Glenn, this could be an opportunity of a lifetime for us," I said. "We understand heavy equipment and this country seems to need everything—road-building equipment, trucks, buses, cars, and farm machinery. When I met the General, he asked what my plans were after we finished the airplane deal, and I told him I was looking for other opportunities."

"Maybe so. But let's get through this one and then see how we feel. I've applied for the license to export surplus military aircraft—both the Nicaraguan Embassy and our State Department have to approve. The U.S. government wants to make sure none of these planes end up in Cuba. The T-28s and B-26s are obsolete here, but they could do a lot of damage if Castro got a hold of them."

The next day when I came home after checking out a B-26 at a northside airport, Pat greeted me at the door. Pat looked both concerned and angry. "What's going on?" I asked.

"Some government man was out here today," she said. "Or at least he said he was from the government. I was picking raspberries behind the house and I heard Sam barking. I came around by the garage and there was a guy in a dark suit near the trash cans. I asked him what he was doing, and he flashed some ID card and wanted to know if you were home. I told him you were not and then he just left. Marie [our next-door neighbor] called about a half hour later. He'd gone over there and asked all sorts of questions about us. God only knows what Marie is thinking."

I hugged her. "Glenn applied for government licenses for the planes; they're probably just checking us out." I tried to sound reassuring but wondered to myself what I was getting us into. Apparently we passed muster, as the export licenses came through within a few weeks.

Glenn located a T-28 at an Indiana airport that sounded like it was in good shape. We drove down and bought it on the spot. I wired DeLarm's expense money to Morgan, asking him to get DeLarm on his way.

Days, weeks, and finally a month went by and no DeLarm arrived. Every time I called, there was a new excuse—bad weather, drop tanks failed to work, waiting for parts, etc. Finally, Morgan cabled that DeLarm was en route. When DeLarm landed, he showed his disappointment upon hearing he was to be put up in our quiet suburban guest room instead of getting to enjoy the bright lights of Chicago. He didn't say much in the car as I drove to our house. "How was the flight?" I asked.

"Good. Plane flew great."

I realized I hadn't seen drop tanks on the plane. "What happened to the drop tanks I told you to bring?"

"Mustang don't roll well with drop tanks," he explained casually, looking out the window.

"What the hell were you doing aerobatics for in my plane?" I asked angrily.

He shrugged.

Glenn and I planned to sell this plane to an Indiana dealer who had handled some Canadian Mustangs. The dealer sent a plane to pick me up and DeLarm flew the Mustang to his field, putting on an impromptu air show there. His flying skills had not been exaggerated. He was a very hot pilot.

The next day the three of us drove to another field in Indiana and picked up the T-28 DeLarm was going to be taking back to Nicaragua. He had never flown one, so we went through the starting procedures and talked about the plane with its owner. I jumped in the back cockpit, and we headed for Chicago's Midway Airport.

DeLarm went through a couple stalls, getting the feel of the plane. Then he rolled it a few times and flew upside down, leaving us hanging in the harnesses. Apparently the plane had come out of the desert, because a dust storm erupted in the cockpits, with sand, cigarette butts, small screws, and bolts raining down. When we landed, I demanded why the hell he was still doing aerobatics in my planes when I'd told him not to. He just shrugged again and looked away.

That night at dinner on our back porch, DeLarm seemed to want to show off for Pat. "I got lots of connections in those countries," he boasted as she put a plate of grilled pork chops on the table. "Can't go in all of them, though, 'cause I did some flying for Somoza and now I got enemies."

Pat smiled politely, "What a shame," she said in a sympathetic tone, shooting me a look. *Who IS this guy?*

DeLarm took her smile for encouragement. "Yeah, I done a bunch of secret missions for Somoza. I brought in stuff for him and his brother Luis in my Lockheed twin. When the FAN guys found out it was for Tachito, no one even looked to see what it was. They just unloaded the boxes at night."

"What do you think was in the boxes?" I asked.

DeLarm dropped his voice dramatically. "No idea. Never asked. Too dangerous." He paused for effect and continued. "CIA stuff is top secret. I told Will," jerking his head toward me, "that I could be a big help to him. I can do anything I want and ain't nobody gonna touch me in Nicaragua."

"Well, that must be very nice for you," replied Pat brightly. Cassie, our tow-headed younger daughter, toddled out on to the porch. "Excuse me for a moment," Pat said, quickly turning Cassie around and marching her back into the house.

DeLarm leaned toward me. "Hey Will, I hear Chicago's got some great joints downtown. You know, girls an' all that."

I ignored the hint. "We'll head out to the airport first thing in the morning so you can get an early start. I'll call Weather again after dinner."

When Pat returned to the table, DeLarm was stabbing his pork chop and looking grumpy. "More iced tea?" she asked, splashing his white shirtsleeve as she poured. "Oh dear," she said and offered him a napkin.

DeLarm took off for Nicaragua the next morning with new charts and a fist full of expense money. I watched the plane grow smaller and disappear in the distance. I sent DeLarm by himself since Morgan said there weren't any Mustangs ready to be brought back up. DeLarm was to wire me when he arrived.

When I didn't hear after several days, I called Morgan. "Your deal's dead, Bub. DeLarm said your plane is junk and left it in St. Louis. He's got something cooked up with one of the Nicaraguan officers to take over your contract."

That bastard. "I can get a '28 down there this week," I said quickly.

"Suit yourself," Morgan said and hung up.

I considered my options. Morgan was a smart guy, and if he said the deal was in jeopardy, it was pretty serious. My only hope was to get a T-28 down fast to Nicaragua before DeLarm could cut us out. Glenn had located another T-28 at a field nearby that was ready to go. But no pilots were available. And we didn't have time to look for one. I decided to deliver it myself.

The military flight manuals that I ordered had arrived. When I bought my first plane, the Navion, it came with a three-page booklet. In contrast, Flight Handbook USAF Series T-28A Aircraft, Revised

39

May 15, 1954, totaled an impressive 131 pages. It described the T-28 in plain, forthright language:

> *The T-28A, built by North American Aviation, is a two-place trainer that is capable of performance equal to that of many fighter airplanes of World War II. From the T-28, you will step directly to a current combat airplane...features of the airplane include dual controls, tricycle landing gear, and a steerable nose wheel.... Approximate over-all dimensions of the airplane are: Length-32 feet, wing span-41 feet, Height (to top of rudder) 13 feet, normal gross weight...is approximately 7425.*

Could I really do this? For the first time, I envied the men who received hundreds of hours of very expensive U.S. military flight training, the best in the world. That night I started memorizing the cockpit, skipping the gauges that had to do with military radios or armaments.

The left side of the instrument panel showed thirty switches, gauges, and buttons; the right side sixteen. For visual, good weather flights most of them were unimportant. If something went wrong, however, knowing how they worked and what they did would be critical. A lot of information on flight characteristics and dos and don'ts followed. The manual stated that inverted spins with the gear and flaps down were not recommended. That was like saying not to use a match to check how much gas is in the tank.

I typed up the pre-flight checklist of thirty-one steps, the pre-take-off checklist of sixteen steps, and a landing list with the gear-down and approach speeds. Since all my flying experience was in retractable gear and adjustable props, I was at least familiar with those aspects of the plane.

I had logged about 2,500 hours in civilian planes. However, flying the high performance and heavier aircraft would be a different experience. I tried to think about it matter-of-factly. The T-28's 800-horsepower engine was a big step up from my Navion's 205-horsepower and my twin-engine Piper Apache's total 300-horsepower. Airspeed was displayed in knots, and I would have a stick instead of a wheel, which meant two hands instead of one–left hand for throttle and right for flight controls. This bird was heavier, faster, and more complicated than anything I'd ever flown.*

I swallowed hard as I looked up at the monster on the tarmac the next day. It was a lot of plane. Yet the cockpit was laid out in a straightforward manner, the procedures made sense, and thousands of men had learned to fly them. By my third time through the manuals, it was all coming together for me. I could do this.

The following morning, Glenn drove me back to the field. I was lost in thought and said little. I would get one of the pilots at the field to give me a check ride and go over the important stuff to keep me out of trouble. After we arrived, while Glenn was finishing up the paperwork with the dealer, I asked the mechanic who was going to give me the check ride.

"There isn't anyone here that knows anything about this bird," he said simply. "The seller flew it in from New York when we took it on trade."

"Oh shit," I muttered. Now what? I wasn't pleased with the prospect of flying a plane 3,300 miles with my only experience having been a short ride with DeLarm.

The mechanic added, "We had '28s where I was stationed, and the guys all said it flew good with no bad habits."

I took heart. "Anything I should look out for?"

"This one looks like it just came from military rejuv'nation. The engine's low time and there's no sign of oil or hydraulic leaks."

If I didn't get this plane down there now, I knew I might as well tear up the contract.

Glenn objected when I told him I was going to fly it without a check ride. "Maybe we should just let it sit until we get a pilot."

"I don't think it'll be a problem. Let me get it started and if everything looks okay, I'll just go ahead."

We walked out on the field with Glenn providing a litany of reasons why I shouldn't fly it. The huge T-28 dwarfed the civilian planes around it. Somehow it hadn't looked so big that day with DeLarm. I reached up and gingerly pulled the external control to lower the flap,

---

*The T-28 stalled at 65 knots, took off at somewhere between 75 and 85 knots, and cruised at 195 knots. The plane would glide with a ratio of 12:1 with wheels up and prop at coarse pitch. With wheels and flaps down, the glide ratio dropped to 6:1.

acting more confident than I felt. Stepping up into the footholds in the flap, I grabbed a handhold and climbed onto the wing. The outside handle slid back the canopy and I dropped into the seat. This wasn't so bad! The rudder pedals were adjustable, a pleasant surprise that made the cockpit comfortable for my long frame.

I sat in the cockpit about twenty minutes, reviewing the gauges and switches, identifying each and what it did. I reminded myself how complex the panel of my first plane, the Navion, had seemed. I adjusted the seat belt and shoulder harness. Time to go. I took out my checklist, taped it to the panel and went through the start-up procedures.

Looking to the side because the big engine blocked my forward vision, I hollered, "Clear!" I turned on the master switch and set the throttle at the suggested one and a half inches forward, the prop control full forward for fine pitch, and made sure the mixture was in the rear, or off, position. I hit the starter button and after a couple of blades went by, turned the magnetos on. The engine coughed a few times as I primed it, which I continued doing until it ran smoothly, and then I slowly opened up the mixture. The indicators on the temperature and oil pressure gauges moved into the green zone. Flaps were down; I moved the flap lever on the instrument panel and raised them full up.

I let the plane roll forward and squeezed the control on the stick to activate the power steering. Taxiing to the end of the runway seemed like driving a car. There I paused, took a deep breath, and then holding the brakes, went through the engine run-up to 2100 rpm. I checked for maximum mag drop of 75 rpm. The canopy was electric and motored nicely into place. Up to this point, the procedures had been much like those for the small airplanes I had owned.

I started down the runway. The plane seemed to accelerate slowly and the 3,000-foot runway all of a sudden didn't seem so long. I resisted the temptation to push the throttle in all the way, which could over-boost and damage the supercharged engine. About one-third of the way down the runway, I eased back on the stick to lift the nose wheel. The transition from ground to air was so smooth I didn't even feel the lift-off. Lo and behold...Look, Ma—I'm flying!

I waited for the nose to swing to the left, but it never happened.* This plane was a pleasure to fly! It felt very stable and was actually easier to handle than a small aircraft. I followed the beautiful Lake Michigan shoreline to Chicago. Glenn had called the Midway tower to alert them I would be landing without radios and would need a light gun.† The moment I turned on my downwind leg, the green light cleared me to land. The Midway tower guys were really on their toes.

As I turned on my base leg and then final, I rechecked the landing procedure: gear down and showing three wheels in the little gear windows, flaps full down, prop control full forward, fuel pump on, and airspeed pegged at 100 knots. I was now looking at 5,000-plus feet of concrete stretching out before me.

While the field was familiar, today I was sitting up much higher than in my Apache, so I knew I'd have trouble judging my height above the runway. I gradually eased off the power and felt the bump as the wheels made contact about halfway down the runway. If I were going to land this at small fields as I planned, I'd better learn how to get it down a lot quicker. I taxied the two-mile trek around the airport perimeter and shut down the engine.

I leaned back against the seat, pleased with myself. For a moment I felt like a super-hot pilot who could fly anything. Then common sense set in. I was lucky the T-28 was such an easy plane to fly. I had just completed a short flight in perfect weather with little traffic and no problems. *Will,* I thought, *don't confuse dumb luck with experience—a seasoned pilot you ain't.* Nonetheless, the day was off to a great start.

The FAA had approved this plane for a ferry permit,‡ but I still asked Midway mechanics to look it over. It checked out fine. The Curtiss-Wright engine had a terrible reputation for excess oil consumption, usually blowing it out along the sides, but this one was perfectly clean.

---

*I learned later that the engineers had designed the '28 as a training airplane to handle much like a jet. They tilted the engine down and to one side, which, together with the five-degree right rudder trim, pretty much eliminated any prop wash and gyro effect.

†A light gun has a long tube that emits a red or green light. It can be aimed at a plane in the air or on the ground. Only the pilot that it is focused on can see it, so there can be no confusion.

‡To be legal, anyone flying a warbird required FAA signoff.

An hour later, Glenn showed up. "Plane feels good to me," I said. "I'll leave for Nicaragua as soon as the weather clears."

Glenn frowned. "You don't have to do this, you know, Will. Remember, you have a wife and two kids. We can just forget about the contract."

"The plane flies fine. I'm comfortable with it," I assured him. "Now I've got to get the charts together." The plane had no navigational equipment. However, I would have sectional charts that identified towns, rivers, railroad tracks, smokestacks, and other landmarks. Flying from Illinois to Texas would not be much of a challenge. My ferry permits restricted me to daytime visual flight, though that wasn't an issue; I had no intention of flying this plane at night without navigation equipment or radios. I didn't like to fly any single-engine plane at night or over water, period.

A fixed base operator in St. Louis called that afternoon, asking when we were going to pick up our T-28. DeLarm had apparently just abandoned the other T-28 at the gas pump there and it was now accumulating storage charges. Glenn made arrangements for a St. Louis pilot to bring it back up to Chicago.

Twenty-four hours later, I was ready to leave. If Pat had reservations, she kept them to herself. She knew how desperate I was to find another business. "I'll see you in two weeks," she said lightly as I kissed her goodbye. I think we both thought that timetable was optimistic.

Out at the airport, Glenn gave me a thumbs-up with probably more confidence than he felt, and I was off. My final destination that day was Brownsville, Texas. I made a leisurely climb to my planned altitude of 8,500 feet. Setting the throttle at 29 inches manifold pressure and the rpm at 2000 gave me an airspeed of 180 knots or about 210 miles per hour. At 8,500 feet, the airspeed indicator would read only about 167 knots due to the lower density of the air. At these settings, gas consumption would be 225 pounds or 37.5 gallons per hour. Allowing for start-up, warm-up, and reserve, I would have a little over 112 gallons for about 600 miles or a little over three hours in the air.

The T-28 has a seven-cylinder engine, with four cylinders

exhausting on one side and three on the other, which gives the engine a peculiar tunka-ka-tunka-ka rhythm. It took some getting used to. Time flew by and I hit my first gas stop right on schedule. I chose small, uncontrolled fields to avoid wasting time with arrival and departure permissions.

I decided I would fly just another hour or so rather than trying to reach Brownsville that day. The map showed a large military base on my route that had been abandoned to general aviation. I decided to take it. The wind was calm and the windsock was hanging straight down, so there was no way to determine the active runway. I circled the field and picked a long runway headed toward some parked cars.

After landing, I was doing my usual walk around the plane, looking for any problems, when a young man appeared. "Jimmy" was embroidered on his coveralls.

"Are you in any trouble?" he asked anxiously. Apparently few planes landed there on purpose.

I laughed and answered, "Not that I know of! I'd like to close my flight plan and get a lift to a motel or borrow a car if possible."

"We don't have a courtesy car. But it's quitting time, so I can give you a ride to a motel."

On the way into town, he explained he was getting some old cargo planes current, but there was little activity on the field. We passed a new-looking motel with all kinds of neon lights. I said I'd like to look for something cheaper. He took me to a place where he said cargo pilots usually stayed.

The 1930s-style motel was a plain one-story white stucco building with peeling green paint around the windows. A VACANCY sign hung on the office door. Jimmy said he would pick me up at seven in the morning for breakfast. Inside, a heavy-set, ornery-looking woman slouched at the reception desk, smoking a cigarette. She looked over her newspaper and grunted, "Room?"

I answered her in kind. "Yeah."

"Three or five?"

"What's the difference?" I asked.

"Two bucks," she replied, tapping her ash.

I must have stared at her for a moment, trying to figure out whether she was trying to be funny because she mumbled, "Five buck room's got a TV."

"I'll take it," I said and laid a five-dollar bill on the counter.

She slid a key across and said, "Number four," and resumed her reading.

I didn't ask about the restaurant across the street. I sensed she felt every word cost her money. In the room, the TV didn't work, but then again she never said it did.

The room was more or less clean, and I threw my bag down, rinsed off my face, and walked across the street to get dinner. That's when I realized how tired I was. It was only four hours of flying time, but I knew I had never relaxed for a minute of it. When I got back to the room, I started rereading the T-28 manual. The next thing I knew, it was morning and Jimmy was pounding at the door. I asked him to give me five minutes and since the water just trickled out of the bathroom faucet, I skipped shaving.

At the field while Jimmy gassed the plane, I walked around it, grabbing surface controls to be sure nothing was loose and looking for leaks. I added a quart of oil, but the hydraulic fluid was right on the mark.

I called the tower at Brownsville, my next stop, with my ETA. I took my time with my preflight review and then looked for traffic. The winds were light and with no clearly designated runway, planes could appear from any and all directions. The takeoff was smooth. I was getting used to the plane and enjoying the 360-degree view from the clear canopy. After raising the gear, I throttled back and reduced the rpm to 2400 for climb. The visibility was clear at 8,500 feet, making navigation with the sectional charts easy.

I had plotted the route with a red marker, and then folded and numbered the large sectional charts so I could slip easily from one to the next. My Piper Apache with its VHF Omni receivers and ADF radio had spoiled me, and I was missing Pat, who usually handled most of the navigation.

When I landed at Brownsville, the wind was blowing and there was a light film of dust on everything. Border towns are different. No one asked questions or expressed any interest in where I was going. It was clear curiosity was discouraged. When I bought the sectional charts for Mexico and Central America however, I mentioned I planned an early start. The man behind the counter looked up at me. "Don't waste your money."

"What do you mean?" I asked.

"Customs across the Rio Grande don't open 'til eight. They'll let you go through earlier and then sock you big for overtime charges."

I thanked him and got a ride to a nearby motel. The next morning I checked the plane more closely than usual, as draining gas or other vandalism was not unheard of in border towns.

Matamoros, the point of entry for Mexican customs, is just a few minutes across the Rio Grande. I was told the Mexican controllers in the tower didn't use light guns, so pilots just looked out for other planes. There wasn't any traffic at eight a.m. I landed and taxied over to the customs shack to present my papers.

The T-28 still had some U.S. military markings, but that didn't seem to raise any eyebrows. When the official asked me a question in Spanish, I told him I didn't understand, and he switched to English without skipping a beat. "Got anything to declare?"

I said no. He waved a subordinate to climb up to check the cockpit. After a fast look around, the fellow shook his head and jumped down. It was clear the customs officer had never seen a T-28: the belly compartment is enormous, but he didn't check it. The head guy stamped my pile of papers and said, "Go."

So far, navigation had been easy with plenty of cities, railroad tracks, and highways as checkpoints. Today would be the beginning of dead reckoning navigation. I took off, jotted down the time, and then followed the coastline of the Gulf of Mexico down to Veracruz. The tower at Veracruz didn't pay any attention to my arrival. I taxied toward the gas pumps and a line boy motioned me to a tie-down spot. He spoke good English and when I told him I would be there overnight and gas up in the morning, he responded pleasantly, "Okay—*no problema.*"

The next morning at the small restaurant in the hotel, I ordered eggs, bacon, toast, orange juice, and coffee. The orange juice and coffee arrived, and then I waited. And waited. After twenty-five minutes,

I signaled the waiter that I needed to get going. He obligingly brought the check. When I protested that the bacon, eggs, and toast never came, he studied the check, scratched off the items, and handed it back to me with a smile.

The airport had a small café, so I hoped I could get breakfast there. No more English was spoken at the airport's restaurant than at the hotel. I managed to get coffee, but realized my meager Spanish wasn't up to the challenge of ordering a full breakfast. Stomach growling, I headed back to the plane.

On my next leg, I flew along the coast, and then followed a railroad track across the Isthmus of Tehuantepec. I was at 8,000 feet, but low clouds were scudding under me, so I descended through them until I was about 500 feet off the deck. When I spotted the field at Ixtepec, I landed, gassed up, and managed to get a cheese sandwich and a warm Coke by pointing at them.

The weather was clearing and when I reached the Pacific coast, I leveled off again at 8,000 feet and trimmed my big fat bird for easy flying.

I had planned to spend the night in Guatemala. But when I calculated my ground speed, I was surprised to find I had a hell of a tail wind. At my speed, I could easily go right into Nicaragua. Morgan said no one flew in the afternoon in Central America, but a mile and a half up, the sky was blue and the air smooth.

I pressed on and when I caught up with an overcast, I pushed the nose down to fly under it. After a few minutes, I realized I was gradually going lower and lower. A dark cloud layer looked threatening, so I swung out over the ocean about six or seven miles. Suddenly I began experiencing violent up- and downdrafts that put my heart in my mouth. The plane was bouncing around in the air and I was now down to 1,000 feet. As soon as I saw a hole, I swung back toward land.

By this time, I had passed the point of no return for Guatemala. I knew I was burning more fuel at the low altitudes, but I wasn't sure how much. I wanted to recalculate my figures, but it was taking all my concentration to fly my bird. Morgan had mentioned a little-used airport at Corinto on the west coast of Nicaragua. I found it and circled the field several times. Cattle were grazing on the runway. They looked up at me placidly; there were too many to buzz out of the way and I wasn't sure they would move anyway. The first splatters of rain hit the windshield.

Now my fuel warning lights were burning brightly. Rain began to pound the canopy, and I was so low I was pulling up for tall trees. I decided to fly along the coast and then turn inland when I calculated I ought to be in line with Managua. Visibility dropped down to a quarter of a mile in spots. I was sitting pretty high in the seat. If I didn't see Managua in three minutes, I was going to turn back and belly in on the beach while I still had power.

My mouth was dry and my heart pounding when I scooted over a little rise and there it was, the Managua runway, dead ahead. I had already slowed to about 100 knots, so I slammed down the gear handle, dumped full flaps, and was just over the runway when the gear-down indicator lights came on. I felt a slight skid of the wheels as they hit the wet tarmac. I taxied the plane over to the hangar and then ran through the driving rain to the terminal.

My arrival created quite a stir. Bringing a plane down in those conditions established me as a Great Pilot or a Damn Fool, depending on your point of view. I suspect Morgan's opinion fell into the latter category. Leaning against a wall across the room, he just shook his head.

The cheese sandwich and Coca-Cola lunch were a distant memory by the time I checked in at the Estrella Hotel that night. I ordered a full meal in the restaurant, ate it quickly, and then ordered a second one. As the waiter brought more food, I looked up to see the entire male kitchen staff peeking around the corner, giggling furiously at the *gringo grande* who ate two dinners.

Chapter 6

A Famous Chicago Gangster

When I arrived at the airport the next morning, Colonel Saavedra greeted me warmly. "Good to see you, Mr. Martin. Colonel Mansfield and Captain Harris from the U.S. Mission are just coming back from test-flying your T-28." I saw the T-28 taxiing toward the hangar.

Both officers wore big smiles when they climbed out. Everyone gathered around the plane. "Mighty nice bird!" commented the colonel. "Handles great."

"And the engine time is low—lower than the contract specs," added the captain. Saavedra beamed. A new plane on any field is always a reason to knock off work and go have a look.

Back in Saavedra's office, I broached the issue of DeLarm. According to one of the mission men, DeLarm had approached a buyer for the planes in Florida, apparently anticipating a good commission plus the contract to ferry them to the U.S. "I understand there's some kind of problem with DeLarm," I said.

Colonel Saavedra dismissed my concern. "We have a contract with you," he said firmly.

"Good." I stood up. "I'm going to get the expense money back from DeLarm and then leave for Chicago tomorrow. I'll send a couple of pilots down in my next plane to bring back two P-51s. There are two ready, aren't there?"

At that moment, the adjunct burst in. "DeLarm," he said breathlessly, "he's taking the new plane!"

A few minutes later, DeLarm strode in with a man he identified as his lawyer. "In lieu of the $800 wages owed by Mr. Martin, my client will be attaching the aircraft recently delivered," the latter announced pompously. DeLarm smiled smugly.

I took a step toward DeLarm, but Colonel Saavedra intervened. He turned very red in the face and snapped, "Get off this field. That plane is the property of the *Fuerza Aérea de Nicaragua,* and I will have you two arrested if I catch you here again!"

"You'll hear more from us, Mr. Martin," the lawyer puffed, but DeLarm looked startled.

"Not here he won't," the colonel bellowed. "Get out before I have you thrown out!" and Saavedra's adjunct hustled the two through the door. When they were gone, Saavedra drank a little water. "They can't do anything," he assured me. He paused. "Just the same, maybe it is best you go back to the States tomorrow."

I had moved that morning from the Estrella to the more comfortable Gran Hotel in the heart of the city, and during siesta time at the hotel that afternoon, I was awakened by a frantic pounding on the door. I opened the door and saw a serious-looking young man standing there, clutching a notebook and pen. "Mr. Martin?"

"Yes."

"I am your friend."

"I betcha. What do you want?"

"I am Alfredo Cortez, star reporter for *La Prensa.*"

"So?"

"I can give you information…you can give me a story." He looked at me expectantly.

"I don't know what you're talking about."

He took a deep breath. "Officials from the labor court are on their way now. They have papers to keep you from leaving the country."

As if on cue, there was more pounding at the door. In burst three government process servers backed by four policemen who bumped into one another as they tried to find a place to stand in my small room. Everyone looked uneasy. I wondered why I merited such a crowd. The leader glanced at the policemen as if to reassure himself, turned to me, and clearing his throat, rattled off something in Spanish as he flourished a sheaf of papers. He then shook my hand and left, his contingent trailing.

The reporter closed the door. "See!" he said triumphantly. "And now, my story."

I opened the door and pushed him through it, "Not today."

In the lobby, the manager and desk clerk were leaning over the *La Nacion* newspaper. "*Mira! Es él, el Señor Martin!*" one gasped, pointing to the front page.

I walked up to the desk and both jumped. They stared at me a moment. I looked at the paper and saw "Chicago" in the headline. "Translate it," I ordered.

The clerk began nervously: "The headline is 'AIR FORCE OF NICARAGUA DOES BUSINESS WITH CHICAGO CRIMINAL.' It says you owe Señor DeLarm $800 dollars and that he has filed a complaint with the labor court." The clerk's eyes grew wide as he read three more columns of colorful details about el Señor Martin, "*un de los famosos Gangsters de Chicago*," according to Señor DeLarm's statement. I dropped a dime on the desk, picked up the paper, and went over to Morgan's room at the Estrella. I banged open the door.

Morgan grinned, a newspaper in his lap. "You sure got yourself into it this time, Bub, didn't you?" he cackled, tipping his chair on its back legs.

"What the *hell* is he talking about?" I exploded. "He owes *me* $700 expense money. I asked you about him before I hired him, and you wouldn't tell me anything. It's a little late now, but suppose you start."

"It was your idea to hire him, not mine," he said with a shrug.

"Get on with it."

"The story going around is that DeLarm'll do anything for anybody if the price is right. He won't overfly Guatemala though, 'cause they'll string him up if they catch him. Seems when he was flying for the CIA during the Guatemalan revolution, he strafed some civilians. He can't go to Costa Rica either. Around here, he's taken care of a few 'jobs' for the General. You won't leave the country 'til this deal is settled, that's for sure," he warned, shaking a bony finger. "Too bad you're not British–they know how to handle these things."

"Can't our embassy do anything?" I asked.

"Go see them and find out." And he shrugged again.

At the U.S. Embassy the next day, Mr. Fairchild, a colorless government official, gave the impression he would prefer no one rock his particular boat. He wore the mandatory dark suit and striped tie. I suspect his goal in life was not to offend anyone. "We have a rather thick file on DeLarm," he began cautiously. "He was involved with various revolutions and at one time, he was a big man here. He can probably prevent you from leaving the country. Let us know if he does."

"I'm letting you know right now that I'm looking to this office for some help!" I thumped his mahogany desk soundly.

"We appreciate your circumstances...."

"Look, I'm asking for a fair trial, nothing more. If DeLarm is a U.S. citizen, and this action took place in the U.S., then this can't be settled in a foreign court. It has to be admitted to the U.S. courts and tried there."

He tented his hands carefully. "Technically, you are probably correct. Unfortunately, the Nicaraguans aren't too concerned with the niceties of law. To further compound the problem, this will be tried before a labor court, scarcely the most distinguished court in the land."

"I'm trying to do business down here. It doesn't help when I make headlines as a Chicago gangster."

"The people who matter know that anyone transporting munitions from the U.S. has to have State Department clearance. You've been checked out." He shut the file and rose, waiting for me to leave.

Instead I remained stubbornly in my chair. "Let's see if I understand. You have just stated that this claim is to be tried, one, in a known kangaroo court where, two, the judge has no jurisdiction, over three, a case being brought forth by the country's leading bandit. And you're telling me the U.S. Embassy isn't going to do anything?

Doesn't the foreign aid we're dumping in here give a U.S. citizen at least the same rights as the local boys?"

"I wish we could help you," he said, dismissing me.

At this point, I realized I was just talking to myself, so I stomped out and headed to the field to Colonel Saavedra's office.

"I can't do anything about this court," Colonel Saavedra said, "but I happen to have a brother who is a lawyer. I think you'd better see him."

Rafael Saavedra, the colonel's brother, also spoke very good English, and he confirmed I wasn't going to be leaving the country. He and his brother put together a retraction from the Nicaraguan Air Force for the afternoon papers. It stated that yesterday's information was inaccurate, and that "El Señor William Martin was prominent in Chicago's business and social circles." *A mobster one day, the toast of the town the next*, I thought.

The preliminary hearing was some weeks later. It was in a labor court concerned mostly with claims brought by peasants against landowners. The case before mine centered on the ownership of fourteen hens and a rooster.

DeLarm and I had each been given twenty questions to answer in writing. My lawyer pointed out to the judge that I did not speak Spanish and that DeLarm's three "witnesses" did not understand English. The judge ruled this irrelevant and told me to post an $800 bond. His decision would be given to me by mail. DeLarm smirked at the judge and His Honor grinned back. About a month later, I received a notice that the judge had ruled in favor of DeLarm and my bond had been forfeited.

DeLarm was a little shit and had cost me real money, but I had to turn my attention back to the contract. In six months, only one Mustang had been ferried to the United States. The whole contract should have been finished. I could have pushed the planes up the Pan American Highway in that time.

It didn't help matters that the planes were turning out to need more work than I had expected. Sitting down with the FAN mechanics assigned to my planes, I outlined what needed to be done. Everyone smiled agreeably and told me "no problema." They seemed eager to begin. I smiled back, happy we understood each other so well.

I gradually realized the mechanics' "no problema" only meant "I heard you," not "I'm going to get right on it." Every morning I was warmly greeted when I arrived at the hangar. Tool boxes would be brought out, parts examined and installed. Then uninstalled. Possibilities debated. Heads shaken. Breaks taken. Everyone was quite pleasant, but the work proceeded at an agonizingly slow pace.

The mechanics quit at noon, free to do whatever they wanted the rest of the day. Certainly the fierce temperatures accounted in part for the shortened workday. Yet when the men wanted to work on extra-curricular afternoon jobs, they showed astonishing energy.

I simply couldn't figure out how to get the mechanics to pick up the pace on my planes. There were successful companies operating in Nicaragua. If they could work with the locals, why couldn't I? Did the military have a work ethic all its own? I'd been hearing some chilling stories about General Somoza. If the men wouldn't work for him, what chance did I have?

I decided to try a bonus incentive. One morning I collared Sergeant Gonzales, the crew chief, and told him I needed to talk to the men assigned to my Mustangs. When they were assembled, I climbed up and sat on a wing.

"Boys, we will have a new deal, a Yankee incentive system. For each plane ready two weeks after you start work, I will pay a big bonus!" There was a mighty cheer.

"We will work afternoons," I continued. Faces fell. "You want to make big money?" The mechanics nodded enthusiastically. "Then we work afternoons. I'll want a list of the parts needed for each plane." There was a murmur of approval. I made a similar deal with the officers.

Everyone smiled and said "*no problema.*"

For the next few days, everybody shuffled a little faster and I took heart. Then one morning I found five of the seven mechanics eyeballing a prop governor. "What's the problem?" I asked.

"We need a prop governor," one announced. "There is nothing we can do until we have it." The rest all heartily agreed, and as far as they were concerned, they were through for the day. It was 9:45 a.m.

I took a deep breath. "I asked for the list of all parts needed for this plane last week."

"We didn't need the prop governor then," another volunteered.

"Why do we need it now?"

Everyone looked at the broken prop governor. "*Se me tiró*," one of the mechanics explained defensively. Translation: "It jumped out of my hand."

What to do? As part of my deal with the FAN, I was to receive all the spare Mustang and Thunderbolt parts. Actually locating them, however, had turned out to be another matter. I'd been told the Nicaraguan supply sergeant, Sergeant Chavez, was the guy to see. I tracked him down and handed him the faulty prop governor. "Have we got one?"

He hefted it and thought a moment. "Maybe," he said.

"Can you take me to the warehouse?" I asked.

"Major Lopez's or the one where the '51 and '47 parts are stored?" he asked.

"The one with the parts."

He climbed in his pickup and I slid in the passenger side. "Does Major Lopez have his own private warehouse?" I asked.

"He has a big business in airplane parts. Uses the air force inventory. He even orders parts for planes the air force don't have, and Uncle Sam keeps sending them."

We drove by the terminal, through an old junkyard of planes, past the bullet-riddled hulks of the B-26s used by the CIA in the Cuban invasion fiasco. We stopped alongside a damaged Mustang. Sergeant Chavez jumped on the wing, reached inside the cockpit and then snapped his fingers. "I forgot. We used that on number six." He turned to leave and then paused. "Wait a minute," he said and unscrewed a hydraulic brake valve. "We'll be needing this soon."

We pulled up in front of a gray frame building. Inside, wooden crates and metal boxes were stacked high, some sealed and others with contents spilling out. "Good God!" I exclaimed. "There're enough parts here to assemble another three airplanes."

"Yup," Sergeant Chavez agreed. "There was a time when the U.S.

got mad and wasn't sending us any more planes. Then the General got mad and bought some P-51s from Sweden, along with these spare parts. It was all catalogued and listed. It got dumped here and the catalogues—I don't know where they went."

"So I see. But right now, I need a prop governor."

"They probably have one here somewhere," he mused. "But it might be faster to order it from Miami. As long as you're here, let's go over to Lanica Airlines. They wouldn't have this type of governor, but we need some prop controls for the P-47s. Lanica has the same type in their C-46 cargo planes."

He spoke to Lanica's chief mechanic. A few minutes later, Sergeant Chavez was handed a box with two controls. The sergeant told me the parts were used but looked okay.

Later that day back at the FAN hangar, when a mechanic installed a control in one of the '47s, the electric block shorted out immediately. We tried the other—same thing.

The guy in charge of the prop shop appeared. "*Qué pasa?*"

"These blocks from Lanica are junk," Sergeant Chavez complained, showing him the faulty parts.

"*No problema!*" the prop shop guy said cheerfully. "We have some new ones." A few minutes later he produced a brand new box of control blocks.

I didn't say a word. The shop fellow had obviously taken them from my inventory and had probably been planning to sell them to Lanica as soon as I was gone.

Sergeant Chavez smiled congenially. "*Sí, sí, no problema.*"

I told him I would order three prop governors from Miami. It was only noon and too early for a drink, but it sure sounded like a good idea.

The next day I looked at the assembled group of mechanics. "While we're waiting for the prop governors, let's get started on those coolant radiators stacked in the warehouse. Each one has to be checked before we install it."

A few minutes later, the crew reported that there were no coolant radiators. I buttonholed the sergeant again.

"Were they yours?" Sergeant Chavez asked in astonishment.

"While you were stateside, one of the officers had them loaded on a truck. I guess he sold them to a junkman."

"Those radiators are worth $400 each!" I exploded.

"Don't tell the junkman that when you buy them back," he advised.

I strode back into the hangar, yanking down an aileron on one of the Mustangs in frustration as I passed. I heard a cry of anguish. One of the mechanics was napping in the cockpit and the aileron moved the stick, whacking him on the head. I continued on, figuring at least one mechanic was awake.

The next day two mechanics got into a fight, each trying to pilfer the battery from the same plane. The major in charge of maintenance simply advised me to order more batteries.

"Why?" I asked. "I brought one down for each of my planes." Rumor had it the major was using my batteries for air force planes.

"One of your men blew one up yesterday," he explained blandly, "and you are short two more besides."

"Funny that whenever a mechanic breaks something, he's working for me, but when I give him a direct order, he's working for the air force," I observed to no one in particular. I cabled for more batteries.

"How can these people get away with this kind of stuff?" I asked a sergeant from the U.S. Mission. "Is it just because I'm a gringo?"

"No, it's not you. They'd steal the front door off the president's palace," he said bluntly. "Ever notice how the mechanics use only one tool at a time? If they need another size wrench for a minute, they have to lock up the one they were just using. Even our mission has problems." He indicated the U.S. C-47 he was working on. "Some SOB stole my polish this morning. But I fixed him. When I got another can, I mixed in half paint thinner. He grabbed that too when I went to the head. Wait 'til he starts polishing his motorcycle," he said, chuckling.

The Nicaraguan military was set up on a strict caste system, usually with a wide gulf between officers and NCOs. I never saw a Nicaraguan officer physically involve himself with any of the planes. Since the mechanics assumed I was wealthy, they were astonished I would get my hands dirty. I often worked alongside them.

Some of the planes were covered with a compound called Bondo, a plastic-like material that sticks well to metal. North American Aviation developed it during WWII to fill the seams on wing panels. This was supposed to streamline the airflow surfaces for greater speed. It was later discontinued since the difference it made proved negligible. For some reason, the Nicaraguans had smeared it all over the wings instead of just the seams. It looked like cheap paint peeling off.

After trying various compounds, I ordered a 55-gallon drum of methylene chloride, a very strong stripper. Morgan asked for the job and recruited some men to help him. But the result looked terrible, and Morgan complained the stripper wasn't working. Since I had used it in the automobile business, I knew it worked. The men just weren't applying it properly.

A glass gallon jug of the stripper was sitting on a Mustang wing in the hot sun. Frustrated with the snail-like pace, I said impatiently, "Let me show you," and without thinking, opened the jug. Pressure had been building up all morning and the caustic liquid exploded in my face. It was a scalding, burning liquid that blinded me almost instantly. I knew there was a water tap just outside the hangar so I flopped on the ground under it, letting the water splash over my face. I lay there, scared to open my eyes.

After a few minutes, I blinked and was relieved I could still see. Morgan just looked away. But one of the mechanics kneeled down next to me and said softly, "*Señor Martin, ten cuidado. No repuestos para los ojos.*"—Be careful, no replacement parts for eyes. I cursed myself for being so stupid, but I was lucky to have gotten off as easily as I did. The work dragged on.

Finally, the second P-51 was ready to go. Inspections, repairs, the painting out of the Nicaraguan insignia, reinspections—everything had been done. The mechanics wanted their incentive money even though the planes were not ready in the designated two weeks. "We didn't have the parts," they protested. I paid.

Chapter 7

Hired Pilots: Part I

After outlining the work to be done on several of the P-51s with Sergeant Gonzales, I flew back up to Chicago. Finding competent pilots to ferry the planes was proving to be a harder job than we expected. Most former military pilots now worked full-time in civilian jobs. So when Glenn found Duane, an instructor with the prestigious Airline Transport Pilot rating, the equivalent of a PhD in the aeronautical world, we thought we had a winner. I told him I wanted him to take a T-28 down and bring a P-51 back up.

I spent hours with him going over procedures and government requirements, particularly related to crossing borders. Any country viewed the transportation of munitions in its airspace as serious business, and I emphasized following the letter of the law meticulously. Duane made no attempt to hide his impatience with my instructions. He kept saying nonchalantly, "Yeah, I know all that. I've flown Mustangs and all the heavy stuff." He reminded me of his ATP license. He flew the T-28 down to Managua and left the next day for the States with the Mustang.

A day later, I received a cable from our customs broker, Bat Corrigan, in Brownsville. Duane had left a message at his office that he had crash-landed between Veracruz and Tampico in Mexico. Since

Bat wasn't in the office when Duane called, he didn't know any details or if he had been hurt. We waited for a call from Duane, but one never came.

Glenn suggested we call the U.S. Embassy in Mexico City. If Duane were in trouble, he might try to contact the officials there. After being passed around, I finally reached a staff member. I started to tell him we thought Duane could be injured when he interrupted, asking who I was, what I was doing flying airplanes all over Mexico, and whether I had import/export licenses. I patiently explained we had filed all the paperwork with his office. It seemed to me that if I were gun running, I wouldn't be telling the embassy about it. Having finally satisfied himself we weren't in the revolution business, he said if the embassy were notified, he would contact us. End of discussion. It was clear there wasn't going to be any help forthcoming.

With a plane down and a pilot missing, we were at a loss as to what to do next. Duane was well known around the airport, but no one knew where he lived or if he had any family. And as it turned out, the address on his license wasn't current.

Bat called again. The news wasn't good. Through a contact in the Mexican Air Force, he learned the Mexicans had confiscated the plane. The plane had entered Mexico illegally with no numbers on it. In fact, they were looking for the pilot to arrest him. "You've got a real problem," he warned grimly. We were stunned.

I called the embassy again in Mexico City. I explained we had been given permission to overfly Mexico, checking in at Tapachula, a border town at Mexico's southwest corner, and again at Matamoros on the northeast side. Since I had been very specific about painting the numbers on the plane, we couldn't understand the identification problem.

The staff member dropped another bomb. "If your pilot was flying an unmarked plane, he might already be in prison." He added that Mexican officials were never in a hurry to inform his office when there was a U.S. national in custody. He echoed Bat's statement, "You've got a real problem. We'll let you know if we hear anything," he promised not very reassuringly.

We had heard horror stories of Mexican jails but didn't know what to do next. We continued to call the embassy every few days, but there was no news on Duane or the plane.

Ten days went by. Glenn and I were at Midway Airport looking over some Packard Merlin engine parts when Duane strolled up. He mentioned casually that he had been back about three days.

"What happened?" we asked in unison.

Duane smiled, unwrapped some chewing gum, and said, "She overheated, and I put her down on the beach."

"How long had you been flying from Tapachula?" I asked.

"Oh I never landed in Tapachula. On the way down, the guy at Veracruz said there was no reason to land there on my return trip and told me I could get gas at his place just as well."

"Don't you remember I explicitly said you had to check in the country at Tapachula and out at Matamoros?"

"Yeah, but I had plenty of gas and was making good time."

"Did you check the engine at Veracruz?" I said, my voice rising.

"Sure. It took seven or eight gallons of water."

"Did you see any evidence of leaks? Did you run it up and check it?" Glenn asked.

"Well, no, actually," he admitted. "I figured if it ran all the way to Veracruz, it would run all the way to Matamoros. And I could always have a mechanic fix it at Brownsville."

"Sure, if it were a gradual leak. But if the leak had occurred in the last ten minutes, what happened was predictable," I pointed out grimly.

He lit a cigarette. "Maybe so."

Glenn asked the next question. "Where did you put the numbers on the plane?"

"Oh, yeah. About that. They told me the guy with the stencil wasn't there that day, and I wanted to get going. Those dumbass Mexicans don't pay attention, so I didn't think it would make any difference."

Glenn and I winced. My heart was sinking. "What happened after the crash?"

"I put it down on the beach and there was a highway about a mile away. I walked over and caught the bus going to Veracruz. Then

I flew to Mexico City. Since I hadn't been there before, I thought I would bum around a few days and see the sights. I really like their music down there."

Glenn and I just looked at each other. Before I could share the choice words mounting in me, our distinguished Airline Transport pilot reached in his pocket and pulled out a fat envelope. "Here're all my expenses. I'd like to get paid right away. Could I get a check today?"

Glenn muttered through clenched teeth, "I'll look them over when I get a chance."

"I'd really appreciate the money today," he repeated, oblivious to the look on Glenn's face.

We waited for an apology or something like, "Yeah, I guess I screwed up." We concluded this guy was so stupid he actually had no idea of the trouble and expense he had caused. Then he asked cheerfully, "Do you have another plane you want me to take down? I could make another trip next week. The T-28 was fun flying."

"I'll let you know," I replied finally. It would be cheaper to set a plane on fire than to let him near another one.

Glenn and I ate lunch in glum silence. Mustangs are notorious for coolant leaks, but Duane hadn't bothered to check the system. He had simply added seven gallons of water. It had been a disaster in the making. The coolant is a sealed system and if it needs water, something is wrong. While degrees and ratings are important, there's more to flying than passing tests. Like a little common sense.

It sounded from Duane's description as though all the plane needed was a new prop and maybe some belly skin. We contacted the Mexican Air Force to arrange to see the plane. There was no response. After a number of letters, I finally received a reply saying that the Mexican Air Force had trucked it to Mexico City.

Thus began a long series of requests beseeching the Mexicans to tell us the location of the plane. Dealing with the United States Embassy in Mexico was a frustrating and disappointing experience. The responses went from we-are-working-on-it to we-can't-find-the-file to why-don't-you-just-go-away? One more problem to add to the list.

Chapter 8

Cockpit Tales

I caught a TACA flight back to Managua via New Orleans. The El Salvadoran airline flew Vickers Viscounts. They were a new kind of aircraft called turboprops. The planes carried about fifty passengers with four Rolls-Royce Dart engines that produced 1300 to 1500 horsepower. The nicest thing about flying them was that although smaller than most airliners, the Vickers Viscounts made much less noise and there was almost no vibration of any kind in the cabin.

After we took off, I told the cabin attendant that I was a pilot and asked if I could go up and talk to the crew. She poked her head through the cockpit doorway and came back and said to go ahead. Up front, I introduced myself and said I had bought the air force planes in Nicaragua. The two men, both Americans, grinned.

"So you're the guy!" said the co-pilot. "We'd heard there was a rich guy from Chicago that had made the deal."

I laughed. "Not so rich! It's a hell of an adventure flying down there, though. Either of you guys ever flown those kind of birds?"

Both were ex-military, but neither had flown fighters. I mentioned I was also selling the Nicaraguans B-26s and T-28s. "Sounds like fun," commented the captain a little enviously. "Who are you getting to fly them?"

"Actually, I'm having a lot of trouble finding good pilots," I confessed. "I take out ads and get lots of responses, but most of them don't have the credentials. It seems a lot of them think all you need is a leather jacket." I made a mental note to ask Glenn to take out some more ads.

We talked shop a little more. It was my turn to be envious. "How do you like flying a turboprop?" I asked.

"It's sweet," said the co-pilot. "If I touch this"–he pointed to a button–"I can feather a prop in about one second. I look out the window and the prop is stopped! Nice in an emergency, eh?" I was impressed. The turboprop could do that because it had no mechanical link to the engine, so if there were a dead engine, the pilot could immediately eliminate all unnecessary drag.

When the plane made a stop in Guatemala City, I went back to my seat, but at the crew's invitation, rejoined them in the cockpit once we were back in the air.

There was a tap at the door. Another passenger poked his head in. "Can I join you too?" he asked. The captain shook his head. "Sorry sir. Only company people allowed up front."

Among the planes I was buying was a rare Trainer-Fighter (TF) dual control Mustang. Texas Engineering and Manufacturing built only fifteen, the last ones in 1951. The rear gas tank in the D model was removed to make way for a second cockpit, complete with instruments and controls, and the canopy was extended so the instructor could step into the back seat. National Guard units around the country used them, and the U.S. eventually gave them to Latin American countries. It was by far the most valuable airplane in my package.

I let it be known that I would like to ride in the TF. Colonel Saavedra ordered Major Gomez to check me out, and he jumped at the chance. Like most of the pilots, he had trained in the U.S., but he had an anti-American attitude that stuck out like porcupine quills.

He handed me a parachute. I had never worn one in my life and didn't have any idea how to put it on. The straps were set for a much smaller man, and I fumbled around trying to adjust them. The growing group of spectators snickered.

The student traditionally takes the front cockpit so I was surprised when the major motioned me to the one behind it. Sitting in the rear cockpit, I felt as though I were tipped back in the dentist's chair. Major Gomez said he would do the takeoff, and we went roaring down the runway. When the tail came up, I could see forward.

At 6,000 feet, the major throttled back and shouted through the intercom, "Go ahead and take it."

I tried gentle turns and then steepened them up, delighted with the sensitive response of this metal thoroughbred. It was as one ace had described—"the perfect union of man and machine."

I told him if he wanted to do a little air work, it was okay with me. I heard a wicked laugh that let me know I'd made a big mistake. He started with aileron rolls at full power in a climbing attitude and finished off with a Split S. On the base leg, he suddenly stood the plane right on its wing tip, cut the throttle, and dove for the field, the engine backfiring all the way down. I sucked in my breath as the ground rushed up. If this had been in the U.S., the tower would have thought it was under attack.

The major then made a low pass and climbed up for another approach. "Go ahead and take it for the landing," he shouted over the intercom.

"Okay!" I replied. Another big mistake.

I started a long final approach, gradually losing altitude. But when a Mustang slows, the nose comes up and forward visibility is lost. From the back seat, I might as well have been in a barrel.

I was at 120 mph about 300 feet above the runway when the major grabbed the stick. "I've got it," he announced and slammed the throttle forward, zoomed down the runway and pulled up sharply. He did a go-around and then landed the plane. When we got out, he said, "You want more instruction?"

"No hard feelings, but I really don't think I learned much," I replied as I unstrapped the parachute.

"Okay. That'll be $50."

"$50? I understood it was part of the deal!" I protested.

When Colonel Saavedra confirmed that absolutely no payment was due, the major told the group loitering there, "He doesn't know how to fly at all."

"What are you talking about?" I asked irritably.

"You were attempting to land and didn't reset the rudder trim in case you had to go around," he sneered.

I didn't know what the hell he was talking about. I was mad but knew better than to show it, so I forced myself to say mildly, "You're probably right," and let it go at that. The FAN officers had a lot of pride and resented the *norteamericanos* as the rich relatives. It was natural, but I sure didn't like it. *

The U.S. had sent down four Lockheed T-33 jets to the Nicaraguans and there was one parked on the tarmac at Las Mercedes. I had been eyeing it, waiting for a chance to go up for a ride and maybe pilot it. I never would have been allowed to do it in the U.S., but rules were more elastic in Nicaragua.

One morning while I was checking a repair on one of my planes, I saw a FAN pilot head out to the jet with a kid who looked to be about sixteen. The teenager was clearly excited as he trotted along to keep up with the officer. Sergeant Chavez was drinking a Coke next to the hangar door and gestured with the bottle toward the boy. "First time to go up in a plane. He looks happy, no?" he said to me, grinning.

I grinned back. The kid was in for quite a ride. I felt a twinge of envy. Well, I'd have to talk to Saavedra. I turned back to my work as the jet engines fired up. Suddenly there was a loud BANG! I glanced over my shoulder and saw what looked like a missile headed straight up from the T-33. "Jesus Christ!" I whispered.

"*Ay Mamacita Linda!*" cried Chavez, dropping his Coke. The rear ejection seat had exploded up right through the tilted canopy, carrying the boy a hundred fifty feet in the air. The sergeant and I stood in the hangar doorway, watching in horror as the heavy metal chair hurtled back toward the earth. There was a loud thud as it landed at the edge of the runway. "*Ay Dios mio, mi lindo....*" said Chavez in an agonized voice. I turned away.

---

* I later learned the major didn't know what the hell he was talking about. There is no need to reset the rudder trim anticipating a go-around, and there is no mention of it in the pilot's manual. Aborting a landing would normally take place while the plane has sufficient speed to fly, so the prop effect would be negligible. So much for my first lesson in a Mustang.

My God. How could this have happened? Pulling the armrest up triggered the seat to eject. Safety pins were always supposed to be in place until the pilots were strapped in and then at the last minute, mechanics would lean into the cockpits and carefully remove them. Obviously no one had taken this precaution, and the kid was probably just trying to get settled in. How could they not have briefed him? Where had the pilot been? I left the airport as the crash truck pulled on to the tarmac.

Chapter 9

HIRED PILOTS: PART II

Several weeks later, I was back up in Chicago. A local pilot contacted us about ferrying Mustangs. Roy was maybe thirty, blond, with a stocky, muscular build. He had owned a Mustang, he said. He brought along a friend, an instructor who was older. Mr. Senior Pilot was a bit patronizing but seemed to have solid experience.

After the disasters with DeLarm and Duane, Glenn and I checked these two out carefully. A fixed base operator at Midway said that while the senior pilot was known for his ego, he had been around Midway for years and was considered reliable. Roy had ferried planes for Morton, the dealer in Indiana who had sold us a T-28. Morton assured us there hadn't been any problems with Roy. I spent an intense two hours going over procedures and then launched the two down to Nicaragua in a T-28. I followed them in an airliner.

They delivered the T-28 without incident. Not surprisingly, the next Mustangs weren't ready, so there was a good deal of time to talk airplanes. One night after dinner, we were sitting around with some of the U.S. Air Force Mission men, swapping stories. Roy and Mr. Senior Pilot were classic intrepid barnstormers who waxed eloquently about their daring and heroic maneuvers. All they lacked were the white silk scarves.

Roy was explaining takeoff procedure in a Mustang. He dramatically demonstrated how to jam the right foot all the way down on the rudder: "You gotta offset that big prop's torque," he explained. "That torque makes the plane want to pull left on takeoff."

None of the mission men had flown Mustangs, since they had gone straight into jets after the T-34.* They listened respectfully as Roy and his partner made it clear that Mustang pilots were a breed apart. I said nothing.

Among the planes the Nicaraguans sold me were two pristine P-47 Thunderbolts. A huge airplane, the Thunderbolt was made by Republic Aviation and was the largest fighter ever powered by a single piston engine. Although we were not using the turbocharger in the tail, its supercharged R2800 2800-horsepower Pratt & Whitney radial engine had enough power to fly at the altitudes we were using.

Ours were one of the late models, the "N," designed originally for the Pacific Theater. Nicknamed "The Jug," the P-47 looked like a sumo wrestler compared to the sleek Mustang. The Mustang's V-12 engine was long and narrow, and the P-51 fuselage measured only two feet eleven inches at its widest point. In contrast, the P-47 looked as though two pilots could almost sit side by side. American pilots used to joke that an evasive maneuver in the '47 was to run around inside the cockpit.

While I had more confidence in the Mustang's hydraulic pitch-controlled prop, I liked the construction and finish work of the '47 better. The manufacturer, Republic, got a lot more for their plane: $85,000 for the '47 versus $55,000 for the Mustang. The "N" model, which we had, was larger than the original P-47s, with an electrically operated full plastic canopy. Like all fighters with a tail wheel, the plane was difficult to taxi; the pilot had to zigzag along to see where he was going. This meant he had to unlock the tail wheel after landing so it would swivel with the rudder pedals. Its extra-wide stance measured nineteen feet between the wheels and it was so tall, most men could walk under the leading edge of the wing without ducking.

One of the Thunderbolts was ready, and Mr. Senior Pilot wanted to fly it rather than a Mustang back. While he and I were looking

*225 horsepower Beechcraft primary trainer

over the plane, I noticed a canvas flap hanging down from the wheel well. Sergeant Gonzales, the crew chief, explained it was just a dust cover. When I looked more closely, I could see only three screws held it in place.

"Looks like it's broken," I said. "Why don't you just take it off?"

"*No problema, jefe,*" he assured me.

The next morning, a minor government bureaucrat came up with more paperwork, so I was delayed getting to the field. When I arrived, Mr. Senior Pilot was taxiing the Thunderbolt out to test-fly it.

I was working on a parts list when I glanced up to see him making a low pass over the runway. His gear was down and as he flew by, the gear came back up. He kept making passes with the gear going down and up. He must have been getting a red light on his panel, but since the plane didn't have a working radio, we couldn't tell him the gear indicator light, not the gear, was the problem. After a number of passes, he left the pattern. I guessed he was burning off some of the 450 gallons of gas to reduce the weight for a belly landing.

I thought frantically. There wasn't another plane available to fly up beside him to try to let him know the gear was working. For lack of any better ideas, I started hunting for a large piece of cardboard on which we could write GEAR IS DOWN and hold at the end of the runway.

Before we could complete the sign, he was back. I watched in horror as he jammed the magnificent machine down on the runway, sliding it about 300 feet on its belly. I climbed on a truck heading out to him and got there just as he was jumping off the wing. He was thoroughly rattled and his face was red. "I had to do it. I had to do it. It was the only thing to do!" he kept gasping.

It turned out there were plenty of hints that the gear was indeed down. P-47s have a hand pump that allows a pilot to pump the gear down if the normal system fails. He said he was able to get it up to 1400 pounds. With that much pressure, even if it weren't completely locked, it would have held for a careful landing. It should have also told him the gear was down and that it was the indicator that was faulty. He also ignored the fact that the tower kept giving him the green light.

The plane was picked up with a fork truck and the wheels lowered. The landing gear was perfectly functional. With the excitement, everyone was through working for the day. The prop was wrecked and much of the underbelly as well. Since Thunderbolt parts were virtually impossible to get, the plane was a total loss.

Sergeant Gonzales was looking at it the next morning when I walked up. "What happened?" I asked. He pointed at the hydraulically operated piston that locks the gear in the down position. The canvas dust cover had jammed the piston, keeping it from sliding into the last fraction of an inch to lock. That was enough to cause the micro switch to give the red "unsafe" light.

I was furious. "Why didn't you fix it yesterday like you said you would?" He just smiled blandly, shrugged his shoulders, and walked away.

When I confronted Mr. Senior Pilot later that day, he said in so many words, "That's not my job."

Technically, he was correct, but I have never flown a plane in my life that I did not first check, especially if there was a work order on it. I realized I was getting bottom of the barrel pilots. Right now though, I didn't have anybody else. Two Mustangs were almost ready, so I paid for them and told Roy and his friend to bring them back. Exhausted, I flew Pan Am home to Chicago.

A week later, I got a cable that Mr. Senior Pilot had crash-landed the Mustang at Veracruz. Apparently he had come in too slow, stalled, misjudged the runway and dropped down hard, so hard that one landing gear broke through the wing while the other completely collapsed. When the nose hit, the front case of the engine and prop broke off. Luckily for the pilot, the canopy remained intact. A bulldozer just pushed the plane off the runway.

Roy delivered his P-51 into Chicago without incident, but Mr. Senior Pilot, now down two airplanes, had to follow in an airliner. Another pilot crossed off my list.*

*Several years later, Mr. Senior Pilot was instructing at Midway Airport and flew into a garage, killing his student and himself.

Chapter 10

B-26 Bronco-riding

I decided to call an instructor whom I had known for years on the off chance he might be available to ferry some planes for me. Albert worked as the full-time senior pilot for a Chicago newspaper, flying a converted Lockheed Ventura bomber. The Ventura was a large twin that served nicely as a civilian aircraft, and Albert was the envy of the other pilots on the field. He was middle-aged, a laid-back man with a quiet dignity about him. No one called him Al. He also moved planes around for dealers from time to time.

We had met five years earlier when he had strolled up and offered to help me tie down my Apache. I had recently bought the twin-engine plane, and I confessed to him that although I had my multi-engine rating, I still wasn't comfortable with it.

"Do you still do any instructing?" I asked.

"Just enough to stay legal," he said.

We started flying together. We would go up to 5,000 feet and then run through drills, feathering one engine, dropping flaps, lowering wheels and so forth. He gave me confidence that I could fly the plane and still deal with an emergency.

At his invitation, I began stopping in for coffee at his hangar. His philosophy of flying made the most sense of any I had heard. When

I asked him which plane was the most difficult to fly, he said simply, "There isn't any such plane. Airplanes are airplanes. Sure, more engines make some more complex, but engineers design airplanes to fly, and that's what they do. The controls are usually pretty logical and the manuals are self-explanatory."

Albert had served as a civilian instructor in the military during WWII. In the rush to train pilots, there was only time to cover the basics, he said. "Some of the best pilots came from farms, probably because they were used to working with machinery and understood how it operated," he commented.

One afternoon he paid me a great compliment. "Will, you've got more practical knowledge about planes than most of my students ever had. You can transfer that knowledge from one plane to another."

While Glenn and I were tracking down bombers, I asked Albert if he would consider taking a B-26 to Nicaragua. He shook his head and said he was tied up through the end of the year. "Will, you can fly a B-26," he told me. I wasn't sure I shared his confidence, but filed that thought away.

Our contract with the FAN called for us to furnish two B-26 bombers with spare parts. The parts list detailing what they wanted grew longer every time I met with them. Finally I offered to give them an extra plane instead of parts. Since parts procurement in Nicaragua typically consisted of stripping the needed item off the nearest parked plane, this made sense to them and was cheaper for me. B-26s in decent condition, however, turned out to be in short supply.

WWII had been over for almost twenty years. Lots of derelict B-26s were sitting on U.S. airfields, having been optimistically purchased with the hope of profitable resale. The market wasn't there and time took its sad toll on the old warriors. The description on the phone was always, "It's in great shape and just needs a little work."*

Shortly thereafter, I spotted a B-26 that was a real beauty parked outside at Midway Airport. I asked the fixed base manager about it. "There's quite a story there, and I know about ten percent of it," he

---

*Some had been converted to civilian use by companies such as Dean Foods. At the time, the '26 could run circles around the old DC-3s still in use. If you wanted speed, the '26 outperformed everything else. However, the '26 had very limited seating versus the DC-3, and thus it was not a practical plane for most corporations.

related. "The pilot ferrying it from California landed for gas. I took my truck out and was filling it when, all of a sudden, customs officers with guns surrounded the plane. The pilot showed them his ferry permit, but the feds announced that it and his export license had been cancelled while he was en route from California that morning. They arrested him on the spot. I don't know what happened to the guy, but the government pays me to run up the engines once a week just to maintain it."

"Is it for sale?" I asked.

"Not sure. Usually the government sells stuff it confiscates. Go take a look in the cockpit if you like."

I looked the plane over. To get up to the cockpit, I made sure to put the correct foot into the initial toehold. If you didn't start with the proper foot and handhold, you would end up facing the wrong direction at the canopy. The manual showed a straightforward instrument panel. I settled into the left seat, started up the engines and was doing a simple magneto check when a black sedan drove up and stopped right in front of the plane, blocking it. I shut the engines down and climbed out.

"What are you doing?" shouted a man in a dark suit and sunglasses. I have never figured out why government men always look like government men, but he might as well have been wearing a signboard.

"Is the plane for sale?" I countered.

"I can't answer that."

I carefully climbed down. "I'm interested in buying it," I said.

He checked my ID, gave me a phone number to call for information, told me curtly not to move it, and drove away.

I subsequently learned that a notorious aircraft dealer owned the plane. His reputation was so bad that a flying magazine had run a detailed article about his shady business practices. Forewarned, I contacted the dealer's attorney directly. We agreed on a price with the condition that the purchase would be handled through the law firm, not the dealer.

Since the paperwork would take awhile, I needed to find another '26 right away. When I learned of one owned by a fire-fighting company in Prescott, Arizona, I called to ask an A&P* mechanic on the field to check it out. The mechanic assured me it was a sound plane and I bought it, subject to inspection. I also asked if any of the firefighters might be available to fly it to Nicaragua. He promised to make inquiries.

On the commercial flight down to Arizona, I studied the B-26 manual, reviewing the numbers and memorizing the placement of essential knobs, handles, and switches. When I arrived at the Prescott airport, I learned there were no pilots available. I remembered Albert's assurance that I could handle a B-26. It looked as though I might have to. I was checking the plane over when a tall, gray-haired, military-looking guy ambled up.

"You the new owner?" he asked.

"Yeah," I answered.

"Ever flown a '26?"

"No, but I hear they handle much like a '25," I answered, hoping to sound authoritative. I'd never flown a twin bigger than my Piper Apache.

"That's right," he agreed.

Standing under the wing, the B-26 looked like a monster. It was fifty feet long, eighteen feet eight inches high, with a wingspan of seventy feet and a weight of seventeen and a half tons. Its two engines of 2000 horsepower each gave it a top speed of 355 miles per hour. What a splendid bird!

The man introduced himself as a retired Air Force colonel and offered to check me out in it. I jumped at the offer.

I continued looking over the plane. When I opened the petcock to drain any water that might have accumulated in the bottom of the gas tank, nothing came out. I concluded it must be plugged up and checked the other side. Same thing. Then it dawned on me I was buying an airplane that had had every drop of gas drained!

I flagged down a line boy and asked him to fill it.

"Yeah, sure, but I have to go back and get the big truck," he said. I understood what he meant when it took 800 gallons.

While waiting for the gas truck, I asked the colonel about the cracks in the tires.

*Airframe and Powerplant, a certification issued by the FAA

"That's nothing to worry about," he assured me. "Those are 20-ply and just look like that normally when a plane's been in the desert. They're fine. It's still daylight," he continued. "Let's crank it up."

Fortunately back at Midway I had figured out the hand- and toeholds that lead up to the cockpit. I climbed up, opened the clamshell canopy, and dropped into the pilot's seat. The co-pilot's seat didn't have a set of controls. The colonel dropped into it and said, "Let's give it a whirl."

We ran down the batteries trying to start it. After hooking up a battery cart, the engines sputtered, groaned, coughed, and finally caught with giant explosions. "Sometimes they're a little hard to start," the colonel observed dryly. Since it was dark now, we arranged to meet early the next morning to fly.

At eight o'clock the next day, the engines started reluctantly, but once going, ran smoothly. The plane was parked with the nose wheel cocked hard to the left. I wanted to go to the right, so I tapped the brake on the top of the rudder pedal. The nose bobbed down, and we were still going to the left. I kept tapping the right brake until the nose wheel finally turned that direction. We looked like the clown car at the circus as we lurched along. I waited for the colonel to tell me what a boob I was, but he seemed perfectly content.

It was an uncontrolled airport, so when I had reached the runway and run through the checks, I just looked around and started off. Once the plane accelerated and the control surfaces had enough air going over them, the controls began to bite and, finally, I felt in charge.

I cruised around in the blue cloudless sky and then set up for the landing. I reviewed my mental checklist—power, wheels, flaps, pumps, props—and aimed for the centerline of the runway. It seemed more like a crash than a landing when we touched down. The impact jarred my whole body. The colonel didn't flinch. The plane wasn't insulated, and the noise of the huge engines made any conversation impossible. When the bird finally stopped, to my surprise he merely said, "That wasn't too bad. Let's try it again." The second time I was more relaxed and made a very acceptable approach and landing. While heading back, I finally figured out that the secret in taxiing is coming down on both brakes gently and then easing off the brake opposite of the direction I wanted to go.

The colonel said casually, "With your experience in '25s, you'll have no problem. Let me just tell you about one thing though. See the little window in the floor? That's so you can see the nose gear to make sure the strut is properly extended. There's something about the '26 design that makes the gear hang up. If it happens, just cycle the gear a couple of times and it'll come down."

At breakfast in the coffee shop, he said the '26 was a popular plane with Air Force pilots, although when fully loaded with fuel and armaments, its heavy weight required extra care. "If an engine died on takeoff, you really had your hands full," said the colonel. "For civilian firefighting, though, they're great—even loaded with fire retardants, a '26 doesn't weigh anywhere near what the combat planes did." The colonel paused. "By the way, do you know the numbers for this bird?"

I recited the minimum single-engine, climb, cruise, landing, and go-around speeds. I added that I was only using 5,000 foot-plus runways. He nodded. "The '26 is a little hotter than a '25, which is why the Air Force keeps the '25 in inventory for twin-engine training." He excused himself to make a phone call.

The minimum speed numbers were important. When I was getting my twin-engine rating, my instructor had warned that the most dangerous time in a twin is during takeoff. He'd explained that if a single-engine plane's engine quits, you are then essentially in a glider and can just ride it down. But in a twin, if one engine stops, the pilot is suddenly in a machine that wants to kill him. The plane turns toward the side of the dead engine. If there is enough airspeed, the pilot can keep the plane under control—while raising the gear, feathering the correct prop, getting on the rudder and hopefully, continuing to climb out. However, if the plane is not yet at that minimum controllable single engine airspeed—140 miles per hour in the '26—although counterintuitive, the pilot must immediately reduce power on the one good engine to maintain the control needed to be able to make an emergency landing.

When the colonel returned, he said, "Well, I talked to my boss and told him the check ride went well. I told him I didn't think you were going to have any trouble."

It dawned on me that the owner of the plane had arranged for the colonel's apparently casual meeting with me and the check ride. I had the feeling if the seller hadn't liked the report, he would have killed the deal. It was one of the few times I encountered a seller who had the scruples to care about the person he was selling a plane to.

The line boy walked by our table in the airport coffee shop. I asked him to top off the tanks, and he came back with a ticket for ninety gallons.

I finished breakfast, paid for the gas and thanked the colonel. The weather forecast looked fine for the first leg of my flight to El Paso, Texas, about 400 miles southeast. I was feeling good about flying the B-26. I now taxied like a pro and the takeoff was smooth. I climbed to 7,500 feet, set the power at 2000 rpm and the manifold pressure for 32 inches. I'd given the El Paso tower my ETA and advised them I would need a light gun. When I turned on my downwind leg, the green light was on me.

I landed and just as I was turning off the main runway, the right engine quit. I stopped the plane and realized the idle was set too low when I pulled the throttles back. It took three tries to finally get it going. I felt every eye at the airport was on me. So much for the new Super Pilot! A jeep with a FOLLOW ME sign took me to an area of light aircraft. A courtesy car deposited me at a motel.

I planned an early start the next morning. After the tanks were filled, the fixed base operator handed me a shoebox full of trading stamps. He was not used to selling 234 gallons at a time. The line boy cheerfully invited me to "come back soon."

My next stop was the old airport at San Antonio to pick up parts I had ordered. The ritual of starting the engines began. After eight to ten turns, nothing happened, so I tried the other engine.

About that time, a mechanic going by in a tug stopped. "Want some help? We got the same engines, R-2800s, and there's a trick to starting them."

I waved him up and the way he expertly climbed the toeholds told me he knew this plane well. I moved out of the pilot's seat, he dropped in it, reached over, and with the electric fuel pumps on, opened and closed the mixture quickly and hit the starter. The engine backfired. When it did light, I thought the rear of the plane was blowing off. He slowly opened the mixture until the engine ran smoothly. He calmly repeated the procedure for the other engine with the same Fourth of July explosion. I looked around, half expecting the fire trucks, but apparently everyone except me was used to this commotion.

"These things just need a little more gas in the cylinders to get going," the mechanic explained nonchalantly. He whacked me on the shoulder, said, "See ya!" and was gone.

Four thousand horsepower was exciting but a little scary. I taxied carefully out to the end of the runway, went through my run-up and reviewed the gauges and trim settings. I went over in my mind the minimum single engine control, takeoff, and the stall speeds. When the tower shot me the green light, I was ready to go. I held the brakes, ran up the power, and then released the brakes, tracking down the runway like a rocket, or so it seemed. When the airspeed hit 100 miles per hour, I raised the nose wheel slightly, but the plane didn't lift off as I expected. Seconds later when it did leave the ground, it seemed forever before I reached the critical 140-mile-per-hour mark and could retract the landing gear.

The day was clear and I climbed to 9,500 feet. A little light rain was predicted, but the air was smooth as glass. The B-26 was a fantastic plane to fly, and I was enjoying it immensely. I could see why it had earned the reputation of being a pilot's plane.

I arrived over the San Antonio airport right on my ETA. The San Antonio controller shot me the green light, and I swung out to make a long base leg for Runway 14. Dropping the landing gear, I waited for the three green lights to appear. Only two came on. I looked through the little window in the floor, and sure enough, the nose gear wasn't down. I left the pattern and raised and lowered the gear three times before all three green lights came on.

I swung back over the field, got the green light a second time, and lined up with the runway. I concentrated on getting the plane slowed up so I wouldn't have to do a go-around. The airspeed indicator read 130 miles per hour when the wheels made contact with the ground;

my touchdown was right on the money. I'm sure my self-satisfied smile went from ear to ear.

Suddenly the plane lurched violently to the left, the wing missing the runway lights by inches. I countered immediately with full right aileron and stood on the brakes, yanking throttles full back. *What the hell was happening?*

This aluminum monster was hurtling down the runway completely out of control. I knew I would stall if I tried to lift off again for a go-around. I picked off a landing light and continued sliding down the runway going like hell toward a road that bordered the field.

When I whizzed by the administration building, my speed was still 100 miles per hour. A trooper was ticketing a girl in a red convertible on the road. They assumed the classic deer-in-the-headlights look as the bomber hurtled toward them, their expressions a combination of disbelief and sheer horror. All three of us were praying this big metal bird was going to stop. Seconds later, the plane slid to a halt about 200 feet short of them.

I sat there in a daze, trying to figure out what had just happened. My heart was pounding and I was soaked in perspiration. This had to be the worst landing I had ever made. I'd be lucky if I got off with just a tongue-lashing from the tower operators. Then I looked down at the left wheel: the tire was shredded and scattered all over the runway! The big engines were idling, and I shut them down. We weren't going anywhere.

Just then two mechanics pulled up in a yellow pickup. "Are you okay? That was some bronco riding, mister!" one said breathlessly. "It looked like you touched down okay and then the tire blew up. When that tire blew, I betcha rubber flew a couple hundred feet!"

The second mechanic interrupted, "You must have a lotta time in '26s to bring it in like that. I've seen one of these things do a cartwheel after it blew out a tire and then catch on fire and blow up! You're one lucky SOB!"

The first mechanic volunteered he had a jack that would fit a '26. When he got the wheel off, we saw that when the brake had locked, it had caught a big chunk of tire rubber under the wheel. The wheel had skidded along on its rubber mat, which not only saved me from ruining the wheel, but more importantly, prevented the bare metal wheel from sparking against the concrete. The wheels are magnesium, and if they catch fire, the plane goes up in smoke. It's almost impossible to extinguish magnesium once it ignites.

The airport manager drove up to tell me the tower wanted to talk to me. I stumbled over to the main building. I had been told the tower guys were touchy because they had not been assigned to a new airport that had just opened nearby. Their only concern now seemed to be why the hell I didn't land when they gave me the first green light. I explained the gear problem and that ended the discussion. No one asked to see my ferry permits, licenses or any documentation. The tower guys acted as if blowing out a tire on a B-26 were an everyday thing. The left wheel ended up about ten feet from the edge of the runway. I said I'd move the plane as quickly as possible, but they said it was no problem—they would just close the runway.

The right tire had burned through all of the plies almost to the tube, so a few more seconds would have blown it off as well. The mechanics directed me to a nearby tire company that had purchased war surplus tires for road graders that also fit a B-26. A huge man mounted tires on both wheels as though the bomber were a baby buggy; he was the kind of guy who could change a tire on a Buick without a jack. At $50 installed, the tires were a real bargain.

I reflected on the close call I'd just had. All the planes we purchased were either in current license or carried FAA ferry permits. A ferry permit requires a licensed mechanic to inspect the plane to certify it for the trip planned. We turned down many planes, even those with licenses, because for one reason or another, they didn't seem right. If the logbooks or paperwork looked suspicious, we passed. I had questioned the colonel in San Antonio about the tires and relied on the word of someone more experienced. I wished I had trusted my instincts. If something doesn't look right, it usually isn't.

That night I had trouble sleeping. It was incredible to me that with only a couple of hours flying time in the '26, I was able to get that thing down without killing myself. The mechanic said I was "lucky." I hadn't believed in guardian angels until then, but maybe the time had come.

Chapter 11

HIRED PILOTS: PART III

When I returned to the airport the next day, the parts I was picking up were stacked in crates alongside the bomber. While the plane was being loaded, a mechanic approached me.

"Hear you're looking for pilots," he ventured.

"That's right. Know of any?" I asked.

"Yeah," he continued. "There's a rich guy, Duke, who hangs around the airport. He heard about you and was real interested. He gave me his phone number to give you."

I called Duke and when he invited me to dinner, I accepted.

Duke arrived in a late-model Rolls-Royce, a guy probably in his early forties, with a deep suntan that he said he acquired at his "little place on the water." His very sexy blond girlfriend listened with rapt attention as he regaled us with stories of Porsche racing and flying adventures. He knew enough jargon to be believable and I hired him. I picked up the tab for dinner.

We spent the next morning going over the rules for entering and exiting Mexico as well as reviewing the B-26 operation, particularly the problems in starting the engines. I had given him the flight manual the night before and he seemed familiar with the plane.

The plan was for him to fly the B-26 to Nicaragua with another pilot, and both would bring back P-51s to Texas. Duke had a "connection" with an insurance company that would cover the P-51s for a very reasonable price on the trip back. The next day, I gave him generous expense money and saw the two of them off. It was a relief not to have to make the trip down myself, since I was still looking for T-28s and parts in the States.

He called the next day from Brownsville to report a burned-out starter on an engine. After running the battery down trying to start it, he had hired a man with a battery cart. He'd then kept turning the engine over and over until the starter had quit.

"Did you start the engines the way I told you?" I asked, exasperated.

"I know how to start these fucking engines," he snapped back.

Normally a plane battery would run down before it would damage the starter. But when Duke put the big battery cart on it and continued cranking it, the starter burned up.* Since the Pratt & Whitney is a common engine, we had no trouble getting a new starter. Electric starters do just that: they start things, and are not meant to be continuously run.

A new starter installed, Duke and the other pilot flew the '26 on to Nicaragua. They checked out the two Mustangs and, surprise, surprise, found they needed some work. Duke announced their time was too valuable to wait for the problems to be fixed and they left without P-51s but with the expense money. The insurance company and I subsequently had a heated argument over a policy that was never actually issued, and I didn't pay their $1,500 bill. I filed Duke under "Rascals I Have Known" and took out another want ad.

It was becoming pretty clear the best pilots weren't interested in ferrying my warbirds. The money was only so-so and they could get better gigs in safer planes. Sometimes I'd have a pilot accept, and then a more attractive opportunity would come along and he'd leave me in a lurch. The lure of the tropics, adventure, and romance did get

---

*Charlie Wilson of General Motors invented the electric car starter. When he presented the design to a class at M.I.T. and told them the turning power "torque" needed, the students unanimously agreed that it would burn up and never work. Mr. Wilson then told them they were looking at the specs of a present day car's electric starter. He said he didn't want it to turn all day—just long enough to start the engine.

the hormones of some racing, and those were the guys who typically answered my ads.

One day I got a call from a couple of charter pilots who said they'd been ferrying Canadian Mustangs down to the States. I hired them on the spot.

My plan was to have the two pilots, Johnny and Jimmy, deliver another T-28 to Nicaragua and then return with two Mustangs. As usual, I sat the two men down and went over charts and procedures. Bat Corrigan down at Brownsville Customs would be available to help with the border crossing at Matamoros. They would next land at Tapachula, the small town on the southern border of Mexico, and observe all protocol in exiting the country. When they arrived in Managua, Morgan would be there. Play it by the book, I told them, no grandstanding games. We then headed to a restaurant where they entertained me over dinner with stories of their flying exploits in Mustangs.

The T-28 has two seats, one behind the other, with dual controls. The accepted practice is for the pilot in the front seat to alternate flying with the man behind him. Apparently the two got into some sort of disagreement, and Johnny refused to relinquish the controls to Jimmy on the way down. They were in bad humor when they arrived, according to Morgan. The next morning, they showed up at the airport and experienced the usual rigmarole getting the planes out. It was decided Jimmy would test-fly the first Mustang.

Morgan reported that Jimmy had asked to have his picture taken in the '51. Sitting on the tarmac and posing for the camera was surely the only glamorous aspect of flying a Mustang in Nicaragua. It was mostly a hot, smelly experience. Because of the sun's heat, the canopy had to be open while you taxied to the end of the runway. The fumes from the short exhaust stacks would swirl back into the canopy. Add to that the smell that rose from the many years' worth of oil embedded in the wooden floorboards, and if you'd had a greasy breakfast, you wouldn't keep it for long.

Jimmy gave a thumbs-up, closed the canopy and started down the runway. When he had gone about 800 feet, he suddenly cut the throttle. The crowd of spectators was used to false starts and wondered what wasn't working now. He taxied back, shut down the engine, climbed out, and started walking quickly in the direction of the terminal.

Morgan caught up with him. "What's going on, Bub?" he asked.

"I've never flown a Mustang in my life and today isn't going to be the day," Jimmy said shortly. He took the afternoon Pan Am flight back to the States.

It was probably the best decision he ever made. The Mustang was an unforgiving plane that killed even experienced pilots. I wouldn't have flown it either.

The beginning of the adventure…

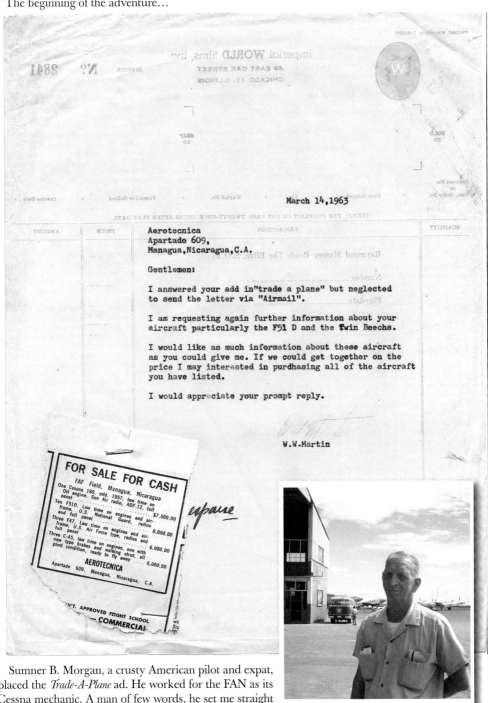

March 14,1963

Aerotecnica
Apartado 609,
Managua,Nicaragua,C.A.

Gentlemen:

I answered your add in"trade a plane" but neglected
to send the letter via "Airmail".

I am requesting again further information about your
aircraft particularly the F51 D and the twin Beechs.

I would like as much information about these aircraft
as you could give me. If we could get together on the
price I may interested in purchasing all of the aircraft
you have listed.

I would appreciate your prompt reply.

W.W.Martin

FOR SALE FOR CASH
FAF Field, Managua, Nicaragua
One Cessna 180, mfd. 1957, low time on
OH engine, Sun Air radio, ADF-12, full
panel $7,500.00
Ten F51D, Low time on engines and air-
frame, U.S. National Guard, radios
and full panel 6,000.00
Three F47, Low time on engines and air-
frame, U.S. Air Force type, radios and
full panel 6,000.00
Three C-45, low time on engines, one with
new type brakes and walking strut, all
good condition, ready to fly away 6,000.00
AEROTECNICA
Apartado 609, Managua, Nicaragua, C.A.

V'T. APPROVED FLIGHT SCHOOL
COMMERCIAL

Sumner B. Morgan, a crusty American pilot and expat,
placed the *Trade-A-Plane* ad. He worked for the FAN as its
Cessna mechanic. A man of few words, he set me straight
on Nica customs and culture.

General Anastasio "Tachito" Somoza Debayle.

Coronel (P-A) FRANCISCO SAAVEDRA O. GN.
Comandante de la Fuerza Aérea de Nicaragua

CNEL. RICARD M. MANSFIELD
JEFE DE LA MISION USAF EN NICARAGUA

Colonel Francisco Saavedra headed the Fuerza Aérea de Nicaragua or FAN, the acronym by which the Nicaraguan Air Force was more commonly called. (*Revista de la Fuerza Aérea de Nicaragua*)

USAF Colonel Richard Mansfield was in charge of the U.S. Mission. Its headquarters were next door to the FAN offices at Las Mercedes Airport. (*Revista de la Fuerza Aérea de Nicaragua*)

One of my
Nica Mustangs
at Las
Mercedes.

One of my two
Thunderbolts.
Neither would
make it back to
the States.

Jerry DeLarm on the wing of the T-28 at Midway Airport in Chicago.

Checking out a T-28 for the first time. I left Midway in it the following day and arrived at Las Mercedes 48 hours later.

DeLarm in front of his Lockheed Lodestar. NBC featured him in a documentary on the CIA, which had hired DeLarm to bomb Guatemalan targets as part of the effort to destabilize that government.

(Photo courtesy of NBCUniversal Media, LLC. *Science of Spying, 1965.* Copyright© 1965 National Broadcasting Company, Inc. All rights reserved.)

Norteamericano dice:

Fuerza Aérea Nicaragüense Hace Negocio con Hampón de Chicago

Un negocio que desde hace algún tiempo está realizando la Fuerza Aérea Nicaragüense (FAN) sin trascen- / der al público, fue descubierto en la mañana del viernes en el Juzgado del Trabajo, cuando un piloto aviador nor- / teamericano, entabló demanda judicial contra otro norteamericano, calificado por el piloto como "uno de los fa- / mosos Gangsters de Chicago", el mismo con quien la FAN está realizando su nego- / cio. El demandante es el señor Jerry Delarm, originario de / Chicago, Estados Unidos, y el demandado responde al Pasa a última Pág Letra A

After DeLarm unsuccessfully tried to take over my contract with the FAN, he went to the local papers and told them the FAN was doing business with "one of the international criminals which abound in Chicago." It wasn't until someone translated this *Nacion* headline that I understood why the hotel clerks had suddenly become so nervous around me!

El piloto norteamericano Jerry Delarm, presentando su demanda laboral ante el Abogado de los Trabajadores, contra el comerciante de aviones de guerra William W. Martin.

Nica mechanics working on the prop governor of a Thunderbolt.

Nica inventory control left a lot to be desired. Although the spare parts were included in my contract with the FAN, it was often easier to just order them from the States than locate them in a Nica warehouse.

Nicknamed "The Jug," the P-47 Thunderbolt was the largest fighter ever powered by a single piston engine.

Replacing a blown-out tire at the old San Antonio airport on the first B-26. A wedged piece of tire rubber prevented the magnesium wheel from catching fire as the bomber and I skidded down the runway, still going more than 100 miles an hour after the tire blew.

View of Irazú's ash cloud from Coco Airport.

My good friend Juan Bonilla. The airport commandant at Coco Airport in San José, Costa Rica, Bonilla was charged with selling his country's two Mustangs. He was honest, charming, and a thoroughly decent human being.

Juan Bonilla and a mechanic with me at Coco Airport. One of the Mustangs I bought sits to the left. A C-46 transport can be seen in the background.

My wife Pat created quite a sensation at the airport. She navigated the B-26 to
Managua and we touched down within 90 seconds of her ETA.

Pat and I visited the mouth of Irazú while we were still in Costa Rica.
Shortly after our visit, a boulder flew out of the crater and landed on someone,
putting an abrupt halt to volcano tourism.

Nica market in Managua. The Nicaraguans were warm and friendly, though as a giant gringo I was an object of great interest.

In the dining room at the Gran Hotel.

Sergeant Gonzales holding his recaptured dinner: iguanas were known as "chicken of the trees" in Nicaragua.

One of my Costa Rican Mustangs next to a KLM Constellation
in SALA's hangar. SALA was probably the best aircraft
maintenance facility at the time in Central America.

Being towed back after the engine glycol cap failed,
filling the cockpit with thick steam.

The impact when my Mustang hit tore loose the 200-pound radiator, seen here in the foreground.

We managed to salvage a few instruments from the cockpit.

What happens when a Mustang hits a fence post.

Chapter 12

Juan Bonilla

Back at the field in Nicaragua, I found no one had as much as wiped the dust off any of my planes. I had two Mustangs moved into the hangar and half-heartedly started a list of work to be done and parts needed. Since a religious holiday was coming up, I knew none of the men would work between now and then.

I decided to go over to Costa Rica, the country neighboring Nicaragua to the south. Word was that Costa Rica was going to sell some Mustangs along with a lot of spare parts. It was apparent I was going to need more parts than originally planned. If I could get them in Costa Rica instead of the U.S., it would save me time and money and I could resell the two Costa Rican Mustangs in the States. I learned that a major was in charge of the sale. I called him, made an appointment, and took the afternoon flight down on Pan Am.

Since it seemed U.S. citizens were always the last to go through customs in Nicaragua, I didn't hurry off the plane when we arrived at El Coco Airport. Juan Bonilla was waiting at the bottom of the steps, a middle-aged, well-groomed man with thinning hair. He was wearing civilian clothes and a great smile. "Señor Martin, come with me please." Unlike his Nicaraguan counterpart, he was unarmed.

I was whisked past the other hot and disgruntled passengers

standing in line for customs. I was conscious of their stares and whispers and felt like James Bond. The major spoke quietly to the immigration and customs personnel, everyone smiled, and we were out the side door. I learned later that he was the airport commandant. I hadn't realized just how tense I had been in Nicaragua's police state environment until I stepped into Costa Rica's friendly democracy. I felt as though a weight had been lifted off me.

The major drove me into San José, the beautiful and modern capital city of Costa Rica. His English was good enough that we could converse easily. Irazú, Costa Rica's long dormant volcano, had recently started spewing volcanic ash, *geniza*, which settled as haze over the valley, explained Major Bonilla. This had been going on for months. All the cattle had been herded out of the area, as the *geniza* coated the grass with an oily slick and the animals couldn't graze. The airport was clear enough to land, but the air had a gritty feel. In the city of San José itself, traffic policemen and anyone working outdoors wore goggles and painter-style masks. Pedestrians wrapped scarves over their mouths and noses. Many carried umbrellas. Shopkeepers hired young boys to quickly open and close doors for customers, and the ash caused on-going maintenance problems for car starters.

Costa Ricans boasted their country had more schoolteachers than soldiers. It had no standing army. The savings had been invested in education and the literacy rate was high. I never saw anyone with a sidearm while I was there.

As Major Bonilla and I were walking toward the warehouse, I casually asked if he had heard of Jerry DeLarm. His face darkened. "He's a son of a bitch," said Bonilla, "a very bad guy. How do you know him?"

I told Bonilla my history with DeLarm. Bonilla shook his head. "DeLarm is one of Somoza's guys." The major went on to explain that the General had backed some insurgents trying to overthrow the Costa Rican government. DeLarm flew a Nicaraguan DC-3 mounted with machine guns.

"DeLarm flew over San José at midday; people looked up when they heard the plane, and he fired on them. Fired on civilians. He killed seven in San José, and three more in other cities. One was a good friend of mine." Major Bonilla paused, his mouth set. "The OAS* got involved and the U.S. sent us four Mustangs. Somoza stopped then and DeLarm returned to hide in Nicaragua," said Bonilla, his voice full of contempt. He paused again, perhaps thinking about the friend that DeLarm had strafed. Morgan's sources had gotten it right, I reflected.

We were now standing in front of the warehouse. "So, we have still two Mustangs, and they are the ones for sale," Bonilla concluded briskly.

I'd heard a little of this history already, though not about DeLarm's role. I knew commercial airline pilots had been hired to fly the Mustangs. They had crashed two almost immediately. Since Costa Rica didn't have a military, it was decided to store the remaining planes. I hadn't known how long the other two had been there; from what Major Bonilla was saying, it sounded like a while. There was a lot of dust on the parts in the warehouse.

We moved on to the hangar. The two Mustangs were in excellent condition and the spare parts inventory looked to be accurate. The major confided that another group had offered an inflated price for the planes, but the government had been suspicious and refused the offer. The bidding would be handled through a formal announcement in the newspaper, Bonilla explained, and he said he would let me know.

"I'm definitely interested," I said, "but since I don't know anyone in Costa Rica, I need some kind of agent to handle this for me. Would it violate any of your government rules if I asked you?" Major Bonilla assured me he would be glad to help. There was no request for a *mordida,* just a handshake between two businessmen. I returned to Nicaragua.

It was several months later when the bids were finally let. It turned out I was the only bidder. I paid a fair price for the planes and parts and told the major I would come over to get the planes underway as soon as I could.

*Organization of American States

Chapter 13

Whither Thou Goest...

My contract called for the Nicaraguan Air Force to provide the labor to prepare the planes for ferrying, while I was to supply any parts not in their warehouse. At this point, I had purchased most of the remaining parts I needed and planned to ship them down in another B-26. I had made a trip back up to Chicago to brief the pilot and supervise the loading of the parts. At the last minute, the pilot informed me he wouldn't be able to make the trip.

"I'm going to have to take a '26 down myself," I announced to Pat. "Morgan says the work on my planes has stopped again, and I don't have a reliable pilot. I have to get the parts down there now."

Pat looked at me. "This is crazy. You told me you weren't going to fly any more of these planes."

"I can't jeopardize the contract by waiting 'til I find a pilot," I explained.

"Oh?" she said skeptically.

"Besides, it's a good plane," I assured her.

"Absolutely," she agreed. "Good for their use—training and flying within seventy-five miles of their base. But it has no radio except the one transmitter and receiver, just a wet compass, the oxygen system isn't connected, and if you hit bad weather...."

"I'll have a parachute," I assured her.

"Fine, if you land in a swimming pool in Acapulco. If you go down in the jungle, Stanley and Livingston combined wouldn't find you." She took a deep breath: "If you fly, so do I."

"It's illegal. I have a ferry permit, but I'm not licensed to carry passengers."

"But I'm not a passenger. I'm a navigator," she pointed out. "Remember, I took ground school with you."

"But what about Suzie and Cassie?" I countered.

"Your folks would love to have the kids."

Pat was a pretty fair VFR navigator, good with radios, and had flown with me for years. No question she would be helpful on this flight. I reluctantly agreed.

Pat was working on the editorial staff of a magazine at the time I met her. She had worked previously for a modeling agency. She could balance her teacup with the best of them at a charity benefit, but behind her gracious manner was one gutsy woman. She shared my sense of adventure. She later confessed to me that her only hesitation in getting married had been a fear of becoming bored. A trip to Central America in an old World War II bomber was not going to faze her.

Although the FAA had already issued the ferry permit, I asked the mechanics at Midway Airport to go over the B-26 thoroughly. They found two problems: cowl flaps that stuck from time to time and a leaky brake. The mechanics assured me both were minor and not worth fixing. I ordered both items fixed. I remembered the B-26 with the blown tire and knew that steering this plane on landing depended on the brakes. This meant taking the left main wheel off and putting in a new hydraulic expander tube, which was more work than the mechanics had planned on.

The problem with the cowl flaps didn't seem too serious. On takeoff and on full-power climbs or other full-power applications, cowl flaps were vital to bring in air to cool the engines. Once the pilot reduced power, he closed the cowl flaps partially or completely to keep the temperature within the prescribed limits. The mechanics simply lubricated the cables.

My dad came out to Midway to see the B-26. He was in his sev-enties, still vigorous, with a head of thick white hair. When he asked what the mechanics were doing on the engines, I told him that the work was minor and that the plane was in very good condition. He just sort of nodded. My dad, like many of his generation, didn't know how to make small talk. I knew he worried this trip was dangerous, but he was no longer in the role of a parent. It would never have oc-curred to him to say, "Be careful." I realized I was finally grown up in the mind of my father.

The Friday before our departure, I was on my way out to the air-port to check something on the plane when the news came over the radio that President Kennedy had been shot. The B-26 was off in a hangar by itself, so I didn't see anyone at the airport. I finished up and as I drove home, I tuned in the news on the car radio just as Walter Cronkite's voice soberly announced: "President Kennedy died at 1 p.m., Central Standard Time, two o'clock Eastern Standard Time, thirty-eight minutes ago." The entire country was in shock. Under that deep shadow, Pat and I finished preparations for the trip.

The next day, Pat caused a sensation at the airport when she walked out to the plane. Pat was quite attractive and in the 1960s, there were few women in aviation. I showed Pat the toeholds and boosted her up to the wing.

This was the only plane I had bought with a working radio—a real luxury. Just as we were about to leave, it quit. Pat and I climbed back out and the mechanics worked on the radio for several hours until they fixed the problem. I wanted to get going. I had promised Colonel Saavedra that I would have the plane there a week ago. The plane's interior was spartan—bare metal without any soundproofing—just as it had been during WWII when the '26 was nicknamed the "hot rod of the bombers."

We stuffed our ears with cotton and wore headphones to dull the noise. Since the intercom wasn't connected, we used a Magic Slate, a child's toy you wrote on and then lifted the plastic sheet to erase the message. There were two or three explosions, clouds of black smoke, a whining noise, and finally a roar with a tremendous vibration as the engines came to life. We made the mile and a half trip from the northeast corner of the field over to the southwest side to runway 4 Right, a whole 6,446-foot-long expanse of concrete. I reviewed my checklist one last time and told the tower I was ready.

"Cleared for takeoff," came the instant reply, "and good luck!" The bomber attracted a lot of attention and no question the controller knew where the plane was going.

Taxiing into position, I set the brakes, advanced the throttle to 30 inches of manifold pressure, lowered the flaps 20 degrees, and looked over at my beautiful navigator. Pat flashed a confident smile, and I released the brakes smoothly, moving the throttles forward to 52 inches, full power.

We took off and were climbing rapidly. I pulled up the flaps at 200 feet, made a right turn with the tower's permission, and we were on our way. Pat marked the time and started unfolding her charts. I'd called the tower at Dallas to advise them we would need a light gun. My flight plan assumed a 300-miles-per-hour cruise, with 75 to 100 gallons of gas just to climb to my cruise altitude and 210 gallons per hour thereafter. The weather was "severe-clear," so I leveled off at 12,500 feet using power settings of 36 inches of manifold pressure and 2200 rpm.

About twenty minutes out from Dallas Love Field, I started slowing up the big bird, dropping 500 feet per minute. We were right over the airport on Pat's ETA. As usual, she was damn accurate. I could see some large planes landing on runway 31 Left, so I expected that would be my runway.

I sailed over the top of the field and swung on to my downwind leg. The tower shot me a green light right away. A small plane flew ahead of me at about my altitude. I assumed the pilot was going to take 31 Right, so I wasn't concerned about overtaking him. Suddenly the plane disappeared. I swung out a little to try to find it, but with the big engine blocking my view, I couldn't see it. I did a 180 turn to the right and came back again downwind. The tower shot me a green light a second time and I landed on 31 Left.

I taxied to the nearest fixed base operator. Before I could shut down the engines, a line boy burst out to tell me the tower chief wanted to talk to me right away. I called the tower from the base operator's office. The tower chief bellowed, "What the hell were you doing making a one-eighty south of the field? We had to delay arrivals 'til we could sort out what you were going to do!"

I explained I'd lost sight of the light plane and had wanted to be sure I wasn't overtaking or turning into it. The tower chief took my license number, hollered some more, and then said they would "be in touch." I walked out with my tail between my legs. I never heard anything more about the incident.

The next morning, as we were paying for the gas and tie-down, the assassination of President Kennedy dominated the news on the small black and white TV in the airport office. The Dallas news affiliate, KRLD, was broadcasting live the transfer of Lee Harvey Oswald from the basement of the Dallas police headquarters to the county jail. Everyone in the airport office had their eyes glued to the screen as the Dallas officials, crowded by reporters and photographers, brought Oswald into view. Just as the news commentator started to speak, a gunshot rang out. Everyone in the airport office gasped as Oswald fell to the floor and a group of men tackled Jack Ruby. Chaos filled the screen. "He's been shot, he's been shot, Lee Oswald has been shot!" the commentator shouted. The room went silent, and then we all talked at once. It was a grim start to our trip.

But Pat and I needed to move on. We climbed aboard our plane, went through our preflight, and started the left engine. The throttle moved about an inch—and stopped. I checked the throttle friction lock, but it hadn't jammed. I looked down the throttle quadrant to see if something had dropped between the levers. "Just a minor problem," I assured Pat as we climbed down. She lifted her eyebrows.

Since it was Sunday, no mechanics were on the field. But the fixed base operator made a few calls and located a man nearby who agreed to come in. When the mechanic showed up, I shared my suspicions that the Chicago mechanics might have disconnected the throttle linkage to get at the cowl cable. In a few minutes, he confirmed it. The linkage had not been properly reinstalled. The cotter pins that kept the nuts from coming off had been left out. I was furious with the Chicago mechanics. I asked the mechanic to check the right cowling as well. He said it was okay.

The B-26 seemed to be a jinx for me. The tire had blown on the first one and now a mechanic's carelessness. *Years later, I related the story to a WWII Air Force captain who had flown B-26s. "Do you realize how lucky you were?" he asked. "If the throttle had jammed on final approach, you would have needed to pull the mixture back to shut down the engine, and if you couldn't make the runway, you'd have had to do a go-around, and that means raising the gear and flaps and feathering the prop. But if you're below 140 mph when it jams, you're just gonna drive it into the ground!" I doubted with such low time in a '26 that I would have had the presence of mind to figure what the hell was going on and go through all those steps.*

Back in the plane, we waved goodbye a second time and left for Brownsville. We met up that night with Roy, who was bringing up another Mustang and had arrived the day before. When he landed in Matamoros across the Rio Grande to check in with Mexican customs, he had pulled off the tail wheel tire.

The tail wheel swivel-design was copied from a German FW-190 captured during WWII. The wheel connected to the control stick. If you pushed the stick forward of neutral and applied the brakes, the tail wheel would be in full swivel. But in the aft position, the tail wheel partially turned with the rudder pedal. If the pilot forgot to push the stick forward when he applied a brake to turn, it was easy to pull the tail wheel off the rim. Luckily tail wheels and tubes were among the parts loaded in our '26, so it was a relatively small problem to fix.

The next morning, we learned we weren't going anywhere, at least not that day. Mexico and the U.S. had closed the border because of Kennedy's assassination and all flights were cancelled. We were considering what to do next when word came through that someone, somewhere in the government, had issued permission for us to proceed. I believe we were the only plane allowed across the border that day, and I never did learn why.

It would be a five-minute flight across the Rio Grande to Matamoros. I had filled up with gas at Brownsville since international credit cards were not always accepted in Mexico. Even with a full load of gas, the manual showed that without guns and bombs, the plane came in more than two tons under the maximum weight. Since Roy had left his plane in Matamoros, I assumed he would ride over with us. "No way, Will," he said, shaking his head. "You can't land a '26 with a full tank of gas. And five minutes isn't enough to let those mag wheels cool off–they're gonna overheat and catch fire," he insisted.

Pat flew with me over the river.

The Mexican customs official was about as wide as he was tall. He eyed the hand- and footholds and realized with his bulk he couldn't climb up to inspect the plane. The usual procedure in such cases was to bring out a ladder. He paused a moment, considered the situation, evidently decided it was going to be more effort than he was interested in, and waved us on. In a few minutes, we were on our way to Veracruz.

At Veracruz, we found a small hotel, too big to be charming, too small to be air-conditioned, so we dropped our bags and headed into the city center. That evening we ate dinner in a restaurant on the town plaza. Sitting on the patio under stately palms in the warm night air, we drank margaritas as we watched a parade of teenaged girls and boys walking in opposite directions around the plaza, flirting as they passed one another. Balloon vendors wandered about the square, their brightly colored wares gently swaying above their heads, and women with baskets of flowers stopped at each table. A woman with red roses nodded at Pat and looked expectantly at me. I bought a rose and presented it to Pat with a flourish, much to the amusement of the flower seller.

Gray overcast skies greeted us the next morning when we arrived at the field. I asked at the gas pump where I could get weather information. The line boy shrugged a don't-know-don't-care shrug. Pilots often ran into bad weather in the 125 miles crossing from the Atlantic to the Pacific at the Isthmus of Tehuantepec pass, which is bounded on both sides by high mountains. If we tried flying under the clouds and the ceiling dropped further, we'd be ducking around mountains. Going above the overcast, we might have to climb above 14,000 feet, an altitude we wouldn't want to hold long without oxygen. A chance tailwind could increase our speed, blowing us out over the Pacific and away from all reference of land.

A Mexicana Airline DC-3 was parked at the terminal, which had a little coffee shop. We went in and found the pilot. "Do you know where I can get weather information?" I asked.

"Whacha need to know?" he replied pleasantly. I explained, and he said he had just come in. He delivered good news: "Overcast only goes to 8,500 feet; pass is clear." We took off ten minutes later.

There's nothing like leaving a gray day on the ground and punching through to sunshine up above. Flying over a sea of clouds with the sun warm on our faces, the world below seemed far away. Pat calculated a southwest heading and Tapachula appeared in short order.

Tapachula, a small sleepy border town, was our designated checkout point for leaving Mexico. Since there were no control towers at the airports we were using, I always flew directly over the field, looking for traffic and the windsock. Just as I was turning on final, a DC-3 loomed up across the field facing me, landing downwind—the wrong direction—on the same runway. I swore and did a go-around, starting the landing procedure all over again. When we landed and taxied up to the service area, the DC-3 passengers were still streaming off the plane. I stomped over, intending to ask the pilot what the hell he had been doing, but thought better of it. In small, non-controlled airports, the locals often made straight-in approaches rather than following conventional pattern procedure.

Since we had been in the air less than ninety minutes, I had plenty of gas. Still, I had found it a diplomatic move to give the local boys business, so I ordered 100 gallons. By now, I had learned to be very precise when ordering gas in Spanish. I had also learned to stand by while the plane was being serviced. The line boys were almost universally friendly, but reluctant to admit if they did not understand.

I had just climbed back up to get my sunglasses out of the cockpit when a heavyset Mexican policeman suddenly appeared and motioned me down. Several more men crowded around the plane, all wearing large automatics on their hips. It did not look much like a welcoming committee. Was there some problem with my go-around with the DC-3?

"You captain of the airplane, yes?" the leader asked ominously in broken English.

"That's right."

"You come with me," he ordered and took me firmly by the forearm. He motioned for Pat to follow. She did not look pleased.

Apparently Tapachula didn't have a police car, but there was a taxi waiting, and we were told to get in. The policeman sat in the front with the driver and half-turned so he could look at us.

"Where are we going?" I asked.

"*Policía*," he answered tersely.

"Why?" I continued, but he just shook his head.

We stopped in front of a small police station. He looked at me expectantly. I paid the cab fare. The station had a dirt floor with chickens wandering in and out. A young girl sat at a shabby-looking desk with stacks of manila file folders. The thought of us becoming part of that stack flashed through my mind. Pat and I were immediately separated and each time I tried to say something, the policeman told me to shut up.

He led me to a small connecting room where a man I assumed was the police chief waited. He stood about five feet seven inches and had a handlebar moustache. There was only one chair, and he took it.

"Why are we being detained?" I demanded, trying to keep my voice from rising.

He ignored my question and ordered, "Write names and addresses of three people in United States who say who you are." I took out my identification, but he waved it away.

I asked again why we were being held.

"President Kennedy is shooted," he announced with a wide flourish of his arm, "No planes permit to fly, but you fly across frontier! We get you now," he concluded triumphantly.

I was momentarily confused. Then it dawned on me: this man thought we were fleeing the country after shooting Kennedy. No doubt he was now anticipating his impending fame from capturing the most wanted criminals in the world. From the determined look on his face, I knew there was no point trying to tell him the assassin had been assassinated.

"In the plane is an export permit to transport munitions," I said slowly, since his English was very limited. "I can show it to you. The American Embassy in Mexico City can verify this."

He shook his head. "Write names of three people and addresses." He left the room.

My brain just stopped working. I knew names and phone numbers, but I couldn't recall exact street addresses. I was conscious of how hot the room had become. Finally I managed to write out approximate addresses for my parents and two brothers. After about an hour and a half, the police chief came back and his deputies brought in Pat. She looked perfectly calm.

The police chief scowled, "Go!" and pointed to the taxi waiting outside. We went. In the cab, I asked Pat, "*What* did you tell them?"

"I wrote down my dad's address and put 'Mayor' in front of his name. I told them they had better release us before my father found out about it because he was going to be very angry. They looked worried when I said that."

Frazee, Minnesota, boasted a population of 1,253 people and Pat's dad, Vernon Daggett, received $20 annually for serving as its mayor. Apparently the clout of Frazee's mayoral office was internationally recognized. And, well, maybe the police chief had finally heard the news about Oswald and Ruby.

Whatever the reason, we were free and we were going to get the hell out of there. Pat climbed in the plane as I got the bill for the gas. The guy had filled it to the top, putting in 200 gallons more than I had ordered.

"Take the extra gas back out—right now," I said angrily.

The man's response was to cross his arms and say nothing. There was no doubt it was no-pay, no-go, or maybe worse. I was furious, but I paid.

I checked the plane over very carefully, and it appeared no one had tampered with it. Settling into the cockpit, I went over the checklist carefully; I knew I didn't have enough time in the '26 to afford any mistakes. In the air, Pat calculated our ETA to Managua. Since we had so much extra gas, I upped the power setting and let the old bomber rip.

It was then that I heard a new vibration and a buzzing sound. I carefully checked the gauges and looked around the cockpit to see if anything was loose. I wrote Pat a note, asking if she could see anything from her side. She got out of her seat and leaned over to look back at the prop and engine on her side. She shook her head, found the flashlight, and crawled into the nose. After a few minutes, she crawled back out, shaking her head.

I kept checking the panel. The only gauge that had changed was the airspeed indicator. Finally I tried pulling back on the throttles to change the power setting. The sounds stopped. I thought about it for a moment and then wrote to Pat, *Cowl flaps vibrate at higher airspeed.* The flaps were in the partial open position, but I didn't want to take the chance of closing them all the way and then not being able to get them back open.

Pat took some estimated distance settings and gave me a new ETA. We landed at Managua in the heat of the day within ninety seconds of her predicted touchdown time.

Most of the air force people had gone for the day, but Morgan was there. His usual sourpuss expression vanished when Pat smartly climbed down from the plane. It was clear Morgan didn't spend too much time in polite society, because he greeted her with "What the hell are you doing with him in this plane?"

Morgan drove us into town. He was making a real effort to use his Sunday manners. Pat insisted on staying at the Estrella, because it was a "native hotel" and she wanted to "experience the culture first hand." I tried to dissuade her. Morgan didn't comment.

When she discovered the bathroom hadn't been cleaned in a very long time, Pat quickly decided she didn't need to become *that* familiar with the local culture. The following day, we checked into the Gran Hotel. It seemed like the Ritz to Pat at that point. Morgan smirked.

The next morning about 5:30 a.m. the sound of gunfire in the plaza jerked us out of our sleep. We lay in bed and listened to the loud popping noises for about five minutes. Then it was quiet again. Pat adjusted her pillow under her head and turned to me. "Do you think a revolution has started?" she asked matter-of-factly. It was clear this was just one more damn thing as far as Pat was concerned. We had talked about using this trip to figure out whether we could really live in Nicaragua. It wasn't looking good.

"Well I'm going to find out right now." I pulled on my pants and buttoning a shirt, headed downstairs to the front desk. After a brief conversation with the night clerk, I returned to our room. Pat was sitting up in bed, waiting for my report.

"Sorry, no revolution. It seems there's a special mass at the cathedral this morning, and the locals were setting off firecrackers to make sure we didn't sleep through it." Pat groaned and sank back down in the bed, pulling the sheets over her head.

The news about Pat had spread quickly. After breakfast, I took her out to the field. A group of FAN officers gave her an appraising eye as we walked up. I knew they were thinking, "Wonder where Will picked up this tootsie!" Faces fell when I introduced her as my wife. Clearly she was off-limits.

Colonel Saavedra was rather frosty when he saw Pat. He said he was surprised I had flown down with a lady. I explained she was my wife, and that I wanted her to see Nicaragua. The colonel then greeted her warmly.

"We are very pleased with the B-26 you brought us," the colonel said. "Our chief mechanic has already run up the engines. I checked it over myself, and it is a very good-looking plane. Does everything work well?"

"Yes," I answered, "but the cowl flaps might need some service."

He dismissed that with a wave. "Just a minor detail." The fact I had flown the plane down with my wife obviously vouched for its reliability.

I looked over the work on the P-51s, and as Morgan had reported, not much had been done. I sat down with Sergeant Chavez and reviewed the list of parts needed to finish up. I planned to go to Costa Rica to check on the work on my Mustangs there and get parts. Morgan was going to Costa Rica on business, so he suggested we go in a Bonanza that he was borrowing.

Since the Bonanza was instrument-equipped, I assumed we would just pop up through the low scattered clouds to the smoother air above. Morgan remained below the ceiling, however, giving Pat and me one of our roughest rides ever. This was typical of the local pilots. They had little use for radio navigation and did all their flying looking out the window.

As we neared Costa Rica, Irazú was still spewing ash. Morgan mentioned tourists could go up to the volcano's mouth to see this phenomenon. When we met Major Bonilla, I asked if he could arrange a jeep to take Pat and me there.

The major was horrified. "Mrs. Martin, are you sure you want to go up to the mouth of an active volcano?"

Morgan couldn't resist. "She married Will Martin, didn't she?" he cackled.*

The following morning, Morgan flew back alone and billed me for the entire trip. I wasn't surprised. Probably I appeared to Morgan as I undoubtedly did to the Nicaraguans: a deep-pocketed American who was fair game.

Work was progressing nicely on the Costa Rican planes. In the process of inventorying the spare parts, I discovered two large gas heaters. Why the U.S. would ship them to a country where the temperature never dropped below seventy degrees was a bureaucratic mystery. When I finished up with the parts, Pat and I flew back to Managua on Pan Am.

That evening we walked down to the local ice cream parlor. While we were there, General Somoza came in with his wife and children. A huge security entourage surrounded him. "Finish up, we're leaving," I told Pat quietly.

Somoza's father had been assassinated, and there were plenty of people who would be glad to get his son. If a grenade were tossed in the ice cream parlor, the customers who survived the initial blast would probably be in little pieces when the Guardia finished unloading their guns. The General was going to enjoy his ice cream without our company.

As we walked out of the ice cream parlor, we saw soldiers, weapons drawn, lining the street. Military jeeps blocked off both ends. A small two-person Guardia helicopter hovered dangerously low over the street, the loud pulsing of the rotor blades drowning out our voices. Pat clutched my arm tightly. I realized any thoughts of moving my family here would take a lot of consideration.

---

*A few months after our visit to the volcano, a rock the size of a Volkswagen flew out and landed on two tourists. The government closed the road to the crater the same day.

Chapter 14

OF TRANSPORTS AND TRAINERS

Among the Nicaraguan Air Force planes I bought were two C-45 Expeditors, a WWII military version of the popular Beechcraft Model 18 commercial light transport. It was made in a number of versions for the U.S. Army Air Corps. The planes were used for navigator training, bombing, gunnery training, utility transport, aerial photography, and mapping. My two '45s, designed for utility transport, were bare bones—canvas seats and no upholstery. They cruised at about 200 miles per hour with a range of 1,200 miles. This model, the forerunner of the D & E Beech-18s, dominated the civilian market for executive transportation for many years. The planes appeared to be in fairly decent shape other than the ailerons needing new covering.

A Miami firm answered Glenn's ad on the C-45s, offering to trade a T-28A modified for long-range flying. I made a deal over the phone and planned to fly one of the C-45s to Miami, taking the long way along the coast rather than flying a straight line out over the water.

The U.S. Mission men had gone through multi-engine training on C-45s, so I asked Captain Harris if someone would check me out. The captain was emphatic. "We don't fly their planes."

"But the planes belong to me," I countered.

"We'd like to help you out, Will," he explained, "but it's been a long time since any of us have flown a twin Beech…." His voice faltered.

"It can't be as hard as flying the DC-3 that you guys got all polished up," I argued.

"Will, no one here will fly that Beech," he said with an air of finality. I was a little surprised by his abruptness, but thought he must feel his men were truly rusty on flying a Beech. Or perhaps, because I was a civilian pilot without any military training, the captain decided it didn't make sense to get involved with me. If I screwed up, it could reflect on the mission. I spent the rest of the day checking over the plane. When I ran up the engines, they performed fine, meeting all the green marks on the gauges.

The next day with the paperwork out of the way, Pat and I loaded our two small bags into the plane and taxied out. I trimmed the nose slightly down, locked the tail wheel and advanced the throttles. With 900 horsepower in the two Pratt & Whitney 985 engines, the acceleration was brisk. It was a beautiful, clear day.

Pat began arranging her charts. Just as the wheels left the ground, the nose suddenly reared up violently at about a 45-degree angle, putting the plane on the edge of a stall. I shoved hard on the wheel to get the nose down, which dipped the left wing. I thought the wing was going to hit the runway, but at the last moment, it came back up and the right wing flopped back down. When I finally got the wings level, I chopped the throttles and made a passable three-point landing.

I was soaked in perspiration. Pat looked pale and was leaning back in the seat with her eyes closed. Shaken, I taxied back to the maintenance area and slumped in the seat. That formation of guardian angels was still flying with me.

Morgan strolled up with his hands in his pockets and in his usual nonchalant manner asked as I shut down, "Having a problem, Bub?"

"Something's the matter with the controls," I explained. "Pat, go back and watch the elevator." I pushed the elevator trim tab all the way forward. "What's it doing?" I called.

"It moved up," she called back to me. Trim tabs are small surfaces connected to the trailing edge of the elevator. When the control is trimmed forward, the nose is held down, and if the trim wheel is moved back, the tail becomes heavy. This takes the effort out of moving the elevator controls and keeps the moving surfaces in a flight position.

But the indicator was still showing the trim set nose down. I had a defective indicator. It had actually been set full nose up, and I hadn't been able to overcome the upward force that the wrong trim had caused. Broken gauge aside, why the hell had the trim been set that way on the ground?*

Standing with me in the tropic sun, Pat asked quietly, "Will, do we really have to fly this plane to Miami?"

I looked at this girl who during all of our married life had joined so enthusiastically in my adventures. "No," I assured her. "I'll have the buyer send a ferry pilot."

The buyer agreed to send a pilot if I would get him through customs and launch him. The next day, Harry got off the Pan Am flight carrying a kit bag containing a rubber dingy. The customs inspector was very curious about the dingy kit and wanted to inspect it. If we had opened the kit however, there would have been a loud pop followed by a fully inflated life raft on the table a few seconds later. With great difficulty, I convinced the inspector to pass it through unopened.

Harry was a real professional. You name it and he had flown it, including many single-engine planes across the Atlantic. He wore a blue business suit that looked as though he had slept in it more than once, and carried only a wet compass, some old charts, and the dingy kit. The next morning when he walked around the plane, he reached up to open the drain and gas ran down his sleeve. He simply shook his arm and a few minutes later he was off, heading in a straight line to Miami.

Pat and I left the following day on Pan Am for Florida. The buyer was pleased with the C-45 that Harry had delivered and showed us a very sharp-looking T-28A with a VHF communication radio. The

*Much later, when a mechanic was taxiing a P-51 that I had preflighted, I finally figured out what had happened. I observed that he moved the elevator trim wheel to full nose-up trim. When I asked why he touched the trim, he replied they always did that "to keep the tail down on the ground." But trim tabs only work with air flowing over the surface and have no effect at taxi speed. These are the kinds of myths that kill pilots and damn near killed Pat and me.

drop tanks were at nearby Tamiami Airport where we would pick them up and then continue on to Chicago. I had never seen a T-28 with drop tanks.

The T-28A had tandem cockpits and Pat sat in the rear, the first time we had not flown side by side. The view from either cockpit was spectacular and we had a real radio that actually worked. We headed for Tamiami.

About seven or eight miles from the airport, the engine started cutting in and out. Pat looked more annoyed than scared: the Nicaraguan mechanical failures were one thing, but we were in the U. S. of A. with FAA mechanics! I had pre-set the Tamiami tower frequency, so I notified them I was having an engine problem, and they immediately cleared me to land. We were high enough that I knew we had sufficient glide to get to the field. The engine kept up the on-and-off business all the way on my downwind leg. When we touched down, fire engines raced alongside of us, trying to keep pace.

I managed to get the plane off the active runway to a fixed base operator, fire trucks trailing. It sounded to me like a fuel problem, and sure enough, the local mechanic found a fuel filter clogged with a sandy material. After the filters were cleaned, the engine ran smoothly. I offered a seat to any of the mechanics working on the plane, but there weren't any takers. Leaving Pat on the ground, I took it up for a test flight, and it performed perfectly.

When they brought out the drop tanks to be mounted, I found what had clogged the filter. The bottom of the drop tanks had a lot of sandy grit. My guess was the last time the plane had been flown, the drop tanks were attached. The rest of the day was spent cleaning out the tanks and hooking them onto the wings.

Each tank held 105 gallons. With its regular tanks plus the drop tanks, the plane had a range of 1,500 miles. The procedure was to fly until the plane's left tank was low and then turn on a valve to direct fuel from a drop tank. Each drop tank had its own electric pump and the main tank gauge would tell you when to stop transferring fuel. Since the Curtiss-Wright engine was notorious as an oil slinger, an auxiliary oil tank had been installed. It had just a pump, with no gauge, so you had to guess at the oil level.

We left in the cool of the morning the next day. I had only put fifty gallons in each drop tank so I could see how the plane flew with the extra gas. The added weight didn't seem to matter. We flew directly across the Everglades to Sarasota. I stayed high, so if the thing quit on me again, I would have time to find a spot to put it down.

At Sarasota, we visited with Dave Lindsay who was running the Cavalier Mustang Rebuilding Company. He was a local publisher who had fallen in love with Mustangs a few years earlier. North American Aviation came up with a lot of prints and data for him. He was removing all armaments, including the machine gun bumps in the leading edges of the wings, and then polishing the planes until they shone. Lindsay believed these airplanes would appeal to wealthy people for executive transportation. His signature modification was to increase the height of the tail similar to the H-model Mustang.

One of Lindsay's biggest deals was remanufacturing a number of Mustangs that went to Indonesia on a U.S.-sponsored aid program. The Dominican Republic and several other smaller countries sent their aircraft for him to rebuild as well. He also built two experimental aircraft for the U.S. government, using overhauled engines from military helicopters, thinking maybe the U.S. would put them into inventory.*

I hoped to sell him some of my Mustangs, but he was only interested in a deal at a cheap price on consignment. I passed, and we enjoyed a pleasant lunch.

I planned to do the 1,000 mile trip to Chicago's Midway Airport non-stop. Since the big T-28A performed so well with the extra weight of the gas in the drop tanks, I put seventy gallons in each one. The drop tanks could not be disconnected, so I would be stuck with their extra weight no matter what. This model cruises at about 225 miles per hour at a power setting of 28 inches of manifold pressure and 2050 rpm. I flight planned for five hours, assuming 44 gallons per hour at cruise. The drag of the drop tanks with the weight of the gas would slow us down about ten percent, but of course we picked up extra range. With 270 gallons of gas onboard, I had a comfortable

*That never happened. As for the two he built, one crashed and the other is in the Air Force Museum in Dayton, Ohio.

margin. There was no indication of excess oil consumption, so I didn't worry about the oil transfer pump.

The T-28A is known for being a ground lover and with the extra weight, it would need more runway to get off. I let the plane accelerate up to a little over 80 miles per hour and then raised the nose wheel slightly, waiting a few seconds until the plane wanted to fly.

It was a beautiful, clear day, and we settled in for the long flight. The intercom worked, so we could talk easily. After I used up the gas in the left main wing tank, I pumped it up from the drop tanks. When the gauge showed full, I stopped pumping. This worked perfectly three times, but on the fourth try, the gauge didn't move. I had been alternately draining one tank and then the other so I didn't have to use a lot of trim to keep the plane level. I kept pumping, but when the trim didn't change, I knew I had a problem.

I reviewed my notes. There should have been plenty of gas in the wing tank. Not knowing what was wrong, I wasn't going to fly into the densely populated area around Midway Airport.

The sun hovered at the horizon. I knew by the time we descended it would be dark. I decided to detour to nearby Joliet Airport, which was surrounded by flat farmers' fields. If I had a fouled line again and the engine quit, I would have better landing options. We landed without incident at the airport.

The next day I had the pump checked. Sure enough, it was clogged with the same sandy material we had found before. Apparently there was enough grit left in the system to foul the pump after it had run awhile. Fortunately, it was only the drop tank pumps and not the main engine pump.

After three weeks away from our children, Pat was glad to be home, and she never made another trip down. Every time I flew, I thought it would be the last time I would be flying these planes. It was the problem of hiring ferry pilots, not the romance of flying that motivated me. I was flying for business, and what a business it was.

Chapter 15

Nica Days

I returned to Managua after the Christmas holidays. It was January of 1964. A lot of people were inquiring about the Nicaraguan spare parts that Glenn had advertised. Joe Friedman, a California parts dealer, flew down to Nicaragua to look over the stock. I helped him through customs and introduced him to Captain Garcia. I had warned Joe that Garcia was a ranking member of the Guardia. The captain, however, was uncharacteristically deferential and actually bowed to Joe, much to our surprise.

The Nicaraguan Air Force invited Joe and me to a party for one of the U.S. Mission officers whose tour of duty was up. We drove to the outskirts of the capital to a restaurant along the Tipitapa River. There was an open bar for about an hour, and then we proceeded to the table for *guapote*, the town's famous culinary treat. The name apparently meant "handsome fellow," an opinion I didn't share: it was a fish that appeared it would swim off the plate had I poured a little water on it.

I tried to figure out some way to politely avoid eating the celebrated main course, but I was seated between Colonel Saavedra and the guest of honor. I glanced at Joe who was busy trying to give away his *guapote* to one of the Nicaraguan officers. "Oh no, Señor Friedman, that is most kind of you. Please!" said the officer, interpreting Joe's eagerness as generosity, and not to be outdone, passed him a second serving. I ordered another drink and, seeing no escape, cut off a bite and ate it. Once you got past the fish stare, it really wasn't bad.

The next day, Joe and I sparred around on the parts. He made a low offer that specified I would pack the parts. I turned the offer down, we shook hands and he left. Organizing the parts would be a hot, gritty job. Managua was a hot, gritty, expensive town, and I think Joe just felt it was too big of a project.

The Gran Hotel had become my base of operation. Just off the Plaza de la República, the main square where the cathedral and the National Palace stood, and a block from Lake Managua, the Gran was in the heart of the city. The old hotel wasn't elegant by U.S. standards, but it was the best in Managua. The original part of the hotel, a two-story pale green building with simple, unadorned balconies, had been built in the 1940s. More recently, a five-story tower with an elevator had been added at the back, bringing the total number of guest rooms to about two hundred. Pan Am had an office in the building.

There was a small curved driveway at the entrance to the Gran Hotel. Inside was a large lobby with a high ceiling; potted palm trees stood near the heavy double doors that never seemed to be closed. Off to one side was a small bar with a very experienced upright piano and five or six wicker chairs. An old-fashioned wooden registration desk stood off to the left. Ceiling fans turned slowly below the ornate molded-plaster ceiling, moving the air and making the lobby a pleasant refuge in the heat of the day. Near the bar area was an enormous, irregularly shaped table, maybe six feet across, made from a single varnished slab of tree trunk, eight inches thick. Chairs surrounded the table and I often met people for drinks there.

Across the tiled floor toward the center of the hotel was an open-air courtyard with a small swimming pool. It was really more of a splash pool for cooling off than exercise, though I suppose someone could have done short laps in it. There were a few metal patio tables shaded by umbrellas on the little raised terrace next to it. I often sat in the courtyard in the evening and enjoyed the night air.

Around on the far side of the courtyard was the main dining room, with its white tablecloths and fresh flowers, usually a single rose, on each table. The menu included the "Yankee Special": a hamburger and apple pie. There was a smaller restaurant as well at the hotel, just past the bar in the lobby. Unlike the main dining room, it was air-conditioned, so heavily it seemed it never got above sixty degrees. It was where the hotel served breakfast.

The Gran Hotel lobby was the gathering place for expat business people, wealthy Nicaraguans, and visiting dignitaries. Top Latin American stars performed at the Gran, and it was not unusual to see wedding parties celebrating there. The U.S. Mission officers seldom came by, however, and when a communications company brought in some American contract workers, they quickly found local girlfriends and rarely showed up at the Gran either. Evenings were usually very quiet for me.

During the day I was distracted by my work, but nights were hard, and I felt very lonely. I tried to sound upbeat when I wrote to Pat. *"The wind is blowing 20-30 knots, and they say it is typical this time of year. I got my library card yesterday and it will help a lot. The selection is limited and somewhat old, but there are a lot of books I haven't read. The monkey is lying outside the window on his pipe rail taking his siesta. I love you. See you soon I hope."*

The hotel staff was professional yet very friendly. They all knew me and welcomed me back warmly each time I returned from a trip. I checked for mail three or four times a day at the front desk, but received little, as Pat's letters always seemed to miss me and be forwarded as I traveled back and forth between San José and Managua. I missed Pat and the girls terribly.

I was surprised when I returned from the airport one day and the desk clerk handed me a letter. She smiled. I wondered what it was; it wasn't an international envelope. Opening it, I pulled out a little note. It was from the hotel's desk staff. *We know how sad you are when you do not receive mail, so we wanted to cheer you up with a letter.* I started to ask her to tell everyone thank you for me but choked up.

I was sitting around the big tree trunk table in the lobby of the Gran one Sunday morning with a group of other foreigners when the subject of firearms came úp. Before I could blink, six guns lay on the table. I felt a bit chagrined that I was the only one not armed. Although guns were more common in Nicaragua than briefcases in the U.S., I'd never thought I needed one.

The proliferation of guns was taken in stride in Nicaragua. A little monkey used to hop around the lobby of the Gran Hotel, amusing the guests. One evening, a guest took out his gun and shot him, and no one skipped a beat in the conversation. Morgan told me about two men in a restaurant arguing loudly over owed money. The debtor, swearing, reached in his pocket. The other man, thinking the first guy was going for a gun, drew his and killed him on the spot. It seems the victim did not have a gun, but was reaching for his wallet. By law, guns had to be concealed while in Managua, but in the countryside they were carried openly.

When I had first arrived, Nicaragua looked like a great place for an energetic American to do business, with the presence of American companies and a welcoming General Somoza. However, over time I had begun to see the cracks in the picture. The country was divided into educated, moneyed families and a mass of people who were little more than peasants. According to Morgan, the local gentry all carried dual citizenship papers. Their money seldom stayed in Nicaragua overnight, but was soon on its way to Swiss bank accounts. With the great gulf between rich and poor, there was a lot of petty crime and many people, including the police, on the take. I was used to Chicago corruption, and although this was more extreme, I just dealt with it.

Somoza and his Guardia soldiers, however, were another matter. The Guardia functioned as the General's personal security force. It always lurked in the background of daily life and could strike at any time with impunity. The Guardia's immigration chief, Captain Garcia, was greatly feared. Every night, an armed guard logged in all the planes, including those of the duster pilots, and a report was sent to the captain. He in turn sent it on to the commandant of the Guardia. If a plane wasn't accounted for, the Guardia took off in search of it. No planes were allowed to fly at night.

General Somoza, so urbane upon first meeting, was turning out to be a pretty grim character. It had become quite clear to me that no one crossed him. If he wanted in on a business, he was in. His political enemies tread carefully. Somoza was known to hold grudges and he took revenge, it was whispered, through hired assassins. The torture of people picked up by the Guardia was commonly hinted at, and I heard of people simply "disappearing." If I mentioned Somoza's name in a conversation, most people clammed up immediately. If someone did talk about Somoza with me, the person was glancing over his or her shoulder the whole time to make sure no one else was listening.

It wasn't surprising that the military men were loyal to Somoza; after all, Somoza gave them their power. But what did give me pause was that many ordinary people, the ones who suffered the most under the Nicaraguan dictatorship, seemed so proud of "Tachito." I guess they figured he was their strongman who fought the Communists and protected the country, but I found it sobering nonetheless.

On one of my trips between Managua and Chicago, I literally bumped into General Somoza out on the tarmac at the airport in Miami. Like a good politician, he instinctively shook my hand. He asked how I was getting on, and of course I said fine. Without the heavy bulletproof vest he wore in Nicaragua, he looked much slimmer. I was surprised to see that little security surrounded him, as he was so cautious in Nicaragua.

One of the U.S. Mission guys had told me Somoza's personal pilot, Teodoro Picado, had made a forced landing in Cuba in the General's Aero Commander a year or so earlier and the Cubans had jailed him. The pilot had recently been released and returned to Nicaragua. Somoza had another Aero Commander, but Picado wasn't going to be flying it. Somoza would never get in a plane with him again according to the officer, because the General no longer trusted him—he thought the Cubans might have corrupted him. Morgan confirmed that story and told me a second one, about a robbery that had happened in another Nicaraguan city while I was on my last trip home. "Not just any old robbery," Morgan emphasized, "it was a robbery with automatic weapons."

In Nicaragua only the military had automatic weapons. "Tachito got real spooked," Morgan continued. "He shut down the whole damn country. The Guardia had checkpoints on all the roads. They were taking mirrors and tilting them under the cars to look for weapons on the undercarriages. The General don't want any revolutions on his hands and had to know where the guns came from and who had them. One day, all the checkpoints were gone." Morgan's tone was chilling. "Guess the Guardia found what they were looking for."

I assumed I was probably safe by virtue of my contract with the FAN; my dealings were primarily with Colonel Saavedra and his officers. Nonetheless, I tried to keep as low a profile as a big gringo could keep and avoided Captain Garcia and the Guardia as much as possible.

Chapter 16

Tico Troubles

Another saint's day was coming up, and work was already slowing in anticipation of the holiday. I headed back to Costa Rica to check the progress on the two P-51s.

With the volcanic ash still drifting down, I was very concerned about grit in the engines. I had my two planes towed over to SALA, a state-owned aircraft maintenance facility, probably the largest and best-equipped in Central America at the time. The manager told me SALA had been in charge of the Mustangs' maintenance. Although the P-51s appeared to be in excellent condition, I decided to do a full inspection of the entire airframes, cables, and hydraulics as well as a retraction of the landing gears.

Usually the volcano spewed out *geniza* at a steady rate, but occasionally it would belch a mighty cloud of the fine, soot-like substance. It was my misfortune that on that particular day, just as the mechanics had completed opening up all the panels on one of the planes, the volcano burped and the wind shifted, sending a whirlwind of fine ash through the open-air hangar. I watched helplessly as the ash settled into all the working parts. Volcanic ash is ground-up rock and not soluble in water. It has to be blown or vacuumed out. If it lands in grease or oil, such as in the wheel bearings, it turns to muck and must be painstakingly cleaned out with solvent. It was a real mess.

I explained to the two mechanics what I wanted done. I had to remind myself that U.S. teenagers at that time grew up repairing lawn mowers and then usually graduated to tinkering with used cars. Oil cans and engines were part of their lives, and they developed some mechanical sense. However many men in Central America had gone from the ox cart to the jet age in one generation. They diligently followed the maintenance manuals when I told them to take off the flat tires and put on new ones. However, the manual did not say *if the wheel hub is full of volcanic ash, clean it out before you put in the wheel bearing.* I requested different mechanics. In two days, I went through four men. After a few more days, when I realized it was going to take much longer than I had thought, I outlined the work to be done and returned to Nicaragua.

A month later, I came back just as the mechanics were trying to start the engine on one of the Mustangs. The engine groaned and growled but did not catch. Fortunately, I got there before they burned out the starter. By now everyone in the area had stopped work and had gathered around to volunteer advice.

There was a little moisture in the ignition harness, which conceivably could cause problems, so I ordered part of it dismantled. After the mechanic working on it broke most of the fittings, the hanger chief and an inspector took over. I poured over the manuals. It didn't look that complicated.

This went on another day with three men leaning over the engine, peering into the cockpit. The starter would engage, the prop would slowly start to turn, and after a couple revolutions, the engine would begin to fire. The minute the starter disengaged, however, the engine quit.

I knew fuel was getting into the engine because a two-foot-long flame was shooting out the exhaust stacks. The mechanic insisted we had spark. He had disconnected one of the wires and when he held the end near any metal on the airframe, he would get a spark when the engine was turning. But when I told him to disconnect the booster coil, there was no spark. I asked them to open up the magnetos' cover and there was the answer: the mag points were broken! No wonder the engine wouldn't run.

Upon closer questioning, I discovered this had been a security precaution against a coup. One of the mechanics, after seeing the broken points, remembered, "They told us to break the points so no one could fly the planes, just in case things went wrong for the administration. They didn't want anyone getting the Mustangs if there was trouble."

It was almost quitting time so the mechanics started to close up their toolboxes. "Oh no you don't!" I announced. "Not after I spent all this time waiting to hear this thing run." Grudgingly, the mechanics got points from the warehouse and installed them. The bird popped right off and all instruments checked out in green. I shut it down and stood for beer all around.

During this time, my two Mustangs were sitting next to a beautiful Dutch KLM Constellation that was undergoing conversion from a passenger to a cargo plane. The Dutch had brought in a bilingual supervisor to translate for the Dutch managers and Costa Rican mechanics. Various scaffolds were set up around the plane.

Most large aircraft have a dump valve to get rid of fuel quickly in an emergency. While the plane was up on jacks for a gear check, someone in the cockpit accidentally hit the gas dump switch. The valve opened, and gas gushed out of a five-inch pipe, hitting the concrete fifteen feet below with a tremendous splash. The entire floor flooded. Electrified light bulbs and power cables from gas engines running generators were lying on the floor, any one of which could have sparked an inferno.

Three Dutchmen raced up the scaffolding, hollering in Dutch, Spanish, and English. The others quickly and calmly began shutting down anything with an electric current while standing in pools of gas as much as an inch deep. By the time the fuel stopped pouring out, I was already about a block away, having torn across the parking lot, half expecting to see the roof sailing after me. I have no idea why the gas didn't explode when it hit the concrete. After the gas had gone down the drains, they flooded the area with water.

With the new points in the magnetos, the engine ran perfectly. When I explained to the mechanics that a pilot was coming from the U.S. and I would not be flying, they seemed genuinely disappointed. That night there was a telegram waiting at the hotel from my pilot saying he had taken another job. Now I had no pilot and no prospects for finding one. Glenn had cabled to say he had a buyer for a Mustang as soon as I could get it stateside. He added cash was running low.

I couldn't wait any longer. I decided I would test-fly the '51. Reluctantly I settled down that night at my hotel with the pilot's manual. During the past months, almost 100 percent of my time had been spent in and around Mustangs. I now knew the circuitry and almost every nut and bolt intimately. That night I worked late in my room, compiling checklists, going over gauges, reviewing procedures and memorizing numbers.

The mechanics cheered the next day when I announced I would test-fly the plane. It was as though a national holiday had been declared; they promptly locked their toolboxes and set up a spectator section outside the hangar.

The location of switches in the P-51 seemed to be an afterthought, as they were arranged with little regard for their operation. The Mustang's primer and starter switches were located on the lower left side of the instrument panel. The left hand started the engine firing and then the right hand crossed over the left to shove the lever down to open the mixture control. I felt like a one-armed paperhanger. To raise the landing gear, the pilot leaned forward, and with the left hand, pulled the handle near the floor in and up. The pilot's head dipped below the instrument panel, which meant for that moment he couldn't see out.

By now, though, the cockpit was familiar to me. I climbed in and taxied to the other end of the field to get to the active runway. Since I couldn't see around the Mustang's big up-tilted nose, I tapped each brake alternately, zigzagging the plane so I could look out the side of the canopy to see what was ahead. Taxiing to the end of the runway seemed to take forever. The controllers in the tower spoke excellent English, the international language in all control towers throughout the world, and cleared me for takeoff. Nervously, I tugged my harness tighter and tried to push away thoughts of men who had died in

Mustangs. I forced myself to focus on the checklists I'd taped to the instrument panel.

Pausing at the end of the runway, I set the brakes and ran the engine up to 2300 rpm, checking for the magneto drop: no more than 120 on the right and 100 on the left. The trim position was at 6 degrees right rudder and neutral on the elevator and ailerons. Flaps were up and the fuel valve was set on the left tank. I carefully ran the throttle up to 35 inches and down again to confirm the engine was running smoothly, but made sure not to exceed 35 inches. Since there was no fuel in the rear gas tank, balance was critical; the plane could easily go over on its nose if too much power were applied with the brakes on. The engine sounded fine. I took a deep breath. So far, so good.

Suddenly all hell broke loose as clouds of hot steam and coolant sprayed over the nose, coating the bird. Thick steam filled the cockpit as I frantically struggled to shut down the switches and get out. The fire truck clanged down the runway with an entourage of jeeps and cars close behind.

Major Bonilla was first on the scene. "We couldn't tell if you were on fire or if the plane had blown up," he said breathlessly.

The plane was towed back to the hangar. I rode with the major in silence. When the engine cooled down, it was evident the pressure valve had let go because the cap on the expansion tank at the head of the engine wasn't closed properly. It wasn't a mechanical problem—just carelessness. I took the rest of the day off. The hotel bar beckoned, but I was pretty sure there weren't any answers there.

The next morning, I had the plane towed out of the hangar again. I taxied to the active runway, waiting for the OK from the tower and then started my rollout, cautiously inching the throttle forward. Moments later, I realized the plane had left the ground. I was flying!

I continued to add throttle until it reached 61 inches. I pulled up the wheels, reduced power and rpm to cruise speed, 36 inches and 2300 rpm. When I leveled off at 5,000 feet, I was indicating 285 miles per hour. I flew in the airport area for about an hour, taking it down to 150 miles per hour and getting the feel of the plane.

I entered the pattern at about 1,000 feet, and when I turned on my downwind leg, the tower cleared me to land. I slowed up, and at 170 miles per hour, dropped the landing gear and put down the first notch of flap. The green gear lights on the panel came on reassuringly as I turned on my base leg. But the plane seemed sluggish when I turned on final, as though it were going too slow. This was probably the most critical part of the flight, and I fought to remember the manual instructions.

At high speeds, the control stick of a Mustang stiffens up and it takes a lot of pressure to move it. At low speeds, it is sensitive and needs only a gentle touch. The stick felt sloppy and I was moving it constantly to keep the wings level. Remembering everything I had read about landing, I resisted the impulse to pile on the power and kept what power I had, steadily holding the nose slightly high and watching the airspeed indicator.

I now had full flap down and the runway was coming up fast. I felt the wheels touch down firmly on a three-point landing. I rolled down the runway, sweat running off my back.

The mechanics gave a mighty whoop. One hollered, "Boss, you looked like a truck falling out of a three-story building!" but it was said in good cheer. I remembered that two local pilots had died in these things, and my flight must have seemed a momentous achievement.

"Calibrate the airspeed indicator. It seems to be reading too low," I told them when the applause died down. They checked the system carefully and assured me the gauge was operating correctly. I just couldn't understand why the stick felt so sloppy on landing.

That night at the hotel, I studied the manuals. What was I missing? Looking at pictures of this powerful machine, the answer came to me: the Mustang is a sleek, strong warrior that doesn't *want* to fly slowly.

I took the plane up again the next day and circled around Irazú, staying clear of the billowing dark gray clouds of smoke. With the orange glow deep down in it, the volcano looked like the mouth of Hell. I didn't spend much time in the area: the engine filters had been cleaned and reinstalled and I didn't want to have to go through that again.

This time when I was ready to land, I started retarding the throttle a long way out. The controls felt sloppy like they had the day before, but I now understood the plane was just reacting to the reduced airflow over the wing surfaces. Like its high-spirited namesake, the Mustang didn't like to be reined in.

Chapter 17

A Gift for the General

A most amiable host, Major Bonilla introduced me to places in Costa Rica I never would have found on my own. Though he did not wear a uniform, he was obviously held in great respect, judging from the deferential treatment given to him.

"Tonight we have a little drink at Connie's, okay Will?" He ended every sentence with a broad smile I found impossible not to return. As we were finishing dinner, he expounded on the beauty of Costa Rican women. "The *ticas* are the loveliest in Central America. You will see," he promised.

We climbed into his little blue Volkswagen with its commandant insignia on the plates. Traffic policemen saluted and waved us through every intersection. The way the major drove, he needed all the clout he could get. Spotting a particularly lovely *tica* on the sidewalk, he suddenly veered across two lanes of traffic, pulled into a no-parking zone and turned off the engine. "A real beauty, no?" he breathed, without taking his eyes off her as she swayed gracefully down the street. Not wanting to seem unappreciative, I leaned forward in my seat and cheerfully concentrated out the window too.

After several more *tica*-watching stops, we arrived at a noisy cantina. Instead of going in the main entrance, he took me to a side stairway and pounded on the door, which opened almost immediately. Around the tastefully furnished living room were more Costa Rican beauties. A group of stunning *ticas* stood three deep at a table, which served as a bar. A combo was playing a sensual Latin melody and there were lots of couples dancing.

Fortified with a Scotch in hand, I squeezed in on a couch between two voluptuous brunettes. "*Noble español*," cooed the olive-skinned girl on my right. Her short white lace dress was tightly cut.

"Uh, I don't speak much Spanish," I said.

"You will learn," she promised. "Me María," and pointing to my drink, purred, "Agua and Scotch." We continued the Berlitz lesson barroom-style until the teacher asked me to dance. It was salsa music—exotic, irresistible, and very much beyond the capabilities of my feet. Maria seemed to enjoy it nonetheless, and as the song ended, in a burst of exuberance, she grabbed all 230 pounds of me and swung me around.

"Maria, I think we need a drink, at least I do," I gasped, and maneuvered her off the floor. There were about six or seven visiting Nicaraguan Air Force men at the bar, but they didn't seem to be fraternizing with the girls. I noticed some couples were disappearing down the hall; I gradually realized that Connie's was taking a low-key approach to the world's oldest profession. There was no hard sell that I could see; for the most part, it was like I was at a well-oiled American cocktail party.

I rejoined Major Bonilla who was surrounded by admiring women. Playfully brushing away a *tica* who was tracing the cleft in his chin, the major leaned over toward me. "These girls," the major explained quietly, "work as secretaries and salesgirls during the day. They come to Connie's to make a little extra money."

About then there was a loud pounding on the door, and a lithe little man with a dark goatee burst in carrying a marimba. The crowd greeted him affectionately and he began to play. Everyone sang and took turns with a solo verse. I couldn't follow the words, but from the laughter, I gathered the central theme extolled the prowess of a lover. Every time the marimba player paused, a hostess poured him another drink, and the tempo increased. About seven drinks later, his enthusiasm got the better of him and he hit the instrument too hard, breaking his sticks.

The party broke up, and now the Nicaraguans who had been patiently biding their time at the bar took charge. They all left with a girl on each arm. If Maria could swirl me around the floor, taking on two of these girls called for quite a man. The major, following my eyes, laughed, "Nica boys must be in good shape, yes?"

Everyone bade us a cordial farewell as we prepared to leave, and it was clear the major was a frequent and popular visitor. It looked to me, however, as with the girls on the sidewalk, he was but an admirer and left it at that.

A few days later, I ran into an oil company engineer outside the Royal Dutch Hotel. "My date's picking me up," he explained. He confided she was a girl he'd met at his company's office earlier that afternoon. "It's gonna probably be an expensive evening," he grinned, "but it'll be memorable."

Just then Maria in her white lace dress drove up in an old Plymouth. Our eyes met, but I said nothing. Ignoring me, she opened the car door and greeted the engineer. "*Noble español!*" she cooed. He smiled a foolish smile and slid into the front seat, winking at me over his shoulder. I gave him a thumbs-up and walked away.

San José was a beautiful city and I enjoyed my visits there. Seeing my interest in the local culture, Major Bonilla suggested we go see a sculptor named Nestor. "He is celebrated for his carvings of Don Quixote," said the major. "Some people say he is as crazy as Quixote," he laughed, as we drove in the blue Volkswagen into the mountains outside San José. We passed people walking alongside wooden donkey carts with brightly painted wheels. I hadn't seen them in the city. Although the carts were transporting goods, the Costa Ricans had made them into colorful moveable works of art.

We pulled up to Nestor's workshop. It was attached to a modest house. A young man came out to greet us. Major Bonilla explained in Spanish that I was interested in his art and Nestor showed us various wood sculptures, wonderfully carved with muted colors. I chose a tall slender seated Quixote with his arms raised above him. I was surprised how expensive it was, but I really liked it. "Good," said Major Bonilla, pleased I had found something that so clearly delighted me. He helped me finish up the transaction and we left.

I returned to Managua with my Don Quixote loosely wrapped, and packaged it more carefully to get it home to Chicago, carrying it onboard in the Pan Am cabin with me. Pat liked it and I decided to make another visit to Nestor on my next trip. Once again Major Bonilla assisted me. This time I bought three pieces, all related to the story of Don Quixote, including Don Quixote alongside his horse Rocinante. I thought they would make a nice grouping back home in our house, a souvenir of a country I found so lovely.

Returning to Managua, I cleared customs and was walking to the parking lot, when two Guardia soldiers approached me. My new Quixotes had the same loose wrapping as the first and the men could see what they were. I felt my skin prickle. One of the soldiers, a Guardia major, touched the largest package. "You have brought a gift for the General, no?" he said, smiling sardonically. "*Very* nice," he whistled as he pulled at the paper to get a better look. "We will give them to the General for you."

I was caught totally off guard. I knew damn well they weren't going to give them to Somoza, but couldn't think quickly enough.

"The General will be very pleased," said the other stepping forward. I looked around but the parking lot was deserted. Reluctantly I released my prizes. "We will give the General your regards," said the major, and the two walked away, laughing quietly. Empty-handed, I continued on to my car, cursing my bad luck.

Chapter 18

THROUGH THE FENCE

The way things were shaping up, it was looking as though I was going to have to fly a Costa Rican Mustang home. Back again in San José, I spread aeronautical charts out on the hotel bed to plan the best route. Leaving Costa Rica, it made sense to overfly Nicaragua, I decided, going directly to the border town of Tapachula, my port of entry to Mexico. With the fuselage tanks full, the Mustang had a good thousand-mile range at a cruise speed of about 300 miles per hour. I compiled a brief checklist to tape on the instrument panel: engine check, trim check, 6 degrees right rudder, zero on elevator and ailerons, throttle lock snug, prop and mixture forward, seat and parachute tight, canopy locked, controls free and easy.

It was June 13, 1964. The day dawned hot and humid, a typical tropical morning. I lined up for takeoff. The plane had its original military radio and sometimes it worked. I tried it, and to my delight, the tower answered. Cleared to go, I gently eased the throttle forward. Steering was easy and the fact that the nose blocked my forward vision no longer bothered me. I held the stick just a fraction aft of neutral as the plane tracked straight down the runway. As sometimes happened, I was airborne before the throttle was full forward.

The speed builds up quickly at that point, and soon I was solidly climbing. I reached down and grabbed the gear handle, pulling it inward and back. By then, it was time to reduce power and rpm. Now I had breathing room to check the instruments, particularly the coolant temperature. I knew it would be high initially, reflecting the takeoff power, but would drop back quickly in shallow climb or level flight.

The Mustang's engine was water-cooled; the radiator carried twenty-one gallons of a glycol/water mixture running through four pipes under the pilot's seat. The temperature usually ran about 100 degrees centigrade in the pressurized system. If the system sprang a leak, it was only minutes before the engine seized.

The coolant doors in the radiator worked in four positions: automatic, manual, open, and closed. Because I was flying in such extreme temperatures, I always used the open position for takeoff and then switched to manual as soon as I leveled off. If there's a coolant leak while the doors are in the automatic position, the thermostat keeps opening the radiator door until the coolant runs out, and suddenly the gauge signals, too late, that the engine is overheating. By flying with the door in the manual position, the pilot can see the temperature start to rise in time to make an emergency landing.

I charted a course northwest to the Pacific, with a right turn to follow the coastline to Tapachula, Mexico. It was elementary navigation, but it worked. The Mustang's cockpit was long enough to accommodate my frame, and by adjusting the rudder pedals, I could stretch out my legs. I had about two hours of flight time in the P-51 and was growing more and more comfortable in it.

Just as I passed over the northern corner of Nicaragua, the engine started to shake and miss. So did my heart. The gauges told me nothing. What in hell was happening? I switched tanks; no change. The vibration grew more intense, and I swung back toward Managua. I tried calling the tower, but the radio had died.

Then the engine quit. The silence was deafening. I tried everything I knew about restarting the engine. I closed the mixture and put the throttle in start position. I flipped the magneto switches on and off. Although the gauges indicated I had fuel pressure, I moved the fuel selector back and forth with the fuel pump on to make sure gas was really flowing. All this time I was losing altitude.

I would have to put it down. I couldn't memorize my own social security number, but I knew this part of the manual by heart. I mentally reviewed the emergency list and worked through the procedures: pulling the prop control back for the least drag, shutting off the master switch, cutting the fuel. I held the plane at the optimal glide speed of 175 miles per hour.

I was over semi-flat terrain and I circled a likely landing spot, noting a tiny town several miles south. I rechecked my harness, pulling it as tight as I could and decreased my angle of descent to start slowing up. I was essentially logging glider time. The greatest danger now was losing too much airspeed and stalling the plane, which would either cartwheel it or flip it on its back.

The ground loomed up. My heart sank as I saw the terrain was hillier than it looked from altitude. I slowly put down full flap and felt the slight ballooning lift. The airspeed indicator read 120 miles per hour. I clenched the stick, *Do not stall, do not stall,* I willed grimly. I eased the plane down until the prop was just clearing the ground. Then I saw the barbed wire fence. Too late to pull up, I gritted my teeth, lowered my head, and flew right through it.

I caught a fence post on each wing, and then banged and bumped along as the plane skidded across the rough ground. I shoved the stick forward to make damn sure I didn't balloon back up.

The front edge of the air scoop caught in a shallow ditch, tearing off the bottom of the plane. The impact sent a shudder through my whole body and dislodged the 200-pound radiator, sending it flying through the air. When the plane eventually came to a stop, I cranked the canopy back, leapt out, and ran about thirty feet before I looked back. There was no explosion. The Mustang lay quietly, prop bent, bottom torn off, and wings with two gaping holes in the leading edges. The radiator had landed about seventy-five feet away. But at least the tanks had not ruptured and no gas was leaking.

I didn't lose consciousness, but I must have been dazed. A while later I found myself sitting on the wing, and I didn't know how long I had been there. My shoulders ached from the strain of the harness. I was parched and wished I had brought water. Strange insects buzzed around me, and the sun's reflection off the sheet metal was blinding.

When my head cleared, I decided I'd better start walking and set off in the direction of the town I had seen from the air. I was in a valley surrounded by low mountains. The turf grass gave way to dusty brownish-red cracked ground. It obviously could not be farmed, but it was clear from the fences that there was some sort of grazing activity. It was high noon in open country now with no shade, and the sun beat down mercilessly.

About an hour later, I reached the town, which consisted of five whitewashed buildings, one of which was a small store. Since I was on my way back to the States, I didn't have any *córdobas*, the local currency. I negotiated a warm Coca-Cola for a dollar that I assured the proprietress would cover the cost. When I sat down on the wooden front steps to drink it, my arms and legs started tingling. The dizziness had passed, but I think I was still riding the wave of adrenalin that had carried me through the intense concentration of bringing the plane down. A pig wandered by, eyed me curiously, and ambled on.

I spotted some telephone wires that led to a small Catholic church with the only phone in town. The priest stopped his window repairing but obviously did not have any idea of where I came from or my situation. After multiple tries, the operator, who spoke only Spanish, got me through to Roberto Vassalli, my customs broker in Managua. He sent a car for me immediately. Since I was supposed to be in Costa Rica, not Nicaragua, I could look forward to a bunch of paperwork and a little chat with Captain Garcia at Immigration.

The Nicaraguans smirked when they heard about the crash: "The Costa Ricans don't know nothin' about airplanes." The irony of that comment didn't escape me. It was important to find out why the engine had quit, so I went out with the mechanics and an officer to look at the wreck.

By this time, the locals had taken their machetes and peeled some of the aluminum skin off the fuselage, as metal was highly prized. My bird looked like the turkey three days after Thanksgiving. A farmer appeared and waved his machete menacingly. *"Mi finca... mi avión!"* The officer in charge brusquely announced that it was FAN property, and that ended the discussion.

Back at the hangar a few days later, the mechanics that had pulled the engine reported the plane crashed because it ran out of gas. There were 265 gallons in the tanks when I left Costa Rica, and I had probably burned off about 50 gallons. Since the mechanics had seen the stripped plane and met the farmer, it would have been obvious to them that the locals had siphoned off the gas. But the official accident report stated running out of gas as the reason for the crash. Apparently it wasn't important the information be accurate, only that the official fill in all the lines. Glenn sent me a cable: *Regret FAA will not accept three minutes P-51 glider time toward type rating, but considering nomination for 'cojones grandes' award.*

When I called the manager of SALA, the Costa Rican aircraft facility that had inspected and serviced the plane, he said he had no idea why the engine quit. I felt thoroughly defeated. Discouraged, I caught the next airliner to Chicago.

Was it ever good to be home—hot water, clean sheets, familiar food, and most of all, my family. But two days later, I woke up with a blinding headache. It was a thundering, throbbing pain that laid me low. Over-the-counter painkillers did nothing. Glenn helped Pat get me to the doctor. He prescribed a powerful medication that alleviated some of the pain and after several days, it passed.

My flight physical was scheduled for the following week. The medical examiner explained that although my head didn't actually hit anything in the crash, the deceleration caused my brain to slam forward against the inside of my skull. Concussions can be felt four to five days after the event. The doctor checked my eye coordination, balance, and reflexes, all of which were normal.

I called England to talk to engineers at Rolls-Royce, the company that had designed the engine. I also contacted other knowledgeable people, including the Indiana dealer who had handled some Mustangs. In the absence of any other explanation, a dried-up carburetor and some type of fuel problem seemed to be the likeliest cause of the crash.

I returned to Nicaragua to meet with the Lloyds of London insurance adjuster who had come in from Panama. He showed up in a dark suit and striped tie, but soon shed the coat. "Yes, old chap, no doubt, it is a total loss. Just dreadful," he announced in his clipped accent. "There's no way of salvaging anything in this jungle. We'll send your cheque out to you as soon as it can be scheduled."

After weeks of waiting, I called Lloyds. Since my policy was for component parts and the accident was "just a partial loss," it was explained, Lloyds would only pay a small percentage for the propeller and an even smaller amount for the fuselage and wing damage. Being screwed is no fun, even if it is in a classy accent. The total check wasn't much more than the premium. Insurance looked like a foolproof business to get into. When the policy ran out, I decided to carry only liability, which I placed with another company.

Chapter 19

Travels with Bill

It was through a U.S. dealer, Jim Morton, that I first met Bill Rolfe. Morton had purchased some of our P-51s and Bill was one of his ferry pilots. A retired air force major, Bill had flown Mustangs at the end of WWII and then jets in the Korean conflict. His jovial hail-fellow-well-met manner notwithstanding, he was a serious professional pilot with a distinguished military record. He was probably in his early forties and getting a little thick in the middle, a pipe smoker with a good sense of humor. A private person, he never talked about his personal life.

We had sold Morton the TF dual-control Mustang. When I mentioned to Bill that I still didn't feel comfortable flying Mustangs, he offered to fly with me in the TF, and I jumped at the chance. This time I sat up front. After Bill made the takeoff, he leveled off at about 7,500 feet and directed me through the intercom, "Put it in a steep bank and keep slowing it up." He kept saying, "More bank— slow it up more."

The plane was shaking like a leaf when he instructed, "Now turn it the other way and do the same thing." After about three 360s each way to practice precision flying, we did a number of stalls; I was surprised how easy they were to recover from. By this time, I was feeling more confident the plane was under my control. This was starting to be fun!

When we turned downwind, he pulled power back all the way and immediately started his turn for a curving base leg on to final. He never added any power. Bill did a three-point landing, setting the plane down as if it were a feather. We only rolled out about 2,000 feet on the runway.

He explained later that in a war zone, there wasn't any time to waste getting down. "You didn't want to get shot, and you or others in the squadron might be low on gas or in trouble."

Bill volunteered to make a trip to Nicaragua. He flew a T-28 down and returned with a Mustang with the fastest turnaround time of any of the pilots. Apparently "siesta-and-fiesta" didn't appeal to him. Both the U.S. and the Nicaraguan military later spoke of him with great respect. When he brought a Mustang into Midway Airport, I asked if the plane needed anything. He said, "Nothing serious," and gave me a list of carefully identified minor problems that needed work. What a class act. Other pilots would gripe, but when I asked them to be specific, then had nothing to say. Bill kept track of expenses in a little notebook and was right on the money down to the last dime. Finally I had a pilot I could trust out of my sight.

The paperwork on the impounded B-26 at Midway Airport was finally sorted out, so I bought the plane and lined up a ferry permit. When I ordered the wing tanks filled, they took almost 800 gallons. The fixed base operator explained with a straight face that "the gas must have been used up when we ran the engines once a week" as designated in their government contract. He knew that I knew where the gas had gone, but there wasn't much point pursuing it.

I suggested to Bill that we deliver a B-26 to Nicaragua and return with two Mustangs. He agreed happily, "Sounds great. Let's go!"

Bill and I met at Midway Airport the morning of our departure. I had ordered the plane to be preflighted, but I checked the oil myself. Instead of looking at the dipstick, the line boy had filled it right up to the top of the tank. We drained it down until it registered just to the full mark on the stick. Oil when it heats up, expands, and if there is too much, can cause fires in flight.

When we climbed into the cockpit, Bill took the right seat, which did not have a control stick. He had only flown with me in the dual-control Mustang, so I was flattered he trusted me in the left seat. Since the noise in the cockpit made conversation impossible, Pat had given me the Magic Slate. The B-26 has two 24-volt batteries, one in each engine cowling. The left one was missing, but we started the engines from the right.

After looking at the charts, we decided to cruise at 32 inches manifold pressure and 2000 rpm. The charts indicated we would burn 171 gallons per hour, but we flight planned figuring another ten gallons to be on the safe side. These numbers would move us along at almost 300 miles per hour, a good traveling speed for the big bird.

Bill suggested we go up to 14,000 feet to take advantage of favorable winds. We were about two hours into the flight when the right engine backfired. I felt as though I had been hit in the stomach. Bill began scanning the gauges and checking the mixture setting. The engine backfired again, and Bill wrote on the Magic Slate, *I think we have a bad jug* [an air cooled cylinder].

I wrote the pilot's universal response: *Oh shit.*

The engine was now backfiring every twenty to thirty seconds. When I eased back on the throttle and dropped down to 13,000 feet, however, the engine ran smoothly again. I looked over at Bill and he tilted his head to one side and shrugged. We'd figure it out later.

That night I took the manual to my room and carefully reviewed the fuel system. I discovered that at higher altitudes starting at 14,000 feet, the engine-driven pump does not put out enough gas to feed the engine without help from the auxiliary pump. In our pre-flight the day before, we had noticed the fuel pump in the right engine's main tank was not working, so we had had to start it with the pump in the right auxiliary tank. That fuel pressure drop was enough to cause the engine to run excessively lean. The fuel pressure gauge, the size of a car speedometer, didn't indicate the problem.

This meant that at altitude, the right engine would backfire if it were running on the right main tank. If we stayed below 13,000 feet, it was okay. This was typical of problems in ferrying old surplus aircraft that had not been flown regularly or maintained properly. Once you knew the problem, you simply worked around it.

7 a.m. at the airfield in Veracruz, Mexico, with the Nica Mustangs that
Bill Rolfe and I delivered up to Chicago.

Bill Rolfe, a former USAF major, was a top-notch pilot and a great travel companion. Here we are loading the B-26 at Midway Airport in Chicago.

When the Thunderbolt's engine quit, Bill managed to put it down on a beach in
Mexico with little damage. The location was so remote, however,
I was unable to salvage the plane.

Bill spread out his chute to block the tropical sun until he was picked up by boat and
brought to a fishing camp and then back up to the States.

153

My Jeep's running board and front bumper after an encounter with Jerry DeLarm's Cadillac.

My brother and business partner, Glenn. After the DeLarm incident, a British embassy official loaned me a gun until Glenn could bring mine down from Chicago.

Chila Lopez welcomed me into her circle of friends. Her father, a Nicaraguan military man, had been murdered by Guardia soldiers.

Scenes from Managua

When my Mustang's engine quit over the Gulf of Fonseca, I barely made it to shore.
Once the tide came in, the plane's wings were submerged.

My man Friday didn't speak English but gestured that the only way out
was by dugout canoe through a mangrove swamp. He holds a machete
in one hand, as was typical in rural Nicaragua.

157

A U.S. Army helicopter pilot brought me back to the crash site the day after the crash.

The crash site from the helicopter: the Gulf of Fonseca can be seen at the top with a strip of white sand beach where I put the plane down.

My "rescuers" decided to take a picture of themselves with the
camera I'd left among my gear at the crash site overnight. When I
got back to Chicago and developed the film, I found this picture.
Note the rifle in the hand of the guy standing in the doorway.

No one had any idea how to salvage the plane out of there, and I had to abandon it.
I carried only liability insurance, so a write-off wreaked havoc with the cash flow.

159

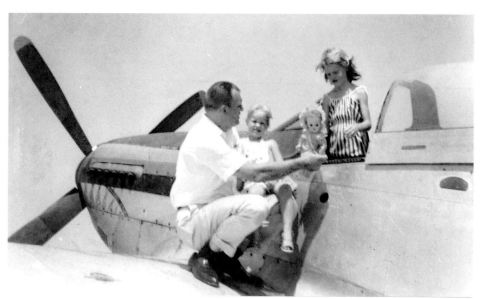

My frequent absences were wearing on my wife Pat and my daughters.
Cassie and Suzie with me on a Mustang at Midway Airport.

The Nica mechanics greeted me with smiles every morning, but my gringo work
standards collided regularly with their casual approach to aircraft maintenance.

Sugar cane makes for a rough landing surface. The Mustang's pilot seat protected me from the stalks that burst through the cockpit floor when we hit.

The almost forty-foot-wide swath cut by my bird.

The FAN posted guards until we had removed the engine and instruments.

The locals stripped the much prized aluminum from the plane.
The woman in the foreground is bringing a Quaker Oats container
that will be filled with siphoned-off gasoline.

Ben Amonds had brought this Thunderbolt most of the way up to the U.S. when it started spewing black smoke. He landed just as the engine seized. A fine pilot, Amonds later went on to fly for United Airlines.

Warbird owner Lou Antonacci loaned me his T-6 so I could log "recent experience" in order to get FAA permission to fly my newly restored but not yet licensed Mustang out of Midway Airport.

On final at DuPage Airport outside Chicago with one landing gear up,
one landing gear down, and zero visibility out the front windshield.
(Photo by Jon Cunningham for *The Aurora Beacon-News*)

Bill Ross, a fellow warbird owner, commandeered a radio in a parked plane and
guided me down after an airborne Cessna pilot lined me up with the runway.

We rolled about 500 feet on one wheel
until the plane lost speed and the right wing dipped.
(Photo by Jon Cunningham for *The Aurora Beacon-News*)

A bent prop and a little wing skin was the extent of the damage.
That night the plane was given the name "El Gato."

The B-26 has a switch that causes three large steel arms to drop down in front of the bomb bay before its doors open. In combat, these arms acted as spoilers and helped the bombs drop aerodynamically instead of just tumbling out. On this plane, because of a hydraulic leak, the arms would deploy on their own without being activated by the switch, creating drag. We took care of the problem by just hitting the switch to retract them, and then re-retracting them every hour or so as they started to droop down again.

Flying with Bill was a real pleasure. He would sit back, light his funny-looking pipe, glance at the chart, and signal a left or right turn. The first time I turned 5 to 8 degrees, and he shot me a pained look. A couple degrees correction was all that was needed. Soon I could sense when he felt I was straying a little off course. He'd shift uncomfortably in his seat, and I would immediately check my heading. I wasn't used to flying that precisely.

We left the States at Brownsville, entered Mexico at Matamoros, and then flew on to spend the night at Veracruz. We landed and headed to a local hotel. I told Bill I was going to take a nap. He said he was going to go for a walk.

I had just woken up when he returned about an hour later. He had picked up a couple of ice-cold Cokes, so we went down to sit in the lobby. "You won't believe what happened to me," he said with a straight face.

I popped the cap off my drink. "Tell me about it."

"Well, I wanted to practice my Spanish. So I see this guy sitting on the ground with his burro standing next to him. '*Qué hora es?*' I ask him.

The guy reaches under the burro and grabs the burro's balls and stares at them for a minute. '*Cuatro y media, señor,*' says the guy to me.

I look at my watch, and by God, he's right on the money! I can't believe what I've just seen, so I say, '*Comó es posible saber la hora así?*'—you know, how can you tell time like that?

The fellow looks at me kind of funny. He lifts the burro's balls again and this time points in the distance beyond the burros's cojones: '*El reloj está ahí,*'—the clock is over there!"

Bill's face kind of twitched, and then he started to laugh and I started to laugh and pretty soon everyone in the lobby was wondering about the two gringos who could have such a good time over just a couple of Cokes.

The battery had seemed weak when we started up at Matamoros. At Veracruz, we had to move the plane to a different spot on the field, which meant starting both engines without time for the generator to recharge. Sure enough, the next morning we didn't get enough juice to send the prop around even once. We found a mechanic with a battery cart who smiled broadly when we said we needed a boost. "Fifty dollars," he announced cheerfully.

"We don't want to buy the battery cart—just use it for a couple minutes," I protested.

"No problem!" he said amiably. "A dollar a minute."

We plugged it in. The engine popped off, and Bill jerked out the booster cable plug. We paid the mechanic three bucks. The left engine started easily when I revved up the right engine to cut in the generator.

Bill believed in running a tank dry when flying with multiple engines. He reasoned that way you could utilize all the gas. When it was time to change tanks, we both watched the fuel pressure gauge. When it started to waver and drop, indicating it was empty, we switched the tank. We got to be pretty good at it and never had an engine quit during the procedure.

We arrived in Managua in the late morning and taxied the plane up to the FAN's main hangar. The next morning Sergeant Gonzales jumped in and tried to start the engines. The left one fired up promptly, but he cranked and cranked the right one to no avail. He shut down the left engine and climbed down.

"Something's wrong with the fuel system," he fumed. Luckily when I tried it, the left engine popped right off, and I showed the mechanics how to cross feed to the right engine.

While our Mustangs were being readied for ferrying, I asked Bill to take one up and do a little air work. I wanted the Nicaraguans to see a U.S. pilot who really knew how to fly a P-51. The U.S. Mission was the object of much derision because the pilots always landed their shiny DC-3 on the main wheels instead of three points. In Latin

America, the pilots often had to go into small fields, so they would touch down on the main landing gear and tail wheel simultaneously in order to use the least amount of runway.

Without much ado, Bill did a test flight, a few smooth rolls and loops, and then brought the plane around for a perfect three-point landing right on the runway numbers. Not one Nicaraguan said a word and for once, everyone appeared to be focusing intently on his work.

When our planes were finally ready, the directional gyros conked out. I scrounged up a couple of small wet compasses, but overnight someone stole them. I couldn't turn up any more compasses, but Bill brushed away my concern. "Hey, Will. No problema. We got maps." We would play follow-the-leader.

Bill took off first. When I followed and tried to come alongside, I came in at a 45-degree angle and damn near ran into him. I jerked the stick back and flew right over the top of him, drifted back and swung out to the side. I eased up so I was about a hundred feet behind him and slightly to his right. So much for formation flying.

We droned on, flying over jungle and along the ocean. When we entered Mexican airspace, we landed to check in with customs at Tapachula and then continued due north another 200 miles to Veracruz for the night. Since we couldn't lock the canopies, we took the parachutes with us. A couple of crop duster pilots strolled over to look at the Mustangs. One eyed the parachutes and then my feet. "Do you fly with those shoes?" he asked.

Puzzled, I asked, "What are you getting at?"

"If you ever jump with those shoes, you'll be barefoot when you land," he pointed out.

I glanced down at my slip-on loafers. I felt even more foolish when he continued, "Ever had any military training?"

I shook my head.

"Well, with your size, about the best you could hope for is a broken leg."

Barefoot in the jungle with a broken leg: a good argument for staying put in the plane.

Bill and I hitched a ride into town and arranged for two rooms.

Over some cold beers in the hotel's cantina, I asked Bill if he had ever jumped. He said he had trained for it, "but the occasion never arose." In a plane built as solidly as a fighter, some pilots figured their chances were better riding it down.

After about an hour, the proprietor came over, wringing his hands. It seemed a large family had just arrived and could-we-do-him-the-favor-of-sharing-a-room-with-twin-beds-and-it-would-be-so-helpful-if-we-could-indeed-be-so-gracious-as-to-accommodate-him, etc. We agreed. Bill moved his stuff into my room.

The dusters came in with another ferry pilot and joined us after they had arranged for rooms. Bill looked at me sideways because a few minutes ago there hadn't been any more rooms. I shrugged, abandoning all notion of understanding Latin logic.

During dinner, the proprietor again appeared, again very agitated. Once more, he had a great problem: would we, looking at all five of us, mind sharing a large room with separate beds for each of us? By this time, we had disposed of quite a few beers and considered ourselves comrades in a foreign land. We took the request in good cheer.

Bill was the only pilot with combat experience. As we all lay in the darkness in our beds, he talked about flying P-38s in the Pacific near the end of WWII, Mustangs at the beginning of the Korean War, and later F-86s. He described an encounter as he was returning from the 40th Parallel and had come up behind a Soviet MIG. He looked directly down at the enemy pilot and knew the pilot realized he was about to be killed.

Almost in unison, we asked, "How did you feel?"

"About what?" Bill asked simply. "The objective was to shoot down the enemy before he shot you." Bill fell silent and with that last story, we went to sleep. I have thought about that night many times.

Years later, flying a T-34 with Ray Morley, a former WWII pilot, we landed in Arkansas. While I watched the plane being fueled, Ray went in the gas shack to settle the bill. He noticed a calendar with a picture of a Mustang. He mentioned a buddy of his had brought some back from Latin America. The flight service owner jumped up and asked, "Is he a great big guy?" Ray said he was, and the man proceeded to tell Bill Rolfe's story of coming up behind the Korean pilot at the 40th Parallel. The flight service owner had been one of the dusters at the table in Mexico.

The next morning, Bill and I followed the coastline up to Matamoros. When I flew with Bill, it felt as though the plane were on rails. I never noticed the plane banking or turning to correct course. The altimeter didn't seem to move either. It was fun to fly with such a skilled professional.

After we landed, I couldn't see any gas in the tank. We hadn't filled the planes since Tapachula about a thousand miles back. Bill reminded me the wing was on a slant and the gas was on the low side. He assured me we had enough for the five-minute hop across the Rio Grande to Brownsville where we could use a credit card for gas.

That made sense and when I followed him off, I couldn't believe how well the Mustang performed. I had never known what it was like to fly a Mustang 1300 pounds lighter. Without the weight of the gas, I felt like I was riding a rocket.

In Brownsville, the planes took within two gallons of each other. We added three or four quarts of 60-weight oil to each. Our next stop was the field at Walnut Ridge, Arkansas. Walnut Ridge had served as the largest facility for dismantling WWII aircraft after the war. By the time we landed, two cars had arrived. The visitors told us that they had flown '51s during WWII, and when they heard the distinctive sound of the Merlin engine, they came running.

In the office, we saw pictures of planes standing on their noses with the engines cut off, waiting for the chopper to slice them up for the smelter. They bore mute testimony to our nation's need to erase the memories of WWII. It was sad to contemplate such an ignoble end for these old warriors.

The battery in Bill's plane had been weak, and it now died completely. The field didn't have any maintenance facilities nor could the gas shack come up with any cables or batteries. We solved the problem by asking our two visitors to drive their cars up close to the fuselage. I connected their batteries in series, so with their jumper cables we had 24 volts. We took the battery connection off and put the jumper cables on, started the plane, and then replaced the cable back on the dead battery. The prop blast made it a little windy, but our visitors seemed happy to relive their wartime flying days.

Midway Airport, our final destination, lay only four hundred miles away. I called the tower to ask for a light gun, and an hour and a half later, Bill and I came over the field and landed on parallel runways. What a great pair of planes! Except for the weak battery, they performed perfectly. There were no gas, oil, or coolant leaks, other than a little oil streak, which was normal after flying three thousand miles.

We sold one of the planes to a research outfit in the East. Bill delivered the other to a doctor in Texas who had experience flying Mustangs.

About a year later, the doctor phoned Glenn. "You got any more of them Mustangs?" he asked. "I'd like to buy another one."

"Yes, but what did you do with the first one?" Glenn asked.

"Well, you see, I was taking off and reaching to pull up the landing gear," he began, "And when I leaned forward, the throttle friction knob hadn't been tightened enough, so the throttle came back. I slammed the throttle forward, the left wing went down from 'torque' and I cartwheeled."

It was pretty obvious what had happened. The doctor had tried to pull a hotdog takeoff and was lucky to have survived. Some pilots think it looks sharp to pull the gear up just as the plane is leaving the runway. Instead of climbing out normally, they hold the plane down and when the gear comes up, they yank the stick back for a great "zoom." But the effect of the prop being suddenly revved up while the plane is flying slowly pitches the nose left and the wing down. And when the plane is close to the ground, the results are disastrous. The doctor's plane wrapped up in a ball of metal. Miraculously, he was not seriously injured.

Another T-28 was ready so Bill took it down. I joined him a few days later in Managua. It turned out the next Mustang and the remaining P-47 wouldn't be ready for another two weeks. Since Morton had other ferrying jobs waiting, Bill flew home commercially, and I remained behind to try to push the work along.

The Curtiss Electric motor in the prop hub that controlled the Thunderbolt's thirteen-foot, four-bladed prop was giving us problems. Conveniently for us, Lanica, the airline located next to the military hangar, was owned by Somoza. Lanica used Curtiss C-46s for cargo, and they had the same type prop and electric controls as the

'47. The Lanica mechanics explained there were small contacts in the controls that corroded over time. Replacing them solved the problem.

The Mustang still needed to be test-flown. I was sick of test-flying, so when Major Gomez who had gone up with me in the two-seater TF volunteered, I agreed. The word spread like wildfire. One of Our Guys would show the *norteamericano* how to fly. A crowd suddenly appeared to cheer on the local hero.

The major swaggered through the onlookers, decked out in his flying togs and parachute. While he was getting himself strapped in the cockpit, Colonel Saavedra's orderly rushed out with the word that no Nicaraguan was to fly Mustangs. The show was off, and the major wasn't going to get extra money. The crowd was disappointed, but hung around.

One more damn thing. I climbed in the cockpit and started adjusting the rudder pedals. Major Gomez watched, hands on hips, legs spread. I started going through the cockpit check. Since one of the hydraulic cylinders had been leaking, I applied steady pressure on the brakes to make sure the master cylinder was holding. I was checking the cockpit gauges when my right leg shot forward and my foot almost broke through the firewall. I shut down the engine.

A disdainful murmur swept through the crowd. I called over Sergeant Gonzales who had shown up to see the fun. He picked a screwdriver from the back pocket of a passing mechanic. This particular plane had a panel for a camera on the left side of the fuselage, and he opened it. He reached in and slowly pulled out a handful of broken rudder cable and held it high for everyone to see. Acid from the battery on the shelf behind the armor plate had leaked down, eating right through the cable. Only a few strands had been holding it together. Although it was on the checklist, it was plain no one had inspected it. If the rudder cable had not given way under the heavy pressure on the brakes, it would certainly have snapped on takeoff.

A hush fell over the men. Without a word, I picked up my chute and strode through the crowd that parted for me. Major Gomez looked pale and avoided my eyes, mindful of what would probably have happened if he had been at the controls. I wanted to vomit.

Chapter 20

A Foreign Affair

Not long after the incident with the rudder cables, it was time to test-fly another Mustang. Everything looked ok on the outside: no leaks, no loose-hanging parts. The instruments checked out and I hoped that for once nothing would go wrong.

As I climbed up in the plane, I noticed there were a lot of people at the passenger terminal building and figured something important was going on. I taxied out to the runway and the tower gave me a green light. I moved about in the seat uncomfortably, trying to ease the tight straps of the shoulder harness and then started forward with the throttle. I had learned to respect it as the most dangerous lever on the plane.*

We began our roll down the runway. I was getting used to not being able to see over the nose on takeoff. Holding the stick slightly aft of neutral, I let the plane gain speed until the tail lifted slightly and the nose began to come down a little. I watched out the window until a few seconds later the wheels left the ground and we were airborne. Once we were at about 200 feet, I ducked down to pull the landing

---

*If a pilot makes a bad landing in a Mustang, the plane can bounce. At that point, it is on the verge of a stall, and many fatal accidents have occurred when the pilot, attempting to recover, adds too much power too quickly. The surge of power causes the plane to veer left...and down.

gear handle up. It was only then that I glanced at the airspeed indicator. It read zero. *Oh shit.*

Had I noticed it wasn't working earlier, I would have aborted the takeoff. Since the plane stalls at 87 miles per hour and the first tick on the airspeed indicator is 50, I typically didn't watch it going down the runway, as the needle doesn't move very far until the plane is really flying. Taking off in this sleek bird isn't like chauffeuring a larger transport where everything is done by the numbers. You *know* when a Mustang is going to fly. However, airspeed is critical on landing, as you can't "feel" your way down.

I continued to climb away from the traffic area and started thinking very hard about what to do. I knew the power settings, manifold, and rpm for climb and cruise, but I had no idea what to set for landing. Landing in a Mustang, as I had discovered on my first flight in Costa Rica, is all about airspeed: the controls become sloppy at low speeds and don't give an accurate signal to the pilot. I had learned not to focus on the engine gauge settings coming in on final, instead concentrating on the airspeed indicator and moving the throttle to maintain 110 miles per hour. Too fast, the Mustang wouldn't land, too slow and it could fall out of the air in a fatal stall.

I drove around a little, practicing some slow flying and then decided to go for it. As I was coming in on final, the airspeed indicator reading a blank, I had a terrible feeling my speed was too slow, so I added a little power. Too much. I pulled the throttle back slightly. By now I was sailing over the runway but not slowing down quickly enough. I had the power full back and the engine was doing its usual backfiring. I thought I could put the main wheels on the runway and carefully go to full braking with stick held back to keep from nosing over.

Wrong. We touched down and—BOUNCE!—sailed back up fifty feet in the air. Now I was on the verge of stalling, so I eased the throttle a fraction and let the plane settle. It landed "firmly"—i.e., no pieces fell off. When I finally turned off the runway, my right tire drove through the dirt at the overrun. I was happy to call it a day.

As I was heading to the parking lot, I ran into one of the American Mission captains who mentioned they were having a cocktail party over at the pool next to the military offices and said I should join them. It was the first time anyone had invited me to one of the U.S. social events. Pleased, I hurried back to the hotel, showered, and put on a clean shirt to go partying.

When I returned to the airport, the party was in full swing. I was chatting with one of the U.S. Air Force officers about my mishap with the airspeed indicator, when a tall German woman marched up to me. She had dark hair and a sturdy Teutonic build. I'd guess she was in her mid-thirties. I started to introduce myself, but she cut me off. "Vair da *hell* did you learn to fly? You embarrassed da whole U.S. Mission today!"

I put my Scotch down.

"Somoza vas at da airport," she continued indignantly, "and he saw dat *terrible* landing. He vanted to know if dat vas one of *his* pilots." She glared at me for besmirching my nation's honor.

"Uh, Will, this is Ute Gardner. She's married to one of our army sergeants," said the officer.

"*I* am glider pilot," she announced crisply. "*I* could haf done better landing."

I had had enough. "I've got glider time too," I replied slowly. "But my glider weighed ten times more than your glider and was going 120 miles an hour when it touched down. By the way, you ever land your glider without a working airspeed indicator?"

She apparently hadn't, as she stared at me a moment and then abruptly turned on her heel and walked away. The U.S. officer said dryly, "Some doll, that Ute. Our gift from Germany. Got a husband who's a real hothead. Word is they deserve one another. First time I've seen her speechless, though." He raised his glass to me.

My social life had been limited in Nicaragua. *Life is pretty dull for a married gringo*, I wrote Pat. Other than my scolding from Frau Ute, I had enjoyed the mission cocktail party very much. There was no American compound in Managua, and opportunities to get together with other English-speaking expats were rare for me.

I was startled when a few days later, Ute walked up to me at the airport and invited me to a party. I figured she was sorry for being so rude and that it would be a chance to meet some more compatriots.

"You should take a cab out to our house, and dair vill be udder people you can ride back mit to da city," she said smiling.

The day of the party I hummed to myself as I shaved and put on a fresh yellow and white *guayabera* shirt over crisply pressed slacks. Downstairs, Ramirez, a cab driver I'd gotten to know a little, greeted me. "Señor Martin, you goin' to a party?"

"Sure am, Ramirez!" I replied. "And I need you to take me there. You know this address?" I showed him the piece of paper I'd written the address on.

Ramirez frowned as he studied it. "Sí, sí, it's outside of town. We will find it."

Away we went. We drove to the outskirts of Managua into a hilly neighborhood. The American-style ranch houses were spaced far apart and there were no sidewalks. Ramirez stopped at the end of a short dirt driveway. "This is the place."

I looked. There were no other cars. "Wait here, will you? Maybe I got the wrong address." I got out and walked up to the front door and knocked.

The door swung open and there was Ute. "I'm so sorry, I must have gotten the wrong day," I apologized.

"Oh no," she said. "You didn't."

"But where's the party?" I asked innocently.

"*You* are da party, Vill," she replied.

It took me a second to register what she was saying. "There's a big misunderstanding," I said bluntly and headed back down the drive where fortunately Ramirez was still waiting.

"You ever hear of the 'badger game,' Ramirez?" I said as we drove back to the city.

"Baa-jer game? What is that?"

"A lady invites a married man to her house for some fun. But after the fun, it is very bad for the married man," I explained.

Ramirez looked momentarily puzzled and then his eyes lit up with understanding. "Ha, ha," he chuckled. "You lucky to get out with your *cojones*." I couldn't have agreed more.

Chapter 21

This Nicaraguan Life

A new class of Nicaraguan airmen had just come back from training in the United States. Their swagger signaled immediately that their aerial skills knew no bounds. As one of the lads climbed into a T-33 jet trainer, however, his I've-seen-it-all demeanor faded and he eyed the runway nervously. While runways in Nicaragua were generally sufficient, they were short in comparison with the miles of hard surface available at U.S. bases.

The young pilot began the roll down the runway. As he increased his speed, he hauled back on the stick, giving the jet a high angle of attack. But the hot weather makes the air thinner and gives less lift to the plane. The T-33 staggered. Realizing he was in trouble, the pilot punched off his tip tanks to lighten the plane, but it was too late. Blasting through a sugar cane fence adjoining the field, the plane shot across a road and disappeared in a cloud of flying turf and flame.

Bells rang, sirens sounded, and everyone ran for a jeep. One of the jeeps nearly ran into the crash truck in the haste to get to the plane. The T-33 was engulfed in flames and when the crash truck got stuck in mud, it damn near caught fire too, saved only by the quick work of another truck driver who hooked on a chain and pulled it away. The T-33's canopy had been jettisoned, and a search began for the pilot's body, during which he was eulogized as the finest and most noble Nicaraguan who had ever gone to a premature death. A priest was called.

About an hour later, a jeep drove up and out sauntered the pilot, perfectly intact. He had jumped out of the cockpit after popping off the canopy, hailed a passing motorist, and gone back to the airfield for a Coke. Making his way through the assembled group, he claimed "engine failure" as the cause of the crash.

Over the months, I had gotten to know Managua a bit. The streets of the city were clean but plain. Unlike San José, Costa Rica, which seemed to be a city filled with flowers, Nicaragua's capital city was grimly utilitarian. The people were warm and friendly, however, and I enjoyed walking around.

One Saturday afternoon I went to the market just for something to do. Saddled horses stood tethered next to parked cars and pickup trucks. A woman with a big pot of what looked like a stew called out to me, "*posole, posole, vas a querer marchantilla?*" I smiled and shook my head.

I passed stands of papayas, melons, onions, flowers, and lots of fruits and vegetables whose names I didn't know, all displayed in large woven reed baskets. A woman slapped tortillas on a sizzling griddle as her young children played at her feet. Dead chickens hung from a horizontal pole alongside iguanas. The intense smells of raw meat, rotting citrus, sweet-scented melons, and smoke from small cooking fires wafted through the street, an oddly exotic perfume—*eau de Managua*. I thought about the plastic-wrapped food back home. It seemed so antiseptic and dull. Then again, the romance of the street market did fade a little when I noticed a cut-open watermelon's "seeds" were crawling!

Nicaragua had made bureaucratic frustration into an art form, something with which I had become well acquainted. I quietly sympathized with unsuspecting newcomers, however. One week, an American band came to town. Sponsored by a local businessman, the band presented concerts nightly for three or four days at the Gran Hotel. I was stopping at the airport terminal for a Coke when I saw the group with their manager, a balding man in his early thirties, slumped on a vinyl couch, looking completely defeated.

"What's the matter?" I joked. "Won't they let you leave the country?"

"Hell, no!" the manager exclaimed. "These bastards have us stranded. They claim we didn't make our contribution to the local union. Our sponsor had the receipt, but the guy in charge was having his siesta, and 'couldn't be disturbed.' Right after our plane took off, the word came through it was all cleared, and we could leave. No apology! No nothing! If there was a problem, why didn't they tell us before we got to the airport?"

Nicaragua 101.

Although the casual work ethic of the FAN mechanics and their supervising officers collided regularly with my gringo expectations, we would enjoy meals together from time to time. I was very pleased one day when a mechanic, Sergeant Gutierrez, invited me to lunch at his house.

We drove to the outskirts of Managua and arrived at a one-story stucco and wood structure with a low-pitched pink roof and a pink screen door, Sergeant Gutierrez's house had dark wooden louvers for ventilation next to windows framed in brown metal, with white curtains visible inside. A tall flowering tree with purple blossoms shaded one side of the house. The front yard was full of colorful flowers; huge red canna lilies with thick fleshy leaves, pink and white hibiscus, and many others I didn't recognize, grew out of the dusty orange soil. A small banana tree stood next to the gate. Surrounding the entire property was a rose-colored wooden picket fence.

We made our way across the bare wooden planks that served as a path to the front door and as we approached the house, the sergeant's startled wife came out. Her husband explained I was a "*gringo importante*" with the FAN and that he had invited me to lunch. Somewhat flustered by her unexpected guest, she smoothed her dress with her hands and greeted me graciously.

After an excellent meal, the sergeant showed me around his

garden. As I was admiring the flowers, he casually mentioned, "I used to have trouble with my neighbor's cow."

"Is that so?" I replied, wondering what kind of trouble cows caused.

He nodded and pointed to his fence. "The cow pushed it down and ate my flowers. I told my neighbor to keep that cow home," he continued, "but when I came home last week, that cow was in the middle of the garden again. So I chased her out and shot her," he said, patting his revolver. "That fixed the problem."

I nodded my head politely and felt a pang of sympathy for the flower-loving cow. It was a sure bet no complaint was filed against a FAN sergeant.

One day as I was leaving the airport, I heard a commotion and stopped to see what was going on. I saw Sergeant Gonzales sprinting down the street. He was a large man carrying a lot of extra weight around the middle, so it was unusual to see him moving so fast. A few minutes later, the sergeant reached toward the ground and I realized he had been chasing his dinner! A two-foot-long iguana had apparently jumped out of the back of the sergeant's pickup truck and had been running as fast as he could down the road, trying to make a break for the nearby jungle.

Beaming, Sergeant Gonzales hoisted the dejected-looking reptile by the tail and put him back in the truck. Iguanas were referred to as "chicken of the trees" in Nicaragua, but that didn't fool me. There were many new foods for a gringo to try in Nicaragua, and I had tried to be open-minded. Blame it on my Midwest steak-and-potatoes upbringing, but I could not eat something that looked like a prehistoric monster. I secretly hoped Sergeant Gonzales wouldn't put me on his dinner guest list.

Although the largest country in Central America, Nicaragua was sparsely populated, and within a few hours of Managua could be found jaguars, alligators, and other wild animals. More than one person in the States asked me to bring back exotic animals from Central America for them as pets. I had no interest in that; not only was it illegal, I thought it was cruel to the animals. However, it was not uncommon in Managua to see a monkey or a wildcat on a leash.

One evening as I was going into the Gran Hotel, I noticed a fat American woman squatting on the ground next to her dachshund. There was the usual line of taxis outside the hotel, with the drivers standing around, waiting for fares. I could see all the drivers were watching the woman intently. I wondered what was going on. Then I saw the ocelot.

A sleek, cream-colored wildcat with black spots, he was stretched out languidly on the sidewalk wearing a collar attached to a metal chain. He probably weighed thirty pounds and apparently belonged to one of the drivers. The woman was pushing the little dog toward the ocelot, repeating, "Get the kitty, go on, get the kitty." The dachshund had far more sense than his owner and was resisting. The ocelot lay perfectly still, eyeing the dog through half-slit eyes while the cab drivers held their breath, waiting for the cat to strike.

I quickly spoke up. "Madam, that's a wild animal, and if you don't pick up your dog immediately, the first swipe of that cat's paw will take out his eyes, and the second will kill him." The woman glared at me and then swept up her dog and marched away in a huff. For a moment I felt bad about hurting her feelings, but I would have felt worse if that dog had been killed. The cab drivers looked disappointed and turned away. The ocelot closed his eyes.

Chapter 22

JIMMY ANGEL'S GOLD

I decided to take the afternoon Pan Am flight to Costa Rica to see how the work was going on the second Mustang and to get a little break from Managua. Pan Am flew DC-7s that were known as "tri-motors" in Central America because they seldom finished a flight on all four engines. I checked out of the Gran Hotel and boarded the plane. It was a full flight.

The Curtiss-Wright engines on the DC-7 snorted, backfired, and blew lots of smoke during their run-ups, which didn't surprise or bother me. But just as the plane started accelerating down the run-way, the pilot suddenly cut power and taxied back to the terminal. The passengers were kept onboard while one of the engines was run up a few times. The plane taxied back out, aborted again, and as it returned to the gate, I saw they had feathered one engine. This time the passengers got off, as the plane heated up very quickly on the ground. The mechanics took the cowling off to work on the number one engine. I had a strong feeling this flight was not a good idea and retrieved my bag.

Although the Gran Hotel was full, the girls at the front desk found a room for me. While I was finishing dinner, the passengers from the afternoon plane trooped in. Pan Am had bussed them to the Gran, having assured them the plane would be ready later that evening.

Whenever I was feeling a bit homesick, I would sit down at the little upright piano in the lobby, and if nobody minded, play for an hour or two. That particular night, home was very much on my mind. I had been playing in the hotel lobby for a while when the Pan Am passengers began to wander in from the dining room. Apparently the plane wasn't going anywhere anytime soon. Everyone was hot, tired and probably thinking of home too.

There were a number of children, so I started to play "Puff the Magic Dragon," a favorite of my girls. The children began to sing along, and the parents were clearly grateful for the distraction. After a while, one of the passengers came up to the piano and spoke to me in Spanish. I answered him in simple Spanish, probably using up all the words I knew.

Meanwhile back at the airport, the Pan Am mechanics were still working on the DC-7. The usual procedure was to keep running the engine up until (1) the problem cured itself, or (2) something broke, which they could then fix by replacing the whole unit. About midnight, passengers were bussed back to the terminal and the plane finally took off. I got a good night's sleep and the next morning took the early flight to Costa Rica, which left almost on schedule.

When I got to the hangar, the crew was working on my '51, and they assured me it would be ready to fly soon. There wasn't much I could do, so I returned to Managua.

Several months later, one of the U.S. Mission men gave me a clipping from a Midwest newspaper. A travel writer had described the Gran Hotel with the piano player in the lobby as a not-to-miss stop in Managua. "*I was surprised,*" he wrote, "*to see a big Nicaraguan wrestler playing the piano there.*"

I don't know what surprised him the most: my size, the wrestling, or that someone in Nicaragua could play the piano. I have no idea how he found out I used to wrestle. I was deeply tanned, but that was the only time anyone ever mistook me for a local.

To save money, I moved from the Gran Hotel to a room that I rented in a nearby house. However I still received mail at the hotel and ate my meals there. One afternoon, I was coming out of the dining room when three well-dressed men and a woman stopped me. "We'd like to talk to you about a business proposition," one of the men explained.

I had just drafted a cable to Glenn, so I said I would send it and then join them in the lobby in a few minutes. This gave me a little time to think. The group appeared to be Americans. I couldn't imagine what kind of deal they were offering. Maybe they were interested in Mustangs and would take delivery here, I thought optimistically.

We sat around a large coffee table with two people on either side of me. The spokesman began. "We know you are a great pilot and own some airplanes. Would you be interested in an adventure?"

"Yes, I own some airplanes," I said cautiously.

"Have you heard of Jimmy Angel's gold?" he asked.

"I've heard stories about lost gold somewhere in the jungle," I answered.

"Let me tell you about it," he continued. "In the early '20s, a U.S. bush pilot named Jimmy Angel met J. R. McCracken, an old Alaskan geologist, in a bar in Panama. At first, Jimmy figured this was just another expat with gold fever. But after more talk, he agreed to fly the prospector to what he said was a mountain of gold somewhere on the frontier between Brazil and Venezuela for $3,000. The arrangements were made and they flew south. McCracken didn't have a map, but just eyeballed it, saying, 'over there' and 'a little to the left' 'til he said, 'land there' and pointed to a mesa. They filled a bag with seventy-five pounds of gold nuggets. They didn't take more because they wanted to get out before nightfall."

I was aware that the other three were watching me intently for my reaction, and I listened without changing my expression.

The spokesman continued. "Then McCracken got sick and died. Jimmy spent the rest of his life trying to find that mountain of gold again. It was on one of his trips looking for it that he discovered the waterfall now called Angel Falls. But he never found his way back to the gold."

At this point, the woman leaned forward and whispered, "We know where the gold is, and we'd like you to fly us there."

Before I could say I wasn't interested, the woman added, "And we know you have some Twin Beeches that would be perfect! They are very simple inside, with lots of room for gold!"

Someone must have told them the C-45s were stripped down with no upholstery or heavy radio gear. I wondered who had talked to them. My curiosity getting the better of me, I played along. I looked at my watch, leaned back and asked, "What's the proposition?"

They looked a little disappointed. It was clear they hadn't finished their pitch. The first guy said, "Put up $10,000 and the use of your planes for a 25 percent share. There's millions of dollars worth of gold just sitting there, waiting. Give us the money now, and we can set up the first trip and meet you in Panama next week."

I interrupted his script. "I imagine you had to pay quite a bit for this information on the location." They nodded solemnly. I stood up. "I am scheduled to talk to my attorney in Chicago tomorrow by radio-phone, and I'll discuss it with him. You're staying here at the Gran?"

"No," the woman said quickly. "We're just passing through. We'll call you." The three men got up with her and headed toward the door.

The next morning, Morgan commented, "I hear the fast-buck crowd worked you over. They come through here about once a year."

Chapter 23

THUNDERBOLT DOWN

The P-51 and the P-47 were finally ready. I cabled Bill Rolfe and he arrived the next day. I had test-flown the two planes. All the essentials were working except the compass on the '51. We had made the trip without compasses before, and as long as I could follow Bill, I wasn't worried. I asked the sheet metal mechanic to cut a hole twelve inches square in each of the empty drop tanks so I could stuff them with small surplus parts. He screwed patches over the holes after I filled them.

Afternoon rains were predicted, so we got an early start. We entered Mexico at Tapachula and went through the usual paperwork. Bill asked if I wanted to fly the '47, but I decided to stay with the Mustang. We refueled, flew up the coastline, and then crossed to the Gulf of Mexico. In front of us was a big black thundercloud. Bill swung out over the ocean, making me nervous because we were past gliding distance to land. We skirted the dirty weather and soon headed back for the shoreline. Flying was easy that day, and I was keeping abreast and a little seaward of Bill.

I was looking north and when I glanced back, Bill was gone. I swung back, dropping altitude as I began searching for him. After about ten minutes, I spotted the plane on the beach. I had been descending from our cruising altitude of 14,000 feet and now I dropped down to the deck. Bill was standing on the beach waving. He had landed wheels up and the plane looked as though it had skidded in without hitting anything.

We had no radios. In my swings, I noticed a small fishing camp that looked as though it were just a few minutes from Bill. There was a short runway with a Cessna off to the side. My drop tanks heavy with parts, and unable to release them, I knew I couldn't put my plane down there. I thought if I buzzed the field and then circled the beach over Bill, someone would figure out that a plane was down. I tried this four or five times, but the people at the field just waved happily.

I circled Bill one more time and headed for Brownsville where I notified the Coast Guard. Since I knew there were all kinds of air/sea rescue planes in the area, I waited at the airport for Bill. After several hours, I learned the Coast Guard still had not received permission to enter Mexico. Five hours later, I found out the Coast Guard had flown a twin-engine amphibian down but decided not to land. They got a message to the fishing camp and a boat was underway to pick up Bill. The men from the fishing camp would bring him back in their Cessna the next day.

When Bill arrived, I took him straight to the hospital emergency room. He could barely walk, with blisters the size of silver dollars covering his feet and ankles. Wearing shoes was out of the question. He explained that after the crash, he had opened his chute for shelter. He'd then taken off his shoes and let his feet hang out, forgetting the blistering tropical sun. Now this was a guy who had gone through military survival training. But because nobody was shooting at him, he was relaxed and got careless. Fortunately, his burns would heal.

Bill explained that the engine had just stopped. No warning, no backfire, no nothing. The Mustang had a glide ratio of 14:1 and I suppose the '47 had something similar. From 14,000 feet, he had had about ten minutes to try to restart the engine. Nothing had worked, and he'd finally realized he was going down. He landed very skillfully on a broad section of beach, wheels up, but with little real damage. The plane could not be salvaged from such a remote location, however, so it was a total loss. Bill asked me if he could bring the Mustang the rest of the way up, so I came home commercially, while Bill stayed in a motel until his feet healed.

Chapter 24

COUNSEL FROM THE COMMANDANT

While I was in Chicago, I helped Glenn wade through the mountains of paperwork: records of parts shipped, FAA correspondence, required forms for the State Department's Office of Munitions Control, aircraft registrations, ferry permits, pilots' expense accounts, log books, and bills of sale. It was a monumental job.

Because telephone service from Nicaragua was so bad—radio-phone to Miami and then regular phone lines to Chicago—we had kept in touch mostly by cable. We used the code word "George" for cash flow, which was becoming increasingly tight. Glenn would cable, "George very sick," meaning, "cash is low, don't write any checks," or "George much better" when we sold a plane and the check had cleared the bank.

The used airplane business was strictly cash-and-carry-and-trust-no-one. We'd had a lot of experience with new and used car dealers when we were in the specialty vehicle business. But never had we encountered the magnitude of the dishonesty and double-dealing that we found with some of the aviation dealers and brokers. As Glenn put it, "We have dealt with many different classes of asses, but these asses are *really* in a class by themselves."

After a quick visit home, I returned to Managua. I found all work had stopped on my planes. I snagged Sergeant Gonzales. "How come nobody's working on my planes?" I asked, dreading the answer.

"It's Air Force Day next week," he explained blithely. "We must all get ready." One more week's delay, plus time for everyone to recover from the festivities. The odds of getting these people to do what they had promised seemed overwhelming. The Thunderbolt crash had hit our bank account hard, but the overall contract could still be profitable. I had no intention of giving up. But if there were ever a Yankee who wanted to go home, it was me.

It caused a lot of concern on Air Force Day when I was seen talking to General Somoza. He was resplendent in a dress uniform that sparkled with medals. He stepped away from his entourage to shake my hand, and we exchanged pleasantries. Any contact with the General started the rumor mill. One of the current stories going around was that I was buying into Somoza's Lanica Airlines, and that I would be its new president. I learned not to comment on these stories because no matter what I said, no one would believe me anyway.

Air Force Day brought a crowd out to the airport. Just as Somoza walked up to the podium, a T-33 jet came out of nowhere and screamed past about forty feet over the FAN hangar. It happened so fast the crowd could only gasp, but it scared the hell out of everyone. As it turned out, it was a planned fly-by to kick off the festivities, not an attack. Somoza cleared his throat and the crowd quieted down. The General began his remarks by greeting the various dignitaries and then lauded the accomplishments of the FAN. In the audience, in a group of civilians, was a young Nicaraguan woman wearing a red dress. She was a knockout, so it was hard not to notice her. After Somoza finished speaking, I noticed him lean over and say something to an aide.

The General's aide made a beeline for the gal in red. After a brief conversation, she got up and left with the soldier. A FAN lieutenant saw that I had observed the series of interactions and chuckled, "Tachito just added to his 'stable.'" Machismo was much admired in the FAN, and the guys with power were viewed as having every right to exercise it. Stories of Somoza's conquests were widespread. His American-born wife, Hope Portocarrero, must have been long-suffering. I did not see her there that day.

The officers' club hosted an elaborate Air Force Day party afterward. All the U.S. Mission people and the Nicaraguan Air Force brass showed up in their military whites, and the president of Nicaragua and I wore business suits. The Nicaraguans did know how to celebrate; it was a good party.

Since no one was going to be working, I decided to use the week to study Spanish conversation with Mrs. Cosina, a local teacher whom I had met through one of the office people at the Gran Hotel. I hoped if I knew the language, it might help me to understand the people. I was not a gifted language student: after one particularly concentrated session, I finally mastered the "j" pronunciation. "*Bueno, Bueno, Señor Martin,*" she applauded generously. "To celebrate, will you have dinner with me tonight? There is a private club we can go to. I would like you to see the nicer side of our city."

She was ready at seven that evening when I arrived. One of the U.S. officers had rented me a retired military jeep so I would have my own transportation. It still had its camouflage paint, but most of its original equipment was either missing or not working. I parked the jeep and hailed a cab.

"Why not take your jeep?" she suggested.

"I wouldn't think of it."

"I've never ridden in a jeep—it looks like fun," Mrs. Cosina said graciously. Her skirt was fashionably tight and definitely not designed for a military vehicle. But with a gallant assist and me looking the other way, she got herself settled, pulling her skirt down over her knees. My "date" admitted to being fifty-two, was pleasant and plump, and taught in a local private school.

When we rolled up in front of the club, the doorman sniffed just as doormen do in the States when you arrive in a junker. Inside it looked like a Chicago nightclub, crowded with small cocktail tables around a raised stage where a band was playing. We had just ordered a drink, when I noticed Jerry DeLarm, my old nemesis, at a table with three other North Americans. It was the first time I had seen him since his court victory.

A few minutes later, there was a raucous laugh. DeLarm had

stumbled up to the bandstand and was fiddling with the mike. In his usual black costume and hat, he looked like the villain in a Mexican B-movie. He struggled through several verses of a popular ballad until the bandleader managed to lead him off the stage. DeLarm noticed me and strode over to my table. "What are you doing in Nicaragua?" he shouted belligerently.

"I'm finishing my contract," I said evenly. "Now you'd better go back to your table."

"You can't talk to me that way," he blustered, rocking back and forth on the heels of his cowboy boots. "Do you know who those men at my table are? They're from NBC."

"What do you want me to do? Tell them the truth about you?"

He grabbed the back of the chair he was leaning on and slammed it down. A hush fell over the room. "You're in my country now," he snarled menacingly as he lurched toward me. "Nobody talks that way to me!"

If we'd been outside, I'd have belted this obnoxious jerk into next week, but I gritted my teeth. "I just did, and I'll repeat it good and loud if you want the whole room to hear. If not, sit down and try to act like a gentleman."

"I'll show you how a gentleman acts when he's insulted," he threatened, his voice rising to an almost hysterical pitch. "I'm getting my gun!"

"Beat it, punk," I ordered and turned back to Mrs. Cosina, not knowing the term "punk" down there was slang for the man that the tough guys used for sex while in prison.

DeLarm uttered a string of oaths and stalked out of the club. Conversation buzzed again and it was obvious whom it was about. Mrs. Cosina looked embarrassed. "I'm sorry," I said, "but that man's a thief and I want nothing to do with him."

The manager appeared and said quietly, "Señor, he is trouble. Perhaps you should leave."

Some of the U.S. Mission people came in and sat at the table next to us. I leaned back and told Captain Wright there had been a little scene with DeLarm.

"You know how these guys are," he scoffed. "Always shooting off their mouths. Don't give it another thought." He paused and added, "But maybe you'd better leave."

I didn't think DeLarm would be back, but we left right after dinner. As I turned the jeep down a narrow one-way street, I noticed an old Cadillac Coupe de Ville following closely. Local driving habits being what they were, I thought nothing of it. Seconds later, there was a jarring bump as we were hit from behind. I looked over my shoulder and recognized DeLarm at the wheel of the Cadillac. The big car banged against the back of the jeep again, this time a little harder. Mrs. Cosina started to speak, but I didn't have time to explain. Hitting the gas, I shot out of the little street and into a large plaza. Crossing it, I whipped to a stop in front of a brightly lit factory warehouse with a guard outside. The Cadillac paused across the deserted plaza, waiting.

"You need to get out...it's the man from the club. Get a cab home!" I said urgently. She sat there, paralyzed. "Mrs. Cosina, get out! Vaya! Out! Out!" I tried to push her out, but she clung to the windshield frame, wailing hysterically. I looked around helplessly. The warehouse guard yawned. Unable to dislodge my passenger, I pulled back into the plaza. Out of the corner of my eye, I saw the Cadillac accelerating toward us.

Just as I shifted from second to third, DeLarm's Cadillac roared up, the beams from his headlights flooding over us. I jerked to the right to avoid being hit broadside, knocking Mrs. Cosina to the floor of the jeep. The Cadillac followed me to the right, coming up alongside to try again to ram me. For the first time, I could see there were other men in the car with DeLarm.

The big car swerved toward me and I narrowly avoided being hit. Knowing how easily a jeep tips, I was trying to keep clear, but just didn't have the acceleration to get away. Not sure what DeLarm was going to do next, I made a desperate calculation. I shouted to Mrs. Cosina to hold on and, gritting my teeth, I slowed slightly and deliberately turned the jeep into the back quarter of the Cadillac.

The jeep's steel I-beam bumper hooked in the Cadillac's right rear wheel well and I slammed on my brakes. There was a hell of a crash. Mrs. Cosina screamed as dirt and pieces of sheet metal flew around and the vehicles skidded across the plaza, locked together. When we stopped, I gunned the little jeep and pulled away, taking a good piece of the now disabled Cadillac's fender for about fifty feet. When it dropped away, I could see my left front tire was still attached and not flat.

Without waiting to find out whether DeLarm had his gun, I floored the accelerator and we took off. Mrs. Cosina was still screaming and didn't stop until the jeep screeched to a halt in front of her door. This time I didn't have to help her. She flew out, knees be damned, shrieking in Spanish to the neighborhood street guard that a crazy man was following us and to shoot him when he came. The guard just nodded and ambled on as though it were all in a night's work.

I zigzagged along side streets back to my room. Parking the jeep down the street instead of in front of my building, I stood in the shadows for a few minutes, but DeLarm didn't show. I went upstairs, poured a sturdy Scotch, and collapsed in bed. By this time, Mrs. Cosina must have pushed all the furniture she owned against her door.

The next morning, I saw most of the damage to the jeep was to the left fender and cowl by the running board. The wheel alignment appeared to be okay, and when I drove it to the field, the steering was loose but no worse than before. I pulled up in front of the U.S. Mission and went in to have my usual free cup of coffee. Captain Wright looked hungover and reported he had a "big head."

"I had a big party last night too," I said. "Want to see how it turned out?" I took him by the arm and steered him outside. I showed him the side of the jeep and before he could ask, I told him the whole story.

"Geez, Will," he said apologetically. "I thought you were only kidding about that nut DeLarm. You coulda been really hurt–these things turn over real easy."

"I know," I agreed grimly. "It's a hell of a thing when you come down here to do business with the air force, and some bum tells you he can rub you out and get by with it 'cause he has clout with the government."

A Nicaraguan sergeant who had been listening interjected, "I guess you haven't heard. The guard at the gate has orders not to let DeLarm on the field. The colonel got really mad when DeLarm told the papers there was something shady about how the air force was buying planes. DeLarm's plane, the one we were working on, got towed down to the other end of the field and now they're charging him storage. He's finished around here."

Captain Wright shook his head. "If I were you, I'd look out DeLarm doesn't pull another court deal and make you pay for a new car."

I hadn't thought about that, but remembering how DeLarm had collected "witnesses" to our so-called contract, I decided the captain might have a point. I headed to the American Embassy. After hearing my latest episode with the Cadillac cowboy, Mr. Fairchild was quiet for a moment. "I'm afraid there isn't anything we can do."

"Look, last time DeLarm came up with all kinds of 'witnesses' saying I owed him money. I'm concerned he'll hire some more 'witnesses' to get me to pay for his car, if he doesn't kill me first."

"Yes, he might do that," Mr. Fairchild agreed sympathetically. He paused. "Do let us know how it comes out," he said.

My next stop was the Presidential Palace, an impressive white building at the end of Avenida Roosevelt on the outskirts of town. It was perched on a hill, "La Loma," overlooking a volcanic lagoon. I spoke to a woman who appeared to be some sort of an administrative assistant. After listening to my story, she picked up her phone, spoke in Spanish too rapid for me to follow, and then hung up. "Go see the commandant of the Guardia."

"What for?"

"Go ahead," she waved. "He's expecting you." She told me where to find him.

Maybe I had made a big mistake. If DeLarm had half the influence he claimed, I was in trouble. As I left, I swore I could hear the rattling of chains from the jail cells rumored to be under the palace. I shot back to the embassy and told Mr. Fairchild where I was going. "If you don't hear from me, better start looking."

La Curva, the Guardia headquarters, was next door to the Presidential Palace. The commandant, a muscular man with black shaggy eyebrows that almost met in the middle, listened to my story, eyeing me as though he were measuring me for a cell. He made a few terse phone calls and then said, "Come back tomorrow at eleven o'clock. We will have DeLarm here."

For the first time, I had hope that DeLarm might be bluffing about his clout. I called Mr. Fairchild and asked him to come to the eleven a.m. meeting. He was sorry, he said, but he had "other commitments."

"Damn it all! You're always out ribbon cutting whenever an American needs help. What else do you do here?"

He evidently couldn't think of anything, because he just said, "Let us know how it comes out."

The next morning, I noticed the three NBC men were having breakfast in the hotel. Acting on a hunch, I stopped at their table. "Gentlemen, my name is Will Martin. May I sit down?"

Coffee spattered; they looked at me in alarm. Not waiting for a reply, I pulled up a chair and leaned in toward them. "I'm sure you realize you were involved in what could have been a nasty situation the other night," I said in a low voice.

"We didn't know he was going to do that. We're just an NBC travel team doing a film on Central America," protested the first.

The second one blurted out, "We just wanted DeLarm for local color because he flew for the CIA in the Guatemalan revolution."

"We don't really know anything about him," added the third quickly. "In fact, we're flying out on the morning plane tomorrow."

I paused. "Perhaps not. I may need you to testify as witnesses, in which case the police will not permit you to leave the country." The three were now speechless. "One more thing," I added as I rose from the table, "I have your names from the hotel register," and I walked away, leaving them staring after me in stunned silence.

DeLarm was chatting with the commandant at the Guardia office, looking cool and confident, when I arrived. The commandant greeted me. "Mr. DeLarm has assured me he doesn't intend to cause you any trouble, so I guess we can just forget the whole thing," he said, starting to rise from his chair.

"Nothing doing," I snapped. "I'm not being set up for a patsy again. We'll settle this right now, and this time, I have the witnesses. And I want the American Embassy involved because DeLarm has an American passport."

The commandant sat back down wearily. He looked at DeLarm, who shrugged. I used the commandant's phone to call Mr. Fairchild and told him I was being set up again. I added that I would demand the three NBC men be held until this was settled. Miracle of miracles, Mr. Fairchild arrived in ten minutes. He took DeLarm in another room, leaving me alone with the commandant.

"You know he's going to come after me again," I said flatly.

His eyes narrowed as he leaned forward. "Shoot him."

I nodded. Here was a problem solver.

In a few minutes, Mr. Fairchild and DeLarm reappeared with a proposition: DeLarm would pay for his own damages if I would not file charges for attempted murder. I agreed. When the embassy official moved out of earshot, DeLarm turned to me, seething with anger, and muttered, "I will get you for this!"

"I'll be ready," I promised.

Back at the field, Morgan reported the word was DeLarm had lost his clout because he couldn't hold his liquor and his tongue at the same time. He'd blabbed about some "jobs" that the General wanted kept quiet. That was the real reason he had been barred from the field.

That night at a British Embassy party, I related my experience. I concluded the story saying I intended to get a gun as soon as I could. One of the embassy staff whipped out his revolver. "Here. Take mine until you can get one from the States." From then on, I carried a gun.

Chapter 25

An Evening with the Dusters

Since the gun given to me at the British Embassy party was only a loan, I cabled Glenn immediately, asking him to bring my automatic down. Years ago I had paid $25 for it. I had shot it once to see if it worked. In a few days, Glenn arrived with it. God, but it was good to see him!

Glenn stood six foot five inches, an inch taller than I was. The Nicaraguans made much of our height. As was Glenn's way, he never criticized anything I had done. I hadn't realized how much I'd missed having someone trustworthy to talk with about plans and problems. His greatest surprise was the sweltering heat and heavy humidity that by now I had grown accustomed to.

Glenn said there was no news on the whereabouts of the Mustang that had gone down on the beach in Mexico. He had been keeping up a steady exchange of correspondence with the American Embassy, and congressmen and senators had made inquiries to no avail. No one in Mexico would admit knowing where the plane was,

The gun Glenn brought down was a 1911 Colt hammerless .38. I showed him how I would carry it in my briefcase. With a cartridge in the chamber, I slipped the gun in the briefcase, leaving the top un- zipped. That way I could reach in and shoot without taking it out of the case. As we stood at the airport waiting for Glenn's flight back to the States, Glenn asked, "Do you think DeLarm is crazy enough to come after you again?"

"Morgan says that's the talk."

He frowned. "I hope it doesn't come to that."

"I hope not too. I've never killed a man," I reflected. "But DeLarm has killed a lot of them if half the stories I've heard are true. And he gets by with it. One more to him wouldn't make much difference. If he comes after me with a gun, I'll shoot."

The Pan Am flight crew walked past and the other passengers began to gather up their belongings and move toward the door. Glenn put his hands on my shoulders. "God damn it, Will. Get on this plane and come home with me."

"I can't."

"You mean you won't."

"Glenn, this deal should put us back into business. I got us into the lawsuit. I have to finish this thing now."

Glenn shook his head and looked sober. "Take care, Will," he said, and then he picked up his bag and walked out onto the tarmac to the waiting plane.

I always did my test-flying within gliding distance of the field. One day, when I was about to take off in a Mustang, a unit of the Inter American Geodetic Survey came through Managua flying a De Havilland Beaver. The Beaver, an older, fat machine, flew as though it were pulling a string of boxcars according to its pilots. It was used for making cargo deliveries and updating maps.

I took off and my temperature gauge started going up fast. I pulled up the gear and flaps and stuck the nose down in a steep glide to run more air through the scoop for cooling. The temperature immediately started to fall. Meanwhile, the Beaver had just taken off. I zoomed by at about 300 miles per hour, flying up and over it.

One of the duster pilots saw me that night and said, "Will, I saw you flying today. Sure looked like fun!" On this particular joyride, the canopy had flown back, creating a suction that picked up the ten-years' accumulation of dirt in the cockpit, blowing it in my face. In the last two weeks during various test flights, the tach had quit, the generator had charged off the peg, brakes had failed, the tail wheel had refused to lock, and during the preflight, the controls had jammed due to a replacement ammeter that had slipped down on the floor and wedged itself against them. Other than that, it was fun.

I joined the Beaver men and a group of agricultural duster pilots for drinks and dinner at the Gran Hotel. Everyone was in for the night because of the no-fly after dark rules. Music from the lobby drifted into the packed dining room, and the conversation was lively over dinner.

Nicaragua used a lot of pesticides on its crops, and while dusting with chemicals was dangerous work, it paid well. The duster pilots acted much like the loggers in the Wisconsin woods that my father talked about. According to my dad, the loggers would work all winter and then blow their wages gambling and whoring over two or three days in town. The duster pilots certainly seemed to be the lumberjacks of aviation.

After dinner, an ag pilot named Henry said, "Will, when you were gone last week, I took one of your Mustangs up for a hop."

I knew that was about as likely as Henry taking ballet lessons, but I played along with the joke. "'Zat so?" I said. "How'd it go?"

"Well, I damn near killed myself!"

Conversation stopped at the surrounding tables and everyone edged forward. Henry went on to relate how he had forgotten what a great experience it was to fly a Mustang, and that once in the air, he was overcome with such good memories that he found himself with a full-blown erection.

He continued. "I said to myself, 'what the hell—why not?' I had to unhook my chute, seat, and lap straps. You know it's a bit tight for me, especially since I gained a little heft since my air force days." There was lots of laughter since Henry was known for being a serious eater.

"I closed my eyes and was really enjoying my fantasy when I suddenly realized this old bird was starting to turn over on her back and I was in immediate danger of falling out through the canopy!"

By now the whole group was in on the joke and offering all sorts of what-ifs. Someone called out, "You know, Henry, it was lucky you grabbed the right stick and righted yourself!"

Another wondered, "Can you imagine the sight of a man being found in the middle of a field in your condition?"

We all laughed 'til we ached. The other men were drinking heavily, but since I was flying the next day, I was pacing myself. We left in a group, still laughing and kidding Henry. Usually I walked back to my room, however that night I was tired and decided to take a cab. I knew most of the taxi drivers who hung around the Gran Hotel, but it was late and they were long gone. A car going down the street did a quick U-turn and offered to take me wherever I wanted to go. I climbed in with a chorus of goodnights from the rowdy group.

My Spanish was still pretty bad, but Mrs. Cosina had helped me perfect certain phrases such as my street address. I gave it to the driver and away we went. After only two blocks, I could see we were going the wrong way. I repeated the address but the driver just nodded and said "*Sí, sí, Señor. No problema.*"

I realized then the driver had sized up my condition based on the rest of the pilots, and I knew I was in deep shit. It was late and in a few minutes we would be on the outskirts of the city.

After the mandate from the commandant of the Guardia regarding DeLarm, I never went anywhere without my gun. I leaned back in the seat, took out the .38 automatic, pulled the slide back that jacked a round into the chamber, and let it bang forward with a loud click. The driver's head snapped around as though it was on springs, and without a word, he made a U-turn and drove directly to my address. He jumped out and rushed around to open my door. The armed guard whom the building owner hired to patrol the street strolled up and said, "*Buenas noches, Señor Martin.*" I shook his hand heartily and went up to my room, my adrenalin pumping. No question the click of the .38 had been worth a thousand words.

It was about a month later at the Gran Hotel when I next saw Henry. He looked a little pissed off, so I invited him to join me for lunch. He slumped in his chair in the dining room. "I just came from a doctor that one of the cab drivers took me to," he announced gloomily. "Guess what?"

It took me a minute to grasp the connection, and then I asked the obvious, "You got a little social problem?"

"Yeah. You remember our get-together? My ride home that night was certainly memorable. We were having a lot of fun, and I should have left it at that. But we weren't flying the next day and someone said, 'What the hell—let's make it a night.' We stopped at that cantina east of town. From then on, things got more stupid. One of the natives there told us about a place where the locals party. We went there and all of a sudden, lots of girls showed up. I know I had a condom, but some of the night is a little fuzzy right now. I'm the only one of our group that seems to have been left with a souvenir, and the doctor the cab driver took me to gave me a shot of penicillin. We're gonna be here until the end of next month, and the first thing I'm doing when I'm back in the States is get with an American doctor to make sure everything's okay with my plumbing."

I didn't laugh, but said very piously, "When God made man, She gave him a penis and a brain, but She only gave him enough blood to run one at a time."

Henry was feeling so sorry for himself I didn't tell him about my run-in with the rogue cab driver that night.

Chapter 26

CHILA

The Nicaraguans operated DC-3s, Cessna 180s, Douglas B-26s, North American T-28s, and several Hughes helicopters. The U.S. gave them many of the planes outright or the Nicaraguans purchased them at salvage prices. The U.S. also provided parts for free.

The Nicaraguan Air Force was getting rid of the P-51s because they were difficult to fly and too many pilots were getting killed. But another reason was the U.S. had exhausted its supply of P-51 parts and couldn't furnish any more. The fact that the Nicaraguans had a warehouse full of parts didn't count. The parts, which had arrived carefully catalogued and indexed, were now all jumbled together in a hodgepodge that defied the best efforts of anyone to locate a specific item.

Most of the FAN officers seemed to have a business on the side, usually at government expense. Supplying parts for duster or other private planes was a cottage industry. The Nicaraguans would occasionally even request parts from the U.S. for planes not in the air force inventory, and the bureaucrats stateside obligingly delivered.

When two of my planes needed radiator thermostats, the Nicaraguans told me they didn't have any. Since this was a small part, I decided I would be time ahead to order them from the States rather than going through the hassle of trying to locate them in the warehouse. After getting the export permits all straight, I used the part number to order from a firm in California. I kept checking with Pan Am's office in the Gran Hotel to see if the package had arrived. José, the young manager at the Pan Am desk, assured me Pan Am never made mistakes, unlike so many other firms. A few days later, on a miserably hot day when the work at the field had gone a little worse than usual, I learned the parts had been shipped to Guatemala the week before and were for all practical purposes lost. I blew my top and just about reduced José to tears.

When I cooled down, I felt like a jerk taking my frustration out on José when he was trying to help. I saw him later when he was leaving work and asked if he would have a drink with me. By this time, he had burned up someone else in the company and had relayed my choice comments on Pan Am's competency. José had only been at Pan Am for six months and his ambition was to be transferred to the States. He learned English from his mother who was an American.

Over drinks, he asked about my work, and I described some of the setbacks I'd encountered. Perhaps because he felt sorry for me, he invited me to the opening of a new nightclub within walking distance. We went to the party with four other people, several of whom were part owners of the place, which was to be a key club. Everyone was excited about it since there were few places to dance other than an expensive country club. About half the people there spoke English, so I could join the conversation mainstream.

The place was jammed. Maneuvering our way through the crowd, José and I made our way to the bar. José introduced me to a friend, Chila Lopez, a petite, attractive woman with short dark hair, dark brown eyes and pale skin. She was probably in her late twenties. She worked for a bank in San Francisco and was home for a visit. She was staying with her mother and spoke of her father in the past tense, saying he had been a much respected man in the military.

"Are you with the American Mission or a private company?" she asked.

When I explained I was dealing with the FAN, her face clouded and she stiffened. The mention of the Nicaraguan Air Force obviously triggered bad memories, and I steered the conversation to the combo. The syncopated Latin rhythms were hard to resist. I didn't have the foggiest notion how to dance to this music, but it carried me along and with the benefit of the Scotch, I felt like Fred Astaire.

Chila seemed to know everyone. When her group left, they offered to drop me at my room. We all piled in a tiny car. "We go swimming a lot," Chila said when we reached my place. "Would you like to come sometime?"

"Sure, that would be great," I replied. I said my thanks and good nights all around and went upstairs, figuring I would never see any of them again. It had been a pleasant evening after a miserable week.

The next day was Sunday. I was sleeping in when I heard a tap on my door. It was my landlady's nine-year-old daughter.

"Your friends are here," she announced.

I looked out from the balcony, and sure enough, there was Chila with her friends below.

"Ready for that swim?" she called.

I pulled on some clothes, grabbed a towel and trunks, and joined them. Sundays were long, lonely days for me, and I was glad to be included.

We drove out past the airport, turning down a narrow unpaved road that wound past a row of dilapidated shacks. When we reached a gate, a man opened it and then ran alongside the car to the next gate. We followed a gravel lane down to a red tile-roofed pavilion.

In front of us was a tropical Eden. A dam had been built on a river and floodgates backed up the water for several miles to form a little lake. Its glass-like blue surface reflected the sky and the lush foliage along the far side. On the near side, close to us, the lake dropped off, spilling in a sheet over the edge of a man-made waterfall, and then tumbled over a second ledge into a swimming basin. The pavilion, an open-air shelter, had an intricate flagstone floor, much nicer than any I'd seen in the city. There were dark wood tables and chairs set up, and an outdoor fireplace stood at the far end of the pavilion. We changed clothes in a modern yellow stucco bathhouse, and then everyone went for a long swim. Afterwards, Chila took charge of the cooking. Fragrant white smoke drifted toward the tables as she grilled bite-sized chunks of beef over charcoal. When she brought the meat over to the table, everyone drew up chairs and ate greedily with their fingers. It was the most delicious beef I'd ever had.

Later, Manuel, our host, joined us and stretched out on a hammock. He was probably in his early forties, very fit, with a swarthy complexion; he had an air that made me think he knew his way around the world. He had served in the U.S. military in WWII and showed me the scar on his back from a wound. When I asked how he had ended up in the U.S., he related a story strange to me but not unusual in Nicaragua.

"A long time ago, I was active in the opposition party here. I was very young," he said by way of explanation. "The Guardia came to my family's house in the night and were banging on the door with their rifle butts. When I came out, they arrested me. I was thrown in jail for a few weeks…they roughed me up a bit… I was lucky it wasn't worse. Then they said they'd let me go if I left the country. I did and stayed away for eight years. But I had some influential friends, and through them, I was eventually allowed to return on the condition I stayed out of politics." Manuel spoke matter-of-factly, without bitterness.

I looked around at his beautiful grounds and farm. "But why didn't Somoza take away your property?"

"He doesn't do that," Manuel said. "I think he doesn't want to set a precedent. If he ever gets thrown out, he probably hopes he'll get to keep some of his holdings. You have to remember there are few industries or properties or usable land here that he doesn't own or control. The night club you were at last night—he owns a piece of that."

Another man, Juan, joined in. "There's a joke going around— it seems some Texans met him in Miami and were bragging about the size of their ranches. They asked the General what he called his ranch. The General replied, 'I call my ranch 'Rancho Nicaragua.'"

"But then how is it you have so many foreign companies here?" I asked.

"Yes we do," Manuel agreed. "But you see, the more successful a business, the more money for the General. So he encourages foreign investors. They can run any business as long as it takes specialized skills. But when it looks to Somoza as though local people could manage it, the foreign investors have got themselves a partner."

"But you have freedom of the press at least. I see all those opposition newspapers in Managua," I said.

"Will, Somoza doesn't care about newspapers...most of the people can't read. The radio stations are another matter; Somoza controls what is broadcast very tightly," explained Chila gently.

I looked around at the group, suddenly feeling very naïve. "So your president then, what's his role?"

"The president! Mr. Schick," scoffed Manuel. "He's a friend of the Somozas. When Luis Somoza stepped down at the end of his term, the family put in a placeholder until Tachito could run. All that happens at the presidential palace is ribbon cutting. General Somoza is where the action is. The president has no real power."

Juan elaborated. "The Guardia is under the direct control of the General. Within the Guardia is another group that operates as a secret police. Captain Garcia is in charge of that—and the cells where political prisoners are kept. Nobody bothers with trials. If Somoza doesn't like someone, they're called a communist and arrested. Of course some of them are, but lots aren't. The Guardia tortures them awhile if they think they have something to tell. Sometimes the Guardia takes prisoners in a DC-3 out over the water and pushes them overboard. Other times they die in the cells." As Juan talked, Chila was tight-lipped. With this last comment, she abruptly stood up and walked away.

I thought about the sharks in Lake Nicaragua and shuddered. The U.S. Mission men must have known about these executions. How could they not?

"Sure, Washington knows about Somoza. It's not much of a secret," said Manuel, reading my mind. "But with Castro in Cuba, it seems the U.S. has figured to hell with human rights...'we'll take Somoza 'cause he can keep control down there.'"

This was the most openly anyone had ever spoken about Somoza in front of me, so I guess I was considered safe to talk to. Somoza was known for having spies or "*orejas*"—"ears"—all over the country.

I was now included in many activities with Chila and her friends. During her visit to Nicaragua, she worked part-time for an insurance agent. With his permission, she arranged for me to use the office typewriter for letters and other correspondence.

My few stumbling attempts to learn Spanish had been terrible flops. Mrs. Cosina had suddenly become very busy after our wild jeep ride, and I had temporarily given up trying to learn the language. Yet I had discovered that in Nicaragua, people who spoke English fluently sometimes would pretend not to. They wanted to put foreigners at a disadvantage, forcing them to stumble along in broken Spanish. Or they hoped the person might reveal useful information unwittingly. When I observed this to Chila, she offered to help me give Spanish another try. When she was busy, her mother taught me.

I couldn't understand why a cab driver didn't realize that "Gran Hotel" in English is the same as it is in Spanish. With patience and persistence, Chila and her mother helped me hear the difference. We worked out simple sentences such as "Please clean my room," which was one I wanted to spring on the maid. (I could always tell when she had been there—one mop track in, one mop track out.) I also learned some phrases to drop among the mechanics that would chatter about the work or me, assuming I couldn't understand them. While I wasn't able to follow the conversation completely, I could now make some comment in Spanish vague enough to give them pause.

I began to try to practice my Spanish whenever possible. Knowing I wanted to learn, people would sometimes give me the Spanish words for things to help me build my vocabulary. While riding with my friend Major Bonilla one wet afternoon in Costa Rica, he pointed to the downpour outside the car window and said solemnly, "Raino."

I was delighted to have learned a new word. "Raino," I repeated, nodding enthusiastically.

"Raino!" beamed the major with satisfaction.

A few days later when I was back in Managua, it started to pour. I pointed out the hangar and said proudly to one of the bilingual Americans, "Raino!"

He looked at me and laughed. "Rain*o*? What language you speakin', Will?"

Crestfallen, I reported back to Chila. "Rain*o*?" she laughed. "Will, I think your friend wanted to practice his English! Raino, *raino…*," she repeated, giggling. "Ok," she said, pulling herself together, "repeat after me, *lluvia….*"

Local etiquette caught me by surprise sometimes. I had learned Nicaraguans don't swear the same way Americans do. The first time some screw-up was so outrageous that I swore, the mechanics slammed down their tools and walked off the job. I quickly learned to watch myself. Chila explained that the "shave and a haircut" rapping on the horn that Americans do when they want a car to move over or to announce their arrival was considered a grave insult, enough to bring out machetes. I never once heard that horn rhythm in Nicaragua.

On her visit home, Chila had some routine surgery. The medical system seemed to work pretty well. Revenue from a state lottery provided medical care for the poor, while the affluent paid for their treatment. I visited Chila in the hospital, a modern building with a balcony for each room. Her family, as was customary, brought food and just about moved in, often staying overnight. Rooms took on a party air with drinks and food. Patients ate their favorite dishes and were surrounded by caring people.

Chila and I met for dinner one evening at a new Chinese restaurant. While we were eating, a group of Guardia men sat down at a nearby table. They were older men and bolstered by the local brew, were joking and laughing loudly. Seeing them, Chila's face suddenly hardened, and she pushed back her chair and left. I threw some money on the table and followed her. I found her outside in the shadows, choking back tears. I didn't say anything, and after a few minutes, she composed herself. "Those men were my father's friends. Those men murdered my father," she said softly. I put my arm around her shoulders, and we walked to the car. I was learning a lot about this part of the world.

Chapter 27

Martinez the Cab Driver

Chila was very concerned about me driving the old military jeep. "Somoza has many enemies, and a lot of people here would be happy to see anyone associated with him killed. Someone could shoot you," she warned, "and it would look like an accident." She had a point. Somoza had already fought back against a number of counter-insurgencies, and although he tried to keep an iron grip, "accidents" did happen from time to time to his soldiers. While I didn't wear any sort of uniform, I was probably well known as the gringo doing business with the FAN, and although I now carried a gun, I didn't have any sort of bodyguard protection. I decided to try to find another vehicle.

It was shortly after that conversation with Chila that I met Martinez, a cab driver. Martinez was a man of means in Managua. His status symbol was his own taxicab, a 1949 Dodge. There was no window on the driver's side, but as Martinez pointed out, the rainy season was still two months away. The car took as much water for the radiator as it took gas, but plenty of water was available. It averaged a flat a week, but when asked about this, he replied philosophically, "Whose don't?"

When he told me he was going to upgrade to a 1952 Ford, I rented the Dodge for $50 a month. I hadn't been concerned about not having a Nicaraguan driver's license. If there was an accident, a gringo was automatically in the wrong, so a license wouldn't matter one way or another. I never filled the tank completely, so thieves would get less on any given day if they siphoned off the gas.

Traffic collisions were a normal part of life. There were few stop-lights, so at intersections, you sped up, honked your horn, and got a good grip on the wheel. It was a battle of nerves as to who would give way first. Flying Mustangs was nothing compared to driving in Managua.

The law favored expediency, and the police improvised. They carried tool kits, and once, when there was a fender bender, I saw the officer simply remove the license plates from both cars and leave. When a serious accident occurred, both drivers got tossed in jail. The police knew that whoever had the most clout would be released, which simplified court proceedings. A death or serious injury was smoothed over with several hundred córdobas to the family. The local jail defied description, and prisoners survived on food brought by relatives.

One day, I forgot the local custom of first swinging left to turn right and vice versa. A small truck ahead of me veered left, and then cut in front of me to turn right, bouncing his right rear bumper off my right front fender. In three minutes, a crowd of "witnesses" gathered, all who agreed that I was in the wrong. The truck wasn't damaged, however, and one more dent didn't show on the Dodge, so I simply drove away.

A week after I rented the car, I decided to fly a plane to Costa Rica for painting. I told Martinez he could use the car while I was gone. He didn't notice the new dent, and when I pointed it out, he simply shrugged and said, "The way of the road."

When I returned, I asked Martinez to drop the Dodge back off at the hotel. He rolled his eyes and gestured wildly, declaring that I had nearly ruined his beautiful car, which was now in the shop for many expensive repairs. The next day, I saw the car going down the street with a new driver. When I cornered Martinez, he said smugly, "So sorry, Señor Martin, your time is up on the car."

With great restraint, I said nothing. I went to Chila's office and sat down at the typewriter with unofficially borrowed official stationery of the Nicaraguan Air Force and typed a formal demand. I asked for the car for the remainder of my thirty days, or a refund of the money. If the car were not returned by nine o'clock the following morning, I wrote, the police would be notified. I also itemized the contents of the trunk.

I waited until Martinez was huddled in a group of cab drivers in front of the hotel, and then strode out, stern-faced, and put the letter in his hand. "There," I said loudly. "It is witnessed that you have received it." Martinez read the letter quickly and caught up with me down the street. I brushed him aside. "We have nothing to discuss. The letter says it all."

Early the next morning, I awoke to a loud pounding on my door. Behold, Martinez. "Your belongings, Señor Martin, they are downstairs," he announced.

On the street were piled my parachute and other gear. He introduced me to a minor government clerk who Martinez announced would be the "Official Observer."

I flashed my copy of the letter. "Okay, Martinez. Where are the rest of the things on this list? And my money? The other chute and the crash helmet are missing."

"That's all there is, that's all there is," Martinez wailed.

"You're wasting my time. I'm going to the commandant."

Official Observer caught my arm as I turned to go. "Please, Señor Martin, is there not some way we can work this out?"

"Sure, pay me what the stuff is worth and refund the remainder of the month's rental money. I'd rather have the car and the goods though. The crash helmet belongs to the FAN, and they will be angry when I tell them Martinez stole it."

"Witnesses!" Martinez interrupted. "I have many witnesses to tell that this was all that was in the trunk!"

"A United States Air Force captain and a Nicaraguan Air Force major were with me when I loaded the trunk. Shall I call my witnesses?"

Official Observer answered quickly, "That will not be necessary. I'm sure we can work this out."

I looked hard at Martinez. "Sure we can. Pay me what you owe!"

Official Observer spoke in rapid Spanish to Martinez. Martinez paled a little and then said, "I will have the car here for you in ten minutes. No more."

"In that case, I'll check very carefully at the field to see if any of these items could be mislaid," I said.

With that, Martinez snatched up the chute and gear and whisked it up the stairs to my room with a speed seldom seen in his country. "I will be right back with the car, Señor Martin."

Official Observer laughed. "You lie a little, we lie a little—everything okay now," he concluded pleasantly.

"No hard feelings," I agreed. His was the best summary of the local business philosophy that I had heard yet.

Chapter 28

INTO THE MANGROVE JUNGLE

Every day new problems turned up. It seemed the last planes would never be ready. While Colonel Saavedra was always polite, he never expressed the least concern about the almost daily disasters-in-the-making that I discovered. I found myself spending more and more time following up on work with Sergeant Gonzales. It was hard for me to understand how the chief mechanic and his men could be so pleasant, yet apparently not give a damn about their work.

I kept trying to find the cause of the engine failures. During my last trip to the States, I had talked to Rolls-Royce and anyone else I thought might know something. The engine salvaged from the Costa Rican Mustang that went down stood off to the side in the FAN hangar with the bent prop still attached, a grim reminder that I needed answers.

When the next Mustang was ready, I took it up for a check ride. I drove it around for a short time and then came in for a landing. As I was on final, I flipped the mag switch from the on position first to left, and then to right. When I turned it right, the engine quit. I immediately switched back to left, the engine caught, and I continued landing. I was elated. Maybe I had found the engine problem.

Back at the hangar, I waved Sergeant Gonzales over. He climbed up on the wing and watched as I turned the switch to the right magneto. The engine stopped.

"The problem is in the mags, right? We are going to change the mags, aren't we?" I said.

"Sure," he agreed with a big smile. "*No problema.*"

When I arrived at the field the next day, the mags had not been changed. The mechanic working on the plane told me the trouble had been in the cable with the wire that ran from the switch on the panel to the mags. When the switch is in the off position, the wire for each mag is grounded. In the left or right position, they open the circuit, breaking the connection to the ground. The sergeant reported that when he started up the engine with the new cable, it ran perfectly as he checked each mag. I was a little chagrined that I had insisted he change the mags.

Among the parts included in my contract were two 110-gallon drop tanks. Bill Rolfe had assured me that Mustangs performed fine with drop tanks hanging off the wings. Although the plane climbed more slowly, the trim didn't change since the drop tanks were attached at the center of gravity.

Bill warned me not to count on the electric drop tank release, however. If the engine quit on takeoff, the drop tanks had to be ditched quickly, and the manual levers were more reliable. On takeoff, once the throttle was fully advanced, Bill told me to drop my left hand quickly on to the two manual release levers on the left side of the cockpit—just in case.*

I considered the drop tanks: they looked new, and if I used them on this next flight, I would have an eight-hour range at fast cruise. I could save time by overflying Mexico and make it to Brownsville in about four hours. The plane would be carrying an extra 1260 pounds of fuel, but without guns and ammo, it still would be well within the weight limits in the manuals.

I had the long-range tanks installed on the Mustang. After the work was finished, I noticed a cable hanging down in the left wheel well. When I questioned Sergeant Gonzales, he said casually that it

---

*The designers also provided an electric switch on the control stick to drop either the left or right tanks or bombs. My Mustangs had only manual switches.

was the tank release. I wondered how in hell anyone would connect the tank without connecting the release. It took another day's work to connect the cable, with the mechanics grumbling about the extra time.

Finally the drop tanks were ready. I wanted to leave before the day got any hotter, but I methodically went over the rest of the cockpit, carefully checking each gauge. As I taxied out, I started to feel apprehensive about the drop tanks. I thought about what Bill Rolfe had said. Mentally I was ready to pull the releases to jettison them if anything happened on takeoff. After a quick mag check, I was ready to go and go I did. It was October 20, 1964.

With the added weight, I used more runway than usual and the climb was slower. I headed northwest to the Pacific coast, climbing slowly toward 10,000 feet. I would be over a good-sized body of water, the Gulf of Fonseca, but at my altitude I wasn't too concerned. After about forty minutes of flying, I started squirming, trying to get comfortable with the bulky parachute, seat, and shoulder harnesses. It was then I felt the first shudder. The engine missed several beats. I sat frozen in the seat, clutching the stick. I was still on the left main tank, the gauges all looked okay, temperatures were normal. Did I imagine it?

Then it missed again, only this time the interval was longer and more severe. "Shit, not another one!" I muttered out loud. I pushed the mixture to full rich, easing the throttle back as the vibration increased, the engine shaking violently in the motor mounts. I hunched over the stick, caressing, encouraging, threatening, and damning it. I looked down. I was at about 7,400 feet over the middle of the gulf and could see two freighters plowing through the dark water below.

By now the engine was barely running. Pushing the stick gently to the right, I banked and pointed the plane back toward the mainland. I was scanning the panel, calculating my options, when the engine quit dead. As the plane began to descend, I was more angry than scared—best case, this was going to be damned expensive. I calculated I had about ten minutes before I crashed either into the water or on to the land. Pushing all other thoughts away, I concentrated on getting me and my bird down in one piece.

* * * * *

The Mustang ground to a halt in the wet sand. I leaped out of the cockpit and ran a hundred feet until I collapsed behind a piece of driftwood. I lay there a few minutes, waiting for the explosion. The only sound was the waves washing up on the shore.

I picked myself up and cautiously crept back, alert for the smell of gas. The plane glinted in the sun, a dented mass of aluminum. I had been intensely focused the last ten minutes on trying to keep the plane flying and then bringing it down without killing myself. Thank God I'd discovered back at the field that the tank release cable had not been attached and that I had stood there to make damn sure it was reattached. If I couldn't have gotten rid of the tanks, the plane would have been a thousand pounds heavier and have glided about as well as a stone. I never would have made it to shore. Now suddenly it was all over. Should I have done something else? What did I miss? I felt a sense of hopelessness alone on the beach.

I spread out the chart on the warm sand and tried to figure my position. During my brief descent, I hadn't seen any signs of a town or road. It seemed one way would be as good as another. I had no wild hopes that the Nicaraguans would launch any kind of search-and-rescue mission. While Pat knew my departure date, she also knew that things didn't always go as planned, so she wouldn't necessarily be worried when she didn't hear from me. By now my anger had given way to feeling sorry for myself. I was going to have a hell of a long walk without a hat, food, or water.

What happened next was right out of *Robinson Crusoe*: my man Friday was coming down the beach! He looked to be about my age, was barefoot, wearing a frayed straw hat, pants rolled up at the knee, and sporting a handlebar moustache. He carried his machete loosely in his hand as Nicaraguans do and smiled as he came closer. He looked at the plane curiously and said something in rapid Spanish. I told him the engine was very bad, and he nodded. I pointed to the chart and showed him the way I thought I should go. I'm not sure he had ever seen a chart or map. In any case, he shook his head and pointed toward the nearest sand dune just east of us. His direction seemed as good as any.

I took my personal gear that I had stuffed into plastic bags in the gun bays and trudged beside him. I was wearing a lightweight flight suit with only underwear underneath. The .38 automatic that I carried after the DeLarm incident was packed with my gear because there was no way to stow it in the cockpit. Since I didn't plan to wear it in the States, I hadn't brought the holster.

From the top of the dune, I could now see a three-shack settlement. A river on the other side paralleled the shoreline and there was a crude boat dock. The dark green I had seen from the air turned out to be a swamp. There were two men standing in front of one of the little sheds; Friday explained to them about my crash. We talked for quite some time—I talked and they talked, though I'm not sure how much was actually understood by either side. I unfolded my chart again and indicated Managua. We established the nearest town was at least forty miles away.

One of the men pointed to a fifteen-foot-long dugout canoe with an outboard motor. It was clear they wanted to help, but they made it plain through gestures that there would be a lot of walking after we got out of the boat. My old wrestling injury had left me with the bum knee and any amount of walking on uneven ground was difficult and painful. However since these guys were the only game in town, I nodded.

I decided to leave my personal gear and camera at the little shack and come back for it later. I left my gun wrapped up in clothing, since it would be awkward to walk with it flopping around in my flight suit pocket. I sat down in the bow and the captain took his post back with the motor. Just as we were casting off, the third man, carrying a small-barreled rifle, took the middle seat. *Oh shit*, I thought with a sinking feeling. No wonder the men had agreed to guide me without setting a price. Morgan used to kid me that the locals would kill me to get the leather from my size 14 shoes. I started to get out of the boat, but the captain hit the engine and we were off. I thought to myself, *Will, you've got a problem.*

It was now about noon and the sun was burning down. I folded my chart and held it over my head to shade my eyes. What the hell was I going to do? I cursed my stupidity in leaving the gun behind.

My heavy laced-up boots would surely pull me to the bottom if I jumped out of the boat. I shook off my dizziness from the hot sun, every muscle tensing as I strained to hear the click of a rifle bolt.

I noticed a rusty machete in the bow of the boat; I started to put together a plan. Casually reaching down, I quietly gripped the machete in both hands. I was ready to whirl around with it if I heard the rifle bolt slide back.

The canoe moved slowly through the dark water, the men brushing aside overhanging branches of mangrove trees; we made so many twists and turns I lost all sense of direction. Unseen animals howled and jabbered. Suddenly the boat made a hard right, and it seemed we were headed to a shoreline. It turned once again and we moved toward a heavy overgrown mass of vines that appeared to be a dead end. My adrenalin racing, I thought, *this is it.* I didn't know how deep the water was, but if I dumped the boat over trying to cut down the guy with the rifle, I might make it to shore. But then what? The jungle looked impenetrable.

Just then the boat slipped through an opening in the overgrowth and a dock magically appeared. A knockdown gorgeous woman in a tight-fitting white pants suit with a very large-caliber pistol on her hip was standing there. She was light-skinned and had long black hair topped with a white sun hat. I was stunned.

We climbed out of the canoe. My guides spoke in Spanish too rapid for me to follow, but I caught the phrase "*el piloto grande.*" The woman said something to them and waved them off. As they turned back toward the water, I stuffed a wad of córdobas into their hands. From their reaction, I had the feeling it was more than they had earned in the last six months.

The woman flashed a fabulous smile and introduced herself and her *encargado,* or ranch manager. "We come to this dock possibly once or twice a month," she said in flawless English. "How fortunate that we came today. It is twenty-five miles through the jungle to the nearest road. Without a gun...who knows?" She shrugged and then asked graciously, "Will you join us for lunch at our home? Then we can arrange for you to get back to Managua."

The odds of her being there were about the same as filling an inside straight in an honest poker game. It turned out her family was one of the largest cotton growers in Nicaragua. There was a cooler in the back of her beige Mercedes station wagon, and two ice-cold Cokes revived me.

I felt like a field hand wearing my flight suit in her elegant dining room at the hacienda. The table was set with linens, fine china, crystal and silver. The rest of the family members welcomed me with great politeness. But I found any mention of the FAN or General Somoza was met with silence or very reserved, non-committal answers. It was apparent I was enjoying the hospitality of people who were wary of the Somoza regime. After some very good Scotch and a magnificent meal, they amused themselves by shooting at wild birds for target practice in their courtyard. Later, the woman's brother drove me back to Managua.

The next morning at the field, the mechanics just shrugged. There wasn't the least bit of interest as to why the engine had quit.

I stopped at Colonel Saavedra's office. As I expected, he already knew about the crash. I needed to get back to the site to see if I could salvage the plane before the tide came in. The plane was sitting in salt water, but if it were dragged back on the beach, rinsed off, and loaded onto a truck, it might be saved. After a few minutes with the FAN colonel, it was clear that although his mechanics had done all the work on the plane, it was my problem, not his.

Next I talked to Colonel Mansfield at the U.S. Mission. He passed me off to Mr. Fairchild, my old buddy at the embassy. He looked pained when I asked for his help. He explained that he was "very busy, you understand" and was due at that very moment in fact at a luncheon, but he would ask his staff to look into my problem "first thing next week."

I returned to the airport and dejectedly sat down on a bench in front of a hangar, trying to figure out my next move. A U.S. Army helicopter that had flown in that morning was parked nearby and its pilot joined me on the bench. I told him what had happened.

"You know," he said thoughtfully, "I think we have a practice mission scheduled right in that area. If we took off now, we might just make it before the tide comes in." This was my kind of guy! He handed me a helmet and I swung into the front seat next to him. The helicopter was a bright red Bell with a big glass nose.

We followed the coastline and found the plane easily. My heart sank when I saw it was already almost high tide. Looking at the roadless terrain, I realized there was no practical way to get equipment in to salvage the plane.

When we got out of the helicopter, we found the Mustang standing in about a foot and a half of water surrounded by eight men, three in Guardia uniforms armed with rifles, three more in civilian clothes who were taking orders from the soldiers, and two of my guides from the little house over the dune. The Guardia men had obviously never run into a situation like this and didn't have any idea what to do. The officer in charge was a captain with minimal English.

The plane was going to be a total loss. I exhaled deeply and thought I might as well play the Yankee benefactor. The group crowded in as I presented my man Friday and his associate with shiny new machetes I had taken from a compartment in the wing closer to shore. The rest looked expectantly. Then I remembered the case of rum stashed in a compartment in the other wing. The captain understood with no trouble when I explained I wanted to make a gift of the rum to him. I drew a diagram in the sand to show how to open the panel, and one of the men waded in, shoes and all. The water was now lapping over the top of the wings. The soldier joyfully held up each bottle to cheers on shore as he unloaded them. The plane was full of gas, which I knew would disappear as soon as containers could be found, so I announced to the captain that the gas was his as well. He beamed and probably concluded the day was turning out better than it had started. There must have been some real hangovers from that beach party.

We cranked up the helicopter and flew back to the airport. The pilot declined my offer of drinks and dinner, saying he had another commitment. Already there were smirks and comments among the U.S. Mission guys and some Nicaraguans about "selling planes to the insurance company." I didn't bother to tell them that after my experience with Lloyds of London on the first crash, I only carried liability insurance. Anyone so stupid as to think I would deliberately crash in this terrain in a plane that touches down going a hundred miles an hour really wasn't worth talking to.

I remembered the tremendous headaches after the first crash, so I decided I'd better get back to the States. Since I didn't have a place to park my gun in Nicaragua, I just threw it in my suitcase. I did take the magazine out and put the cartridges back in the box of ammunition Glenn had brought down with the gun. Just as a precaution, I put the cartridges in a separate bag.

I caught the next airliner out to Miami. At U.S. Customs, the inspector asked me to open my suitcases. I slung the bags up on the counter. The two little old ladies next in line stopped their chitchatting and peered around me to see what I had. The inspector unzipped the zipper that opened the whole side of the large bag, revealing the black steel .38 lying on top of my shirts. There was an audible intake of breath behind me.

The inspector ignored the gun and moved the clothes around a little, I suppose looking for liquor or cigarettes, and rezipped the bag. He checked the smaller bag and then asked for my passport. He flipped through it, glanced at the many foreign entry and exit stamps, took out his ink stamp, and punched it down on a page. He handed the book back with a smile. "Welcome home, Mr. Martin." We both turned to look at the shocked biddy hens that were staring with great round eyes. I picked up my bags and the inspector winked at me. "Step up, ladies, you're holding up the line," he said sternly.

The headaches started the following day, but were not as severe as the ones from the previous crash. I thought I ought to have my head examined on general principles for ever getting into this deal.

When I developed the film in my camera from the trip, I discovered my two beach guides had taken pictures of themselves, one of which is in this book.

Chapter 28

Yankee Blues

The plane crashes were taking a toll on our cash flow. Planes not delivered didn't get paid for. We had tried to get a line of credit, but as soon as a banker would find out the planes were in Nicaragua, the discussion ended. It had been some months since my move from the Gran Hotel to the cheaper rented room in a nearby house. I tried to live as frugally as possible, but Managua was an expensive town. Glenn kept a close rein on cash flow up in Chicago, and Pat had pared household spending to the bone. It was tight, and we were just managing. However, "George" looked like he was turning the corner, and we were guardedly optimistic for "his" recovery as long as no more planes went down.

One day when I went to the Gran to pick up my mail, there was a thin airmail letter from Glenn. I was shocked when I read it:

> *Just got notice from Fraud and Complaint Dept of Criminal Branch of State Attorney's Office saying a warrant is being issued for my arrest. Priester signed complaint. Said our check for his T-28 bounced. Going before judge next week to explain. Glenn.*

I was stunned and immediately called the operator to get put through to Glenn by radiophone. By then he had figured out what had happened: the check we had received from the buyer of our last two Mustangs had been returned for insufficient funds. Having assumed it was good, Glenn wrote against it to buy the last T-28 we needed to fulfill our end of the contract with the FAN. We'd bought it from George Priester, the owner of Priester Aviation Services, a well-regarded operation at Palwaukee Airport, north of Chicago.

Although a jovial guy, George knew the plane had left the country, and when our check bounced, all the pleasantries disappeared. He wanted his money immediately and had gone to the courts to enforce payment. Glenn met with Priester, and then after somehow convincing the aircraft dealer he was going to get his money, began trying to chase down our Mustang buyer for payment. Glenn sounded calm over the phone. I knew he was trying very hard to keep the pressure off of me.

We had started this project in 1963. It was now 1965, and we had delivered the last of our B-26s and T-28s, which the Nicaraguan Air Force had enthusiastically accepted. Many had less engine time than called for in our contract. Of the twenty-six Nicaraguan planes and two Costa Rican planes that we purchased, five Mustangs plus two P-47s had crashed due to mechanical failure. The '51 that went down in Mexico was still being held by that government. There were six that still had to be readied and ferried to the States. We had almost two years invested in a project that Colonel Saavedra had promised could be completed in a matter of months.

With his usual good sense, Glenn pushed me to abandon the deal. His voice echoed over the radiophone: "Will, each time you go down there, you tell me it's your last trip. How much longer is your luck going to hold? Let's call it quits while you're still in one piece. I'm trying to keep you out of the obituaries."

"We're so close to the end," I countered. "It'd be a shame to walk away from it now. Besides, I think the work has improved."

"That's what you said before the last crash. How many times have you said, 'This is the last time I'm going to fly'?"

Glenn was my best friend as well as my brother. He was worried, but knew in his heart I was going to finish the contract. I promised him I would be home soon and hung up.

Pat never asked me to walk from the contract, even though she was aware of DeLarm and the crashes. But I knew my absence was wearing on her and the girls. One day I opened a letter from her and found a drawing made by our three-year-old daughter, Cassie. It was a picture of a family, but with only a woman and two children. *I asked Cassie why there was no father in the picture,* wrote Pat, *and she replied, "he ran away."*

I stared at the letter. My eyes smarted with tears. I had committed just about all the money I had in the world to this deal. My kids were growing up without me. I had put Glenn in hock. How much longer could Pat hang on? How much longer could I hang on?

That letter was the closest Pat ever came to protesting.

Years later, she explained it by saying simply, "I thought finishing it was important to you." She did say if I had disappeared on a flight, she had planned to post a reward with Bat Corrigan, our customs broker in Brownsville, which would be big enough to get the duster pilots out. Pat realized they were the only ones who could do low-level flying. She added that she would have offered two rewards: one if they brought me in alive, and a lesser amount if I came home in a body bag.

As I lay in my bed in Managua that night, I thought about what Glenn had said. I thought about Pat and the girls back home. Then I thought about the New York lawyers. God damn it, I was not going to be beaten again. I was going to get the last planes out.

It was late January of 1965. Relations with the Nicaraguan mechanics were not improving. There was an undercurrent of complaints that I was faultfinding and picky. I had tried gifts, incentives, and bonuses with little success. The mechanics would focus on the reward without making any effort to earn it.

One morning, Morgan strolled by as the mechanic who was the prop expert was checking the new prop on a Thunderbolt. The starter was grinding hard, but the mechanic continued running it until the battery died.

"Bub," Morgan said, "You are now observing the Nicaraguan

Repair Technique. If it doesn't work, keep grinding it, and maybe the trouble will stop. If it does, don't look for the cause. Why fix the roof on such a sunny day?"

"Morgan," I said with a sigh. "I'm going to have to bring in American mechanics to finish up."

"Told Saavedra yet?" he asked.

"Nope."

"He won't allow it," Morgan predicted. "He'd take it as an insult, like his men aren't any good."

"They're not," I pointed out.

"Everybody knows that. But look, Bub, you've got lotsa planes outta here already. Did you see those T-6s they got torn apart over there in the hangar? They've been overhauling them for four years! By their standards, it's going great."

"I guess I can't afford their standards," I said as I motioned the mechanic on the P-47 to stop. He was now attaching a battery cart, which would just burn up the starter as well. "Get someone to find out why it isn't starting," I ordered and sighed again.

The following day, I stopped at Colonel Mansfield's office at the U.S. Mission. He greeted me cordially, and turned up his air conditioner a notch for my benefit.

"Colonel Mansfield," I began, "I've got to talk to an American. If I stay there in that hangar much longer, I'll start to think like the Nicaraguans."

He grinned knowingly and lit a cigarette as I continued.

"When I took this deal, I assumed since the pilots and mechanics were trained in the States, with the U.S. military, at U.S. expense, and since there is a U.S. Mission here on the field, that the work would be done according to U.S. standards. I just came from flying a plane they said was ready to fly: the brakes failed, the prop controls locked, the seals weren't tight—and on and on. These are their air force planes. How can you put up with this? It apparently goes on all the time."

The colonel took a deep drag on his cigarette and exhaled slowly. "Will, not one of my men will put foot in a plane that a Nicaraguan has as much as cleaned the windshield of. My men are fly-guys. They hate desk work, but they can find lots of it rather than get in a Nica plane."

I persisted. "I realize they don't have the same mechanical background as our guys. But they don't even try. It's Holy Hannah Day so nobody shows up for work, and then they're hungover the next day. At noon, they stop work and go home. I know the U.S. supports their air force with monthly payments. Can't you influence them to at least stay awake on the job?"

"If you figure out how to get them to work, let me know," he answered. "But this is the best life most of them have ever had. They have uniforms, shoes, food, and prestige." He paused. "You understand, technically our mission is here by the invitation of the Nicaraguan government, and we can only advise."

"Then why don't you?"

"Martin, I've got enough problems of my own without yours too. Good luck to you." He turned his air conditioner back down and I left.

Chapter 30

EL GATO

Rumor had it the FAA was not going to license warbirds after July 1, creating a new pressure. If I couldn't get my last planes to the States to license before then, I might as well put them on the scale and sell them for scrap.

When I told Colonel Saavedra this latest development, he tsk-tsked a bit and suggested, "Why don't you see Major Amado?"

The upshot was I added Major Amado to the payroll. The major was enthusiastic about the project and assured me he would supervise on a daily basis. Fourteen mechanics would complete their air force responsibilities in the mornings and work for me afternoons, Saturdays, and Sundays to get my five remaining planes finished. The mechanics would receive a $500 bonus for each plane ready to ferry by April 30.

I went back to prodding and pushing mechanics and checking every nut and bolt. Parts continued to be a problem. No one ever asked for a part until it was needed. I would cable the States, coax it out of customs, and then it would turn out to be the wrong size. Dysentery plagued me. It seemed as though the most activity on the field was in my bowels. Major Amado never once showed up at the field and when I complained to Colonel Saavedra, he said it was between the major and me.

In the evenings, I wrote letters to Pat. *The days are blending into each other so smoothly I never know what day it is. I feel like I am living two lives, one here and one at home. I know today is Friday because the pool is being filled at the Gran. Yesterday was a day like I have never had before. First, Bob [Vassalli] gave me the news of the latest outrageous [shipping] costs and terms. When I went to Chila's office to borrow her typewriter and cool off in her office, I accidentally parked my car in a no parking zone and the police towed it off. It cost thirty córdobas. I was going to stay home but the landlady and her daughter were going to see Dr. No and asked me to go along. I did and after I bought the tickets, I found out we had a one and a half hour wait so we went for a drive. Anyway, to finish off the day, my landlady's car ran out of gas. My day was complete.*

On my last visit back to Chicago, Glenn and I had composed a letter to Colonel Saavedra that detailed our original deal and described the slowdown after we had delivered our T-28s and B-26s. The letter pointed out the disappearance of a C-45 engine and the P-51 radiators and the fact that Major Amado never showed up in the hangar after he was paid. We emphasized that all the planes we had delivered had met or exceeded the terms of our contract, each licensed by the U.S. and thoroughly inspected for ferry permits. I had been holding the letter. Frustrated and out of ideas, I finally sent it to Saavedra.

When I didn't get a response, I sent a copy of the letter to General Somoza. He fired it back to Colonel Saavedra and told him to settle it.

The atmosphere was tense at the meeting in the colonel's office. The FAN officers were mad I had complained to the General. I looked at the unsmiling group and began. "You said I could get these planes out of here at the rate of one a week. I've been here for two years, and I think this nonsense has gone on long enough."

"Do any of you officers remember me saying that?" Colonel Saavedra asked. No one remembered. "According to the contract," he said smoothly, "we agreed to get these planes ready to ferry. But the contract doesn't say when." There was an ominous silence.

They had me. What could I do? Sue General Somoza? If I didn't keep the heat on, I couldn't get the last five planes out. *All right, you bastards*, I thought. *All bets off.* We had another round of negotiations, and they thought of a few new fees. After the meeting, I was marked as fair game and someone had his hand out all the time. According to one of the mission officers, the mechanics had figured any gringo would give up and leave after a few planes. They never thought I'd have the staying power to finish the contract.

The whole air force seems to know I've been to see the General, I wrote to Pat. *In a cab today, a drunk and dirty man with a rooster got in the front seat. I don't mind dust, but I didn't want the rooster to do what the Nicas are doing to me.*

When I told the mechanics to move the last Mustang into the hangar to start working on it, Sergeant Gonzales explained that it had been so badly damaged it could not be repaired. "It's going to be mounted on a pole as a gate guardian…that's all it's good for," he said glibly.

I walked around the plane. "I don't see any damage."

"Major Gomez decided," he said, closing the subject.

There was nothing wrong with the Mustang. By then I had been in Nicaragua long enough to predict what was going to happen: they were swapping out this Mustang for one in far less pristine condition. I cursed inwardly. As I guessed, my "substitute" plane turned out to be one that had been partially stripped for parts and needed much more work.* There was nothing I could do.

I knew if I returned to the States this time, I might as well give up hope of completing the deal. The only activity would be the pilfering of parts. I grimly settled in. Thus began five long, tedious months of unrelenting frustration. The tempo and quality of the work never varied—crises daily and disasters at regular intervals.

Every night I wrote a letter to Pat. *Boy it's hot. It should start raining soon. Chila has helped with a lot and I would like to extend an offer for her to visit us in Chicago. She is returning to Cal[ifornia] in June. I never see or talk to Morgan any more. I am dragging at night and moving slowly in the daytime. If I weren't so close I'd say to hell with it all. Send a helmet if possible with Bill [Rolfe]…. Hope I beat the next letter home.*

---

*I learned about a year later that the FAN did turn around and sell the first plane. So much for the gate guardian.

During these months of pushing, pushing, pushing every single day, I test-flew planes and survived broken rudder cables, a canopy unlatching, a throttle friction lock coming loose, tail wheel steering unlatching, prop control failing, airspeed gauge quitting after takeoff, a battery fire, brake failure, and a generator giving out.

The crazy part was, with all the mechanics' incompetence and indifference, they were always smiling. I knew now that "Sí, Señor" didn't mean a damn thing. But it was hard to stay mad at people as friendly as these men. They greeted me warmly every morning and were unfailingly cheerful. They just didn't work much. When I left the field, the officers would pull the mechanics off my planes to work on one of their projects.

The Mustang DeLarm flew up to the States had been the only one with a full set of working instruments. The others had no radios and none of the gyro flight instruments had been operational. I didn't like test-flying without a radio and considered spending a thousand dollars or so for a portable one. However, there really wasn't much that anyone on the ground was going to be able to do if I did radio with a problem. The crash truck always stood by anytime I flew.

Weeks dragged by. Finally, another two '51s were ready. Or so the mechanics said. After a half hour of test-flying the first, the engine started to run rough. I landed and the mechanics began checking. They reported that they had found and replaced a bad magneto switch. I flew it again for an hour, and it ran fine. Problem solved.

The repair facility in Costa Rica had quoted me a good price to remove the paint and Bondo from the wings and then repaint the planes. I decided to take the two Mustangs to them.

A duster pilot, Pete, offered to fly one of the planes. Just before we left, he drew me aside. "Will, I dunno if something's fishy around here or not. One of the mechanics just asked me which plane I was going to fly. I told him and he said, 'Be sure you do.' You don't suppose they're settin' you up, do you?"

"After all the times they've almost killed me accidentally, I don't think they could do much worse if they tried deliberately," I assured him. With the bonuses I was paying, I figured it was in their best interests to keep me alive. "But in case there's a problem with either plane, the other one follows him so at least he knows where to send help," I added.

It was the morning of May 1, 1965. I wanted to leave before it got any hotter. I had learned to stand on the wing and lean over to arrange everything I could before climbing in. A plane would have to be on fire or without wings before I would jump, I had decided. The manual warned that because the Mustang's tail surface was very close to the cockpit, if you bailed out, you had to leap toward the wing tip in order to avoid hitting the back of the plane. Still, I wore a parachute. The military seat pack parachute made the cockpit uncomfortably tight. I jiggled the seat adjustment and tightened all the seat and shoulder harnesses.

By now the sweat was pouring down me; the metal sides of the cockpit were burning to the touch and the seatbelt buckles felt as though I were holding hot pokers. I methodically went through my checklist, sweating in the 100-plus degree heat. The prop blade slowly rotated. The engine gave a couple asthmatic coughs, the instrument panel began its St. Vitus dance; as the cylinders began to fire off, the various vibrations smoothed into a uniform roar. At extreme low idle, the gear train for the overhead valves would click and clank as though it had been assembled the wrong way. Above all this racket, I listened for but heard no indication of trouble.

We took off, and I flew slightly behind the other plane. Pete was a very experienced ag pilot and knew the area well. The sky was clear blue with the predicted afternoon thunder showers still a long way off. I felt well acquainted with Mustangs and was alert to any unusual sound. I didn't have long to wait. Thirty minutes out the engine started running a little rough. I increased the rpm and manifold to try to clear it. It didn't. The panel gauges, those that were working, told me nothing. Probably plug trouble, I thought. I came alongside Pete, waggled my wings, and motioned that I was in trouble and headed back. Ten minutes later, the vibration took on a much rougher tone. This was sounding just like my previous engines before they failed. For engine problems, the manual instructed to lean the engine, switch tanks, or reduce power. None of that worked. Then the engine stopped. I looked around to signal Pete I was going down, but he was nowhere to be seen. Apparently he had abandoned me. I was furious.*

I'd been concentrating on trying to keep this bird aloft and had not looked at the terrain. I was at less than 1,500 feet now. I glanced around and saw nothing but hills and trees. I remembered Morgan's comment: "*If you go down in the jungle, the trees just open up and close after you.*" Out of the corner of my eye, I glimpsed a tiny sugar cane field. It looked like my best bet.

I stood the plane over on its wing to line up with the field, shoving the nose down while turning to keep it from snap rolling. I was at about 300 feet and my airspeed was down to 150 mph. "My GOD!" I shouted aloud, as I realized with horror I was now in a ravine and the sugar cane field was *above* me. I dumped full flap, felt the quick lift, and rode the plane up to the rim of the hill. I put my head down as the Mustang hit the ground, my helmet banging hard back and forth against the canopy. Sugar cane stalks two inches thick burst through the floor like spears, filling the cockpit, and I was completely blinded by flying dirt and sugar cane. When the bird finally stopped, I was in a sugar cane jungle. Miraculously none of the stalks had stabbed me.

It was deathly quiet. I sniffed for the smell of gas but the tank was apparently intact. Cautiously, I rolled back what was left of the broken canopy and climbed out, flexing my arms and legs. Everything seemed to be working. I was perspiring profusely yet was cold at the same time.

I stood there in a daze, my mind trying to comprehend this disaster. The wings had cut a swath through the sugar cane about forty feet wide. The plane teetered on the edge of the hill and a little push would put it over on its back. It was crumpled from the radiator to the spinner. Cables hung out like withered snakes.

Minutes later I heard shouting. Across the ravine a Nicaraguan on horseback appeared. A crowd of farm workers quickly surrounded the plane. A European rancher arrived in a jeep and offered to take me to his place. There his cook made a pot of strong coffee for me. The rancher said he would take me to the nearest town where I could

---

*Later, Pete told me he knew the shortest route back to Nicaragua was over the roughest terrain and he wasn't going to chance it.

then get a ride back to Managua. A mile or so down the road, we met a 1938 Ford truck loaded with soldiers.

I climbed on the truck and rode back to the site. I heard a plane overhead and saw Somoza's Aero Commander circling. I stood on the wing and waved to let them know I was okay.

About an hour later, a helicopter arrived for me. It was then I got a good look at the countryside: there wasn't any other spot between the place I crashed and Managua where you could put down a plane. I had chosen well with the sugar cane field.

When we landed at Las Mercedes, a crowd of several hundred surged forward, each trying to touch me. An eerie thought came into my head. There was a local superstition that anyone touching a person who survived after being marked for death would have good luck. Had the plane really been sabotaged as Pete feared? Was DeLarm behind this? He knew the mechanics, he spoke the language. He had the motive and the means. I tried to push the thought away. It could have been just another mechanical failure. But then why was everyone trying to touch me?

From somewhere in the crowd came the shout: "El Gato! El Gato!" Everyone joined in chanting, "El Gato, El Gato!" I was the cat with nine lives. I pushed through the crowd, refusing Colonel Saavedra's offer of whiskey.

Chapter 31

WHEELS UP

I hadn't been home since Christmas. It was the longest six months of my life. I lived for Pat's letters and missed my family terribly. *May 30, I have been ill last week but I think I might be over it. If it doesn't clear up today I will go to a doctor on Monday. I may have a mild case of malaria. I am so tired I haven't got the energy to fight this deal much longer. How I miss your meals, the quiet evenings, the children, Sam [the dog]. The nights are becoming longer and longer. I realize how much time I've been away by the exploits you write about the children. They seem to be growing up so fast. How is our Wonder Dog Sam doing? Please continue to write even though I expect to leave next week. Your letters are the only thing that keeps me going.*

There are 30,000 barking dogs in Managua. I know as I counted them last night. They yipped, howled and barked the night through. I feel I could serve a jail sentence easier than spend more time here. I was really sure I wasn't going to have to write anymore and that I'd be home.

One morning in early June, I was out at the field sitting in a P-51, trying to jerry-rig some kind of clamp to hold my charts in place. I was facing the terminal and noticed passengers being loaded on a C-47 transport plane. I thought at first it was a Lanica airliner, but it was unmarked. There were maybe fifteen, twenty civilians with some

Guardia soldiers mixed in. I didn't pay much attention until I heard shouting and looked up to see two of the civilians tearing across the runway as fast as they could.

Nobody was chasing them, but the soldiers were shouting and milling about, radios to their mouths. The two men were out of sight when I heard a couple short rat-tat-tat-tat blasts. I remembered the .50-caliber machine gun placements on the other side of the field.

I climbed down out of the cockpit. Sergeant Gonzales came up to me and with frightened eyes ever so slightly shook his head. I looked around and all the mechanics were concentrating very hard on their work. No one was looking toward the field. A sick feeling came over me. I slowly climbed back up into the cockpit. The soldiers resumed loading their human cargo on the C-47 and it took off. A few minutes later, a truck drove around the perimeter of the airport toward the area in which the two men had disappeared.

The soldiers had avoided shooting in front of witnesses, radioing instead over to the machine gun operators. No one in the terminal would have paid any attention, as it was a quasi-military field and a gun going off was not unusual. But the mechanics knew what had happened. For the first time, I felt a deep sympathy for them. They had to live here knowing violent death could come to those who crossed the Somozas, and that just by being in the wrong place at the wrong time, it could come to them or their families. Any plans I'd had for settling here had long ago been shelved. Now I just wanted to finish up and get the hell out of Nicaragua.

Finally, the last five planes were ready. It was June 18, 1965. A car dealer in Florida had bought the P-47 that Mr. Senior Pilot had crashed. He had been able to find a prop and some belly skin for repairing the plane and then bought it from me, FOB, Managua. He sent down Ben Amonds, a duster pilot in his twenties, to bring it up to Miami. Ben was a likeable, clean-shaven young man who was building up his flying time in order to join United Airlines. I lined up three more pilots. George, another duster, was a competent pilot by day but an alcoholic by night. I knew of his drinking problem, but it never seemed to interfere with his ability to fly. Dave Lindsay at

Cavalier, the Florida remanufacturer of Mustangs, had recommended two former USAF captains who rounded out the group. They had flown Douglas Sky Raiders, a huge, single-engine fighter, in Vietnam, and could and would pontificate on anything and everything related to Mustangs. They were competent pilots, so I put up with the egos. Pete, the ag pilot, asked to fly one of the Mustangs back to the States, but I took a curt pass on his offer.

I assembled the men, outlining the routes and regulations. Navigation would be simple. We would fly down the coast and land at our port of entry on Mexico's southwest border. I reminded them we were flying with full tanks and that they were to take off on the left fuel tank and switch to the tank right behind the cockpit after twenty-five minutes of flight. One of the captains announced he didn't want gas in his or his buddy's rear tank. He went on to lecture me about the center of gravity and how problems could develop "when pulling Gs with tanks behind the pilot."*

I looked them straight in the eye. "I don't give a rat's ass what you do with your own planes, but you are not going to be pulling Gs in mine. It's straight and level for 3,000 miles—no aerobatics, got that?"

They sulked and mumbled a few snide remarks. I told the men they could pick any plane and I would take the remaining one.

I checked each plane the day before departure. The next morning, I paid the bonuses. An hour later, right before takeoff, I noticed three compasses had disappeared. When I confronted the Nicaraguans, everyone looked the other way. If we wanted to leave that day, it would have to be with three planes lacking this most elementary navigational equipment.

One plane was also low on hydraulic fluid. I pointed this out to Sergeant Gonzales, but he just shrugged. I borrowed fluid from Pan Am. The mechanics leaned against the hangar and watched me spill the hydraulic fluid all over myself as I added it without a funnel. Each

---

*To extend the P-51's range, the military added an 85-gallon tank just behind the pilot. This additional weight of 510 pounds moved the center of gravity back from that of the original design, causing an unstable condition in combat maneuvers. The procedure was to use up the gas in the rear tank as soon as the pilot could switch from the left main tank, which had to be used for takeoff and for about the first fifteen minutes of flight. (The gas in the carburetor return line flowed to the left tank.)

pilot climbed into his bird and one by one, the planes rolled down the runway with me bringing up the rear. As my wheels left the ground, I felt a tremendous relief.

We flew in loose formation, those of us in the planes without compasses keeping our eyes glued on those with. When we passed Guatemala, we saw clouds with heavy weather and dropped down to the deck for a short time. After we resumed our altitude, I was startled to see a Mustang on both my right and left sides, closer than any plane had ever been to me. The air force captains then switched positions, one over the top and the other below. It was obvious they had planned this. I had other things on my mind and ignored them.

We arrived at Tapachula. It was then we realized we hadn't decided who was going to land first. We had no radios and after circling a couple times, George landed. He confided later that he was glad none of us saw him land because he leveled off at about five feet above the runway and then dropped for a real bone-cracker landing. The rest of us followed, one by one.

We checked each plane for coolant and oil leaks, and I asked each pilot if there had been problems. Other than one hydraulic leak, the birds performed fine. It was about 4:30 p.m., and when we closed our flight plans, we learned from the inspector for immigration and customs that we were now into overtime. The charges would be $75 per plane. The fun began. By this point my Spanish was pretty good, but when I resisted the charges, suddenly no one could understand me. It boiled down to paying the charges to ensure that "details" would be slid over. If not, our ships would have to be very carefully inspected and "mucho, mucho" documentation would need to be filled out.

After more discussion, I finally negotiated a lesser sum and paid it. When I asked for a receipt, the customs officer responded with many gestures and much eye rolling. The gist was a receipt would take a "long, long time" to prepare. We left without a receipt and piled in a cab.

The next morning as we were preflighting the planes, I noticed a mother holding a young boy at the airport fence. He was pointing to the plane with great enthusiasm. I walked over, and without a word, picked up the little boy and deposited him in the cockpit.

His excitement overcame his shyness and he blurted out, "*Cuando soy mayor, seré piloto!*" After a few minutes, I returned him to his mother who thanked me profusely. Mothers are mothers the world over.

The hydraulic fluid was down quite a bit on one plane. No one saw any leaks, so I asked the line boy for fluid. He smiled and said, "Very, very expensive, Señor."

I had just bought between 500 and 600 gallons of gas, and when he quoted me an exorbitant price on the fluid, I had just had enough. I got a paper cup and a pair of pliers. I asked each pilot to get in his plane and step on the brake. I opened up the bleed fitting on the brake assembly and took a little fluid from each plane. The brake hydraulic system fed from its same reservoir, which left a healthy reserve. My pilots thought I was crazy, but they weren't paying the bills.*

We agreed on a takeoff order—and if we were still all together—a landing sequence. The Vietnam hotshots left first, George followed, and then Ben. I was last as usual. When I caught up with Ben, I saw his P-47 was spewing dark smoke in a steady stream. I pulled alongside and pointed to his tail. He immediately did a 180-degree turn and went for a straight in, downwind landing back at the Tapachula airport. I made a high-speed pass right over the little office building, hoping to alert the crew there to the problem. I saw Ben make the runway, and I landed on the same strip as fast as I could.

Ben was down safely, but on his landing rollout, the prop locked up. When the engine of a heavy bird like a '47 seizes and the prop stops turning, the plane falls like a rock. The manuals have no suggestions other than to jump if there is enough altitude. If it had happened while Ben was still airborne, he would have been in big trouble.

Ben was pale but composed as he climbed out of the cockpit. He managed a weak grin as I observed matter-of-factly, "That could have ruined your whole day." We looked at this old wounded warrior, hoping that if the owner could find a new engine, it might not be destined

*I knew the mechanical uplocks would keep the wheels retracted even if all the fluid leaked out; I just wanted to get the gear up for the next leg of the flight. The wheel weight will cause the gear to drop down when the cockpit handle is put in the down position. I learned this trick after a hose broke on my Navion at a small airport in Ohio. I rigged a temporary car hose by cross threading the fitting, knowing the large springs of the Navion would push the gear back down when I got to my home base, even if all the fluid had leaked out.

for the scrap heap. It was a piece of history worth saving.*

Ben wanted to fly a P-51 back to the States so I gave him mine. It was going to a dealer in Texas. I took a feeder flight into Mexico City and then booked a seat on Mexicana to Chicago.

The Mexicana plane was a De Havilland Comet, a beautifully sculpted aircraft with the four engines tucked into the wings. After the passengers boarded, the doors were closed and the engines started. But before starting to taxi, the pilot suddenly shut down the engines and announced first in Spanish, and then in English, "This airplane is going to Chicago, United States. If you are not going there, get off the plane!" Two people stood up and got off. The door slammed shut again and we finally departed.

And so I settled back into my life in the States. My brother Glenn joined a large insurance company in downtown Chicago. I opened my own consulting firm dealing primarily in mergers and acquisitions.

A few years later, I faced a particularly tough negotiation with a seller's lawyers. I was standing with my buyer outside the conference room when he turned to me and said in a low voice, "Will, these guys are real sons-of-bitches; we've got to look out."

I turned and gave a little smile. "I've put together deals where I was the only one at the table without a machine gun. This is nothing."

He looked sideways at me. I just laughed and walked into the meeting.

---

*The buyer subsequently sent mechanics down with a new engine. Ben went back to fly it out, but bad luck continued. On his next landing, on the west side of Mexico, the engine caught fire on final approach. He was still high enough to bail out and with his air force training, that's what he did. He landed in brambles, was a little beat up, but suffered no serious injuries. The '47, of course, was junk. Even though it was no longer my plane, I felt sad to see this beautiful warbird with only 200 hours destroyed.

Epilogue

I finished the FAN contract in June of 1965 and left Nicaragua for good. Although General Somoza did not stage a coup as the State Department and President Schick had feared he might, Somoza was determined to win the next election when Schick's term was up. *La Prensa*, the conservative press, accused Somoza of early campaigning for the 1967 presidential election in violation of the Nicaraguan constitution, as his post as Guardia chief was supposed to be apolitical.

In January of 1967, with presidential elections on the horizon, a coalition of Nicaraguan liberal and conservative groups opposed to Somoza organized a massive protest in the Plaza de la República. Tens of thousands of people began marching up Avenida Roosevelt toward the Presidential Palace in the late afternoon of January 22. Alarmed by the crowd, the Guardia fired into it. Some of the protesters shot back and fighting broke out.

The total number of protestors that died is disputed, but at least forty demonstrators were killed and more than a hundred were wounded. Three Guardia members also died. The National Telegraph Office was bombed and many demonstrators ran for cover into the National Palace. Somoza ordered tanks into downtown Managua and some six hundred insurgents took over the Gran Hotel, seizing a hundred people hostage, most of them Americans. The U.S. Ambassador, Aaron Brown, and Catholic Church officials negotiated with the insurgents for the release of the hostages. Once the crisis was contained, Somoza cracked down brutally.*

The next month, Somoza was elected president by a wide margin in a highly irregular election. He retained his title as military chief of the armed forces and consolidated his power.

During this time, I received a newspaper clipping from Chila. It showed a picture of a B-26 that the Nicaraguans had crashed. "Good!" Chila had scrawled across the bottom of the picture.

A powerful earthquake on December 23, 1972, destroyed an estimated 80% of the commercial buildings in Managua and left approximately 10,000 dead, 20,000 injured, and 250,000 homeless. The five-story wing of the Gran Hotel collapsed, and much of the Plaza de la República was in ruins. General Somoza diverted most of the foreign relief that poured in from around the world for his own use, drawing worldwide attention to his increasingly corrupt regime and receiving widespread condemnation in the international press.

Then in 1978, Pedro Joaquín Chamorro, the publisher of *La Prensa*, was assassinated. Somoza denied responsibility, but Nicaraguans were outraged. The U.S. ambassador, Mauricio Solaún, characterized the killing as the "detonator" that marked the turning point for Somoza's regime.† The following year, Americans watched in horror as footage of ABC newsman Bill Stewart's execution by Guardia soldiers was broadcast on their TV screens.

Bolstered by growing opposition and U.S. President Jimmy Carter's withdrawal of support for Somoza in the summer of 1979, the *Frente Sandinista de Liberación Nacional* or FSLN, a left-wing socialist/Marxist party, overthrew Somoza's government, forcing Somoza to flee the country. He was assassinated a year later in Asunción, Paraguay, by Argentinean Marxists who fired an RPG-2 rocket into his white Mercedes sedan.‡

*Bernard Diederich, *Somoza* (New York: E.P. Dutton, 1981), p. 79-80. Clifford L. Staten, *The History of Nicaragua* (Santa Barbara, CA: Greenwood Press, 2010), p.70.
†Mauricio Solaún, *U.S. Intervention and Regime Change in Nicaragua* (Lincoln and London: University of Nebraska Press, 2005), pp.103-5.
‡Claribel Alegria and Darwin Flakoll, *Death of Somoza* (Willimantic, CT: Curbstone Press, 1996), p. 132-4.

Today, the old Las Mercedes airfield has been expanded and renamed the Augusto C. Sandino Airport. The part of the Gran Hotel still standing has been turned into a cultural center. Sadly, I never heard from Chila again after the earthquake. Her mother's house was a few blocks from the Gran Hotel and the heart of the earthquake, and Chila was most likely there for Christmas. Morgan, old and in poor health, left Nicaragua shortly before Somoza's fall, and died soon after in Miami. Francisco Saavedra was promoted to the rank of general and continued to head the FAN until 1968 when he retired and joined Lanica Airlines. He was the general manager of Lanica when the Somoza government collapsed in July of 1979. He managed to escape with his immediate family who were already in Guatemala, and then traveled to Miami. His brother Rafael, my attorney, was not so lucky, however. A Sandinista commando attacked his house and set fire to it. Rafael's newly married daughter and her husband managed to get away, but Rafael and his son were taken prisoner, shot, and their bodies burned in the street.

Roberto Vassalli, my customs broker, and his family escaped, airlifted to Panama from where they then made their way to Florida also.

Nicaragua, having suffered so terribly as Somoza and the FSLN struggled for control, subsequently staggered under the double burdens of the Sandinistas' incompetence and corruption as well as the United States' economic sanctions and clandestine support of the Contras. A stability of sorts has re-emerged in recent years, and many exiles from the late '70s have returned. The damage has been great, however, and Nicaragua today is the poorest country in Central America and the second poorest in the Western hemisphere, behind only Haiti.

My Costa Rican friend Juan Bonilla and I lost touch over the years. I learned recently that after retiring from the airport, he had joined his oldest son in the construction business, building commercial warehouses for U.S. companies in Costa Rica. He died of cancer much too young. I wish I could have had one last lunch with him.

My encounter with Jerry DeLarm at the embassy in Managua was the last time I saw him. In 1985 he was convicted in a U.S.

District Court in Florida on three counts for his role as a pilot in a drug-running operation out of Jamaica. He was sentenced to five years in prison and served two before being paroled. He died in 2000.

In the years that followed the completion of my FAN contract, I kept trying to track down the Mustang that had landed on the beach in Mexico. The flood of letters, phone calls, and telegrams to the U.S. Embassy in Mexico City proved futile. Friends with contacts in Mexico, U.S. senators and congressmen, all made inquires without results. In 1972, I attended a business conference in Mexico City at which the U.S. ambassador was scheduled to speak. Before the event, I met with an embassy staff member. I told him I planned to stand up during the reception and relate my experience with our inept embassy and the indifferent Mexican government.

The next evening at the reception, when I gave my name in the receiving line, the ambassador said, "Ah, Mr. Martin. You are the young man who has the airplane problem. Could you be at my office at ten o'clock tomorrow?"

The next afternoon, I finally saw my old warrior. The hot dry climate had preserved it, and outside of a bent prop and some ruptured belly skin, it looked to be in good shape. The Mexican charge for storage was $5,000. I had expected there would be a *mordida*, and I was just grateful it wasn't more.

I called a number of Texas transportation companies before I found one that agreed to put it on a standard flatbed trailer and bring it to Chicago. They said they had a Mexican affiliate and could transport it all the way up. Most firms said they would transfer it at the border. The dispatcher assured me their firm handled fragile cargo all the time.

Months went by. Finally I learned that the plane had been trucked to the border, offloaded onto a high-sided trailer and transferred to a train. My instructions had been to deliver it to a hangar at Midway Airport. At the appointed time in Chicago, a burly driver strode in and asked, "Where do you want me to dump this loada scrap?" I was horrified to see heavy chains had been used to tie my Mustang down, crushing the aluminum. Loose parts were tossed helter-skelter.

I could have wept. The plane had managed to survive a crash landing, only to be done in by a truck ride. When I refused to pay the shipping bill, the court ruled that the trucking company worked only as an agent and was not responsible.

I eventually restored the plane. Al Heinz, a young A&P mechanic, worked evenings with me in a hangar at Midway Airport along with other aircraft mechanics. For Al, it was much more than extra money. There is something about Mustangs, an aura really, that makes working on them a labor of love. The months rolled by. We took out the extra gas tank behind the cockpit to fit in a second seat and sent the engine to the West Coast to be rebuilt. It took almost two years, but the '51 was finally restored to its former glory.

By now a circle of warbird owners was following the restoration. One of them, Lou Antonacci, gave me a heads up that the FAA was going to require recent experience before giving approval for flying an unlicensed plane out of Midway. Mustang owners would sooner loan their wives than their planes. Where was I going to get "recent experience"? Then I heard flying a T-6 would qualify for recent experience and Lou offered his. Wally Sedgewick, who had been a popular WWII instructor and now did check rides for the FAA, gave me a thorough refresher ride that included wheel and three-point landings, full stalls with power on/off, slow flight with steep turns, and then for fun, some rolls.

An FAA inspector examined my plane and signed off on its airworthiness, but told me it would not get its limited license until it had been flown. So I gathered my logbook, accident reports, and a flight manual, and headed out to the FAA office at suburban DuPage Airport.

The DuPage FAA examiner paged through the flight manual and spent the next hour asking detailed questions about Mustang innards. Since I had worked hands-on with Al for two years, I knew the systems well. I showed him the signoff on my flight in Lou's T-6 by Wally, who was one of their best examiners. But when he looked at the accident reports on my three crashes, he said, "Three accidents? That's not much of a recommendation."

"If you can figure out how to keep an airplane up when the engine quits, then you're wasting your time at the FAA," I retorted.

A lot of jockeying and jostling with the FAA followed, providing ample evidence of the FAA's unofficial motto, "We're not happy 'til you're not happy." The bottom line was the FAA would not sign off on the plane without recent P-51 experience, and I couldn't get the P-51 experience without flying the plane.

Glenn had sold one of our Mustangs to a fellow named Junior Burchinal in Paris, Texas, that Burchinal then converted to dual control for instruction. Since he was an FAA examiner, I borrowed an Aero Commander and flew down to get certified.

Junior and his Flying Tiger Air Museum were famous, or infamous, depending on whom you talked to. He was a colorful character who always wore a red baseball cap and was missing a front tooth. At one point he served time in prison; some maintained he got a bad rap. Just about everyone agreed he was a skilled pilot. He had flown historic aircraft in a number of movies. His raggedy collection of WWII planes varied over time, but at that point included a Corsair, Wildcat, B-17, B-25, and T-33 jet that were available to fly to anyone with cash. A wrecked P-38 was relegated to a corner. He operated out of a little duster landing strip.

I assumed I would fly from the front cockpit, but Junior motioned me to the rear seat. Its panel boasted a stick, throttle, and two stubs of extensions of the rudder pedals—no brakes, speed indicator or any other instruments. "We'll start off with some spins," he announced enthusiastically.

"Oh no," I told him. After all I'd been through, I was not going to deliberately put a Mustang in a spin. "I just want to get the recent experience qualification."

We did some 360s, steep turns, full stalls, a wheel landing, and a full stall landing. After about an hour of flying, Junior scrawled a statement on the back of his business card that said I was a competent P-51 pilot. The FAA then licensed both the plane and me. I did the test flight, and all was right with the world, at least my portion of it.

But my adventures with crash landings were not over. A group at DuPage Airport had planned an air show honoring WWII aces. They asked if I would bring my Mustang and speak at their program.

I decided to fly over the day before to go through the schedule. Al asked if one of his friends, Sonny Major, who had never flown in a plane before, could ride along for the ten-minute hop from Midway to DuPage. It was March 15, 1975.

The DuPage tower cleared me to land and although I had flown it only three hours since we'd finished the restoration, the plane felt good. I was relaxed and enjoying the ride. My only problem was the radio, which broke up from time to time. As we approached the airport and had the runway in sight, I heard the tower operator telling someone his landing gear wasn't down. I glanced at my panel and was reassured by the landing gear indicator's three green lights.

By now I had full flaps down, the prop in low pitch, and was easing back on the throttle, ready for a neat three-point landing. The tower operator was frantically shouting, "One gear isn't down!"

I finally woke up and asked, "Are you talking to the white Mustang?"

The controller screamed, "YES!"

I rammed on as much power as I dared without rolling the plane and slowly eased the flaps up. Heading west of the airport, I radioed the tower, advising I was going to try to shake the landing gear down. A pilot in a Cessna 182 flew alongside to warn me of any traffic. He called the tower to urge them to foam the runway.

Banking hard, I put the plane in a steep turn again and again, hoping the G-force would snap the balky gear down. With all the gyrations, why Sonny, my poor passenger in the back seat, didn't get airsick, I will never know. Al Heinz had joined the controllers in the tower with the Mustang manuals and was frantically trying to figure out what had gone wrong with the gear.

As I strained to pull up on the gear handle, it broke in half and stuck in the down position; cycling the gear to try to drop it was no longer an option. I thought it might help if I dumped the pressure in the hydraulic system, but when I pulled out the hydraulic dump handle, the pressure just dropped and came right back up. I considered breaking a line in the cockpit, but knew hydraulic oil spraying into the cockpit could blind me. Now I was left with one gear up, one gear down, and no possibility of bringing the plane in on its belly.

After about an hour had passed, I realized the best I could do was burn off as much gas as possible and put the Mustang down. My Cessna-guide had to land to refuel, handing me off for the time being to a passing helicopter that hovered to watch for other aircraft.

Just as I thought things couldn't get any worse, the engine started leaking oil that flowed over the windshield, blocking all forward vision. The Cessna was soon back, and I radioed the pilot that I needed him to fly alongside me to line me up with the runway. I throttled back to 120 miles per hour so the Cessna could keep up. The airport lacked the facilities to foam the runway; I was going to have to bring it in dry. The tower closed the airport to all other traffic.

Meantime, Bill Ross, a pilot friend and warbird collector, commandeered the radio of an airplane near the runway to try to talk me down. I was facing a landing with one wheel up, one wheel down and limited vision. I called Sonny on the intercom to tell him once the plane stopped, to get out and away from it as fast as he could. The Cessna pilot and Bill lined me up with the runway. "Keep coming. Keep coming," Bill intoned. "You're lining up nicely."

Once I could see the runway peripherally, it was just a matter of easing down. I kept the right wing up as long as I could with the ailerons as we rolled down the runway on one wheel. When the wing finally dipped and the prop hit the runway, the plane swung to the right and skidded to a stop. Mercifully, there was no fire.

The headline the next day in a local newspaper, the *Beacon-News*, read AIRPLANE TRAGEDY AVERTED.

Skillful flying kept two men from tragedy Saturday afternoon at DuPage County Airport.... When Martin discovered the right landing gear wouldn't go down, ...he circled the field in the P-51 Mustang, a converted World War II fighter plane to burn off gas.... He landed at 4:12 p.m. in a manner witnesses said looked like it was an ordinary landing, it was done so expertly. The plane went about a quarter of a mile on the runway, using only the left landing gear, until it lost speed and finally veered off the runway on to the grass at the right of the landing strip. An FAA spokesman said the men's chances had not been good. It is a hard to maneuver plane.

A woman listening to an aviation monitor heard the conversation between Martin and the pilot of another plane in the air assisting him. She said the pilot of the disabled plane "exuded calm and confidence. It was more exciting than "Airport '75."

The right flap, a wing tip, and the prop of my beautiful plane were damaged. At the time, the parts cost half again as much as the price of a new Cadillac. What the hell—who needs a Cadillac-and-a-half?

The culprit was a gear door that was missing a cotter key located where an inspection would not have seen it. The green lights came on because we had changed the gear lights and apparently made a mistake on one down-lock micro switch. The oil came from the nose of the airplane where the prop governor seal, which is under very high pressure, had a pin-size leak. The gear handle broke due to a WWII design flaw, a metal not strong enough for the job having been specified. The hydraulic pressure would not stay off because of a missing bracket near the dump valve. Any one of these problems would not have been serious; together they proved nearly disastrous.

That night, Al said, "Will, I think the guys in Nicaragua had it right. You are the cat with nine lives. We should name this plane 'El Gato Rápido.' Few guys survive one Mustang crash, and you've had four." And El Gato Rápido it became.

Mustangs had become popular as high-performance sports planes in the years between El Gato's landing in Mexico and when I restored it. It seemed every time I landed, someone made me an offer to buy the plane. To get rid of them, I would name a ridiculous price. To my dismay, one day a man from Florida said, "That sounds fair. I'll take it." It was an offer I couldn't refuse. And before I knew it, El Gato was gone.

Subsequently, I bought a derelict Canadian Mustang that had been spared the jazzing-up and "improvements" that were the recent fate of many P-51s. I started restoring it in a shop building at our home. About ten great guys volunteered every Saturday. Some were A&Ps, and others were just in love with Mustangs. One man said, "This is the only P-51 I will ever have a chance to work on, and I'm going to do it right." He polished his area of aluminum until it looked like a mirror. When new recruits showed up, they were assigned the dirtiest job we had: applying paint remover to clean the Bondo off the seams. If they came back after that, they could join the team. Pat provided lunch, during which there was always a lot of hangar flying and good-natured kidding. We were well underway with its restoration when again, there was an offer I couldn't refuse, and it was gone.

I now fly a T-34, a great plane. My aviation activities are more and more involved with Squadron Four, an offshoot organization of the Warbirds of America, a group of men and women dedicated to preserving these old warriors. When we sponsor air shows or static displays of these historic legends, great crowds come to see and learn about the history of these machines and the role they played in our country's defense. Warbirds are part of the Experimental Aircraft Association (EAA), sponsor of the world's largest airplane convention held at Oshkosh, Wisconsin, each summer. Pilots, homebuilders, vintage, ultralight, aerobatic, and general aviation enthusiasts come from all over the world. Without the EAA's active promotion of historic aircraft preservation, I suspect the FAA would have long ago restricted these famous planes to museums.

* * * * *

When I took off for the last time from Las Mercedes, I was so glad to be leaving Nicaragua, I never wanted to think about the place again. But I did, of course.

General Somoza was a useful U.S. ally on the international stage in the fight against communism, and we were all worried about communism in the early 1960s. Through the airplane contract, however, I had naively stumbled behind the stage curtain, where I witnessed Somoza's harsh regime up close. Even for a tough guy from Chicago's South Side, it was pretty grim. And as it turns out, when the international press began to focus on Nicaragua in the mid-seventies, I learned there had been much, much more I hadn't seen.

Astonishingly, the period I was in Nicaragua would later be characterized by Ambassador Solaún, the last ambassador before

Somoza's overthrow, as the country's "golden years," during which modest social and political gains were made under the presidencies of Somoza's brother Luis and René Schick. In fact, during the first half of the 1960s, Nicaragua had the strongest economic growth of any Central American nation.* Yet even then, it was a very difficult place for most Nicaraguans, and much of the corruption I encountered, in retrospect, was the response of people just trying to get by.

I think of the many fine people I met in Nicaragua. Chila had welcomed the big gringo into her group of friends when I was lonely and homesick. Bob Vassalli, my customs broker, had proved a reliable agent time and time again, helping when the Mustang went down in Nicaragua, ushering my various pilots through the red tape maze, and looking out for me as a friend. The staff at the Gran Hotel, the officers who invited me into their homes for meals, Morgan, even crusty Morgan, they all had tried to show me the better side of Nicaragua. Thanks to them, I managed to carry away a few good memories.

People have asked me why I survived my three Nicaraguan crashes. There were probably three reasons. One, growing up in the car business, I developed a fair amount of mechanical sense. I understood the workings of the P-51. Two, I read and believed the military aircraft manuals. In very clear, simple language, the manual authors had written, *do this or you will die.*

And most important of all, three, I was damn lucky.

*Bernard Diederich, *Somoza*, p. 76.

Acknowledgments

The transformation of my story from a pile of notes and a box of 50-year-old slides into this book has involved many people and I am grateful to all of them.

A great thank you to Ann Howard Creel, Neil Russell, James Coates, Jr., Carlyle Singer Jones, and my daughter Cassandra Moran for their unsparing and insightful critiques of the manuscript, and to Colonel Darrell L. Anderson, U.S. Air Force, Retired, for his close technical reading of it. And a big thank you to my daughter Suzanne Martin for her tireless editing and painstaking backstory research.

Thank you also to Jorge Fernandez and Victor Bello for their assistance with both language and cultural references, the limited Spanish vocabulary I acquired fifty years ago having completely disappeared. Thank you too, to Christopher Winters of the University of Chicago Map Library for helping digitize a fragile 1963 newspaper and locating the 1979 CIA map that appears at the front of the book, Benna Solomon for deciphering the legalese of the archived appeals documents related to Jerry DeLarm's drug-running conviction, and Jennifer Crewe, Margaret Hivnor and Gary Marenzi for generously offering their contacts and advice. My son-in-law, Hart Weichselbaum, with his many years in the advertising world, provided welcome input on matters from book design to marketing channels.

I am greatly indebted to Dennis Cartín Esquivel, of Costa Rica's *Asamblea Legislativa. Dirección del Departamento de Servicios Bibliotecarios, Documentación e Información*, for locating the family of my friend Juan Bonilla. I then had the pleasure of meeting one of Juan's children, Federico, who told me about his father's later years after I left Central America. I am also grateful to the late Roberto Vassalli, Jr., the son of my Nicaraguan custom's broker, Bob Vassalli, for not only providing the information on Morgan's last years, but also making an introduction to Rosario Saavedra Roman, Francisco Saavedra's daughter, who shared what happened to her family after Somoza's fall.

The beautiful picture quality of the book's photos reflects the efforts of Patricia Andrews, Tony Kuligowski and Erik Smith at Gamma Imaging in Chicago, who took on the task of cleaning and digitizing my five-decades-old, non-standard size slides. Patrick Aylward did the excellent interior layout. My marvelous granddaughter Claire Weichselbaum designed the website, soiboughtanairforce.com, which she continues to host for me, and it was her initial design that the very talented art director Christopher Gyorgy then transformed into the book's cover. Many thanks to all.

Finally, my greatest thanks go to my favorite navigator and intrepid wife, Pat Daggett Martin, for her on-going assistance throughout the writing process in organizing my notes, critiquing my writing, and most of all, for her unwavering conviction that I had a story worth telling.

INDEX

A

Amonds, Ben 164, 236, 239, 240
Antonacci, Lou 164, 245

B

B-26 4, 28, 30, 33, 36, 56, 64,
        73–82, 83, 106, 107–112, 117,
        149–151, 203, 224, 229, 242
Beechcraft Model 18 119–120
Bonilla, Major Juan 95, 103–105,
        118, 135, 138–141, 208, 243,
        254

C

C-45 27, 33, 121, 186, 229
C-45 Expeditor 119
Cavalier Mustang Rebuilding
        Company 123, 237
Chamorro, Pedro Joaquín 242
Chicago Yacht Club 10, 11
CIA 4, 38, 52, 56, 196
Corrigan, "Bat" 60, 85, 225

D

Daggett, Vernon 115
Dallas Love Field (Dallas, Texas)
        109–110
DC-7 15, 183, 184
D & E Beech-18 119
De Havilland Beaver 199
De Havilland Comet 240
DeLarm, Jerry 34–35, 37–39, 44,
        50–54, 69, 90, 154, 191–197,
        199, 201, 218, 225, 234
    Costa Rica 104–105
    drug-running conviction 243
    Guatemalan revolution 52
    NBC documentary 91
DuPage Airport (DuPage, Illinois)
        165, 245–248

E

earthquake, 1972, Managua
        242–243
El Coco Airport (San Jose, Costa
        Rica) 95, 103
El Gato 166, 228–234, 249
Estrella Hotel 25, 49, 51–52, 116

Experimental Aircraft Association
(EAA) 250

F

Frazee, Minnesota 115
Frente Sandinista de Liberación
Nacional (FSLN) 242–243
Friedman, Joe 125
Fuerza Aérea de Nicaragua (FAN)
13, 26, 28, 30–31, 38, 54, 56,
57, 67, 74, 88, 92, 117, 130,
145, 162, 168, 180–181, 190,
203, 204, 210, 212, 214, 220,
224, 229, 230, 241, 243, 244

G

German FW-190 111
Gore, Bob 22–23
Gran Hotel 25, 51, 116, 126–128, 179,
182, 183–186, 191, 200, 201,
204, 208, 223, 241–243, 251
Gulf of Fonseca 5, 157, 158, 216

H

Heinz, Al 245, 247
Howell Airport (Crestwood, Illinois)
16
Howell, Willy 16

I

InterAmerican Geodetic Survey 199
Irazú Volcano 95, 97, 104, 118, 136

J

Jimmy Angel's Gold 183–186

K

Kennedy, John F. 3, 4, 108, 110,
111, 114
KLM Constellation 99, 133

L

La Nacion 52, 91
Lanica Airlines 26, 29, 57, 172–173,
190, 235, 243
La Prensa 51, 241, 242
Las Mercedes Airport 24, 67, 88, 89,
90, 234, 243, 250
Lindsay, Dave 123, 237
Lockheed T-33 67, 178, 190, 246
Lopez, Chila 155, 203–209, 210,
229, 230, 242, 243, 251

M

Mansfield, Col. Richard 28, 50, 88,
220, 226
Matamoros, Mexico 47, 61, 62, 85,
111–112, 167, 168, 171
Midway Airport (Chicago, Illinois)
21–23, 38, 43, 62, 69, 72, 74,
77, 107–108, 123–124, 149,
172, 244, 245, 247
Morgan, Sumner B. 13–14, 24–30,
33–34, 37, 39, 48–49, 52, 59,
85–86, 87, 105, 106, 116–118,
120, 128–130, 186, 197, 199,
218, 225–226, 230, 233, 243,
251
Morton, Jim 69, 148, 172
Mustang
Canadian 37, 85, 249
canopy 85
cockpit 143
control stick 136
coolant leaks 63
crash landing 5–6, 72, 144, 217
drop tanks 37, 215
engine 70, 132, 143
glide ratio 188
H-model 123
instrument panel 134, 142, 231
landing 66, 174, 175
landing gear 134

propeller 70
range 142
rudder trim 67
takeoff 70

N

Nestor (sculptor, Costa Rica) 140–141

O

Organization of American States
(OAS) 105

P

P-47 Thunderbolt 13, 25, 27, 28,
33, 56, 57, 70–72, 89, 92, 93,
153, 164, 172, 187–188, 190,
224–226, 236, 239
P-51 TF (Trainer-Fighter) Mustang
65, 148, 173
Picado, Teodoro 129
Priester Aviation Services 224
Priester, George 223, 224

R

Raymond, Bruce 19
Republic Aviation 30, 70
Rolfe, Maj. William 148–156, 151,
152, 187–188, 215–216, 230
Ross, Bill 165, 248
Rubinkam Airport 17–22

S

Saavedra, Col. Francisco 28, 30, 31,
32, 33, 50, 51, 54, 66, 88, 108,
117, 125, 130, 173, 214, 220,
224, 226, 228, 229, 234, 243
Saavedra, Rafael 54, 243
SALA 99, 131, 146
Schick, René 207, 241, 251
Somoza Debayle, Anastasio 4, 26, 29,
31–33, 38, 55, 88, 104–105,
118, 128–130, 141, 172, 176,
190, 206–207, 210, 220, 229,
241–242, 243, 250, 251
Somoza Family 3–4, 29, 236
Somoza Garcia, Anastasio 29
Somoza, Luis 4, 29, 251
Stewart, Bill 242

T

T-28 28, 30, 33–35, 36–49, 50, 60,
63, 64, 69, 84–85, 90, 149,
172, 203, 223–224, 229
T-28A 119, 121–124
TACA Airlines 26, 64
Tapachula, Mexico 61–62, 85,
113–114, 142–143, 169, 171,
187, 238–239
Texas Engineering and
Manufacturing 65
Tipitapa River, Nicaragua 125

U

U.S. Mission 28, 50, 58, 88, 119,
125, 127, 129, 168, 176, 184,
191–192, 194, 207, 220–221,
226

V

Vassalli, Roberto (Bob) 145, 229,
243, 251, 254
Veracruz, Mexico 47, 60, 62, 72,
112, 151, 167, 168, 169
Vickers Viscount turboprop 64

W

Walnut Ridge, Arkansas 171
Warbirds of America 250

Z

Zumallen, Al 18

ABOUT THE AUTHOR

WILL MARTIN holds a commercial pilot certificate and multi-engine and instrument ratings. Flying "El Gato," the P-51 Mustang he restored, he has performed in many air shows, including those at the Experimental Aircraft Association's Oshkosh Fly-In Convention (now known as EAA AirVenture Oshkosh), the Chicago Air and Water Show, and the Texas Commemorative Air Force. Martin is the founder of the EAA's Squadron Four Warbird chapter and has been a featured speaker for numerous aviation and business groups. He and his wife Patricia live in a suburb of Chicago.